MEN AND SOCIETY

Clyde W. Franklin II
THE OHIO STATE UNIVERSITY

THE NELSON-HALL SERIES IN SOCIOLOGY

Jonathan H. Turner, *University of California, Riverside*
CONSULTING EDITOR

Nelson-Hall  Chicago

For my daughter, Alison

May your world become
increasingly less sexist

Cover Painting: *Father and Child*, Chicago artist Ann Ponce

Library of Congress Cataloging-in-Publication Data

Franklin, Clyde W.
    Men and society / Clyde W. Franklin, II.
      p.   cm.
    Bibliography: p.
    Includes index.
    ISBN 0-8304-1148-8
    1. Men—United States—Social conditions.   2. Sex role—
United States.   3. Men's studies—United States.   4. Masculinity (Psychology)   I. Title.
HQ1090.3.F74   1988
305.3′1′0973—dc19   88-9841
                                             CIP

Manufactured in the United States of America

10 9 8 7 6 5 4 3

 TM The paper used in this book meets the
minimum requirements of American
National Standard for Information
Sciences—Permanence of Paper for
Printed Library Materials, ANSI
Z39.48-1984.

Contents

Acknowledgments

Many have contributed to this book directly and indirectly. I am indebted to the men and women at The Ohio State University who have taken my Sociology 635 class, *Men in Society*, and my Sociology 101 class (many of whom entered this introductory class fresh out of high school with numerous challenges to myself, as a profeminist man), to my personal friends, men and women, to Vicki Saunders who typed the first chapter, and to Dianne Small who typed the remainder of the book. To all of you, and especially Dianne who assisted me throughout the project and with the acknowledgments, I give a warm thank you, for without your help this project would not have been realized.

1

Discovering the Study of Men

*No feminist vision can move women
from the margin to the center by ignoring men.*
—Harry Brod, 1986

In an eastern city a man is ordered to undergo psychiatric examination for beating his girlfriend and burying her alive. The girl, a high school honor student and college scholarship winner, appeared to have been beaten, put into a plastic bag, and buried in a shallow grave in the man's backyard. Police said that when she was uncovered less than ten minutes after the burial her body was panting for air and her legs were moving. She died approximately one-and-a-half hours later.

A middle-aged businessman in a small midwestern community is photographed engaging in sexual activities with a two-year-old girl. The same man had carried on an affair with the little girl's mother until she was jailed for child abuse.

A young female model in New York gets involved in a dispute with her landlord over an $800 rental deposit. The landlord, allegedly, with the aid of two other men, cut up the model's face with a razor, causing injuries requiring over a hundred stitches.

The mayor of a suburban community resigns his position after being charged with public indecency for the second time in less than two years. The year before, the mayor had pleaded no contest to a public-exposure charge and had been found guilty. In the latest incident, a young woman tells authorities that this is the same man (married and the father of several children) who exposed himself close to her apartment on several previous occasions.

Few persons reading the above accounts of true incidents that occurred in a so-called civilized society would not be appalled. Still, many are unlikely to recognize the threads of commonality linking all four accounts. Most of us will agree that the crimes are heinous ones. We may also recognize quickly that the perpetrators are males and that the victims are females. But, there is an additional characteristic which holds the accounts together; a "dimension" of traditional masculinity can be found in all four. Traditional masculinity, as I discuss in later chapters, includes, all too often, male violence toward both females and other males; male social domination of females; male domination of the heterosexual sexual arena; male isolation of sex from other aspects of life; and male objectification of women, fixation on their body parts, and conquest of women, among other things.

What all of the above suggests is that the tendency to describe the incidents at the beginning of this chapter as social anomalies or pathologies must be avoided. Instead, social phenomena like heterosexual and homosexual rape, male child abuse, wife battering, and destructive male physical, social, and psychological competition must be viewed within a special context. The context within which these phenomena are *best* seen is one which implies that all are logical outcomes of a society's socialization process that teaches males to become men by engaging in and supporting behaviors which, if internalized fully, logically lead them to interact destructively with others.

Men who rape and/or batter women, abuse children, physically and psychologically wound each other, or engage in other acts destructive to self and others are not beings from another planet. They are products of our society and have very much in common with numerous other men who have not yet been discovered committing such acts. Some portion of the emerging Men's Studies discipline is devoted to emphasizing this precise point. What is it about masculinity, especially traditional masculinity, that perpetuates men's destructive and hurtful behaviors? Why is it so difficult to define masculine other than to say it means "not being feminine"? These and numerous other questions are critical ones to answer for those interested in Men's Studies.

The development of Men's Studies to this point owes a tremendous debt to the following statement constructed by courageous men at the Berkeley Men's Center in the late 1960s and early 1970s:

Berkeley Men's Center Manifesto

We, as men, want to take back our full humanity. We no longer want to strain and compete to live up to an impossible oppressive masculine image—strong, silent, cool, handsome, unemotional, successful, master of women, leader of men, wealthy, brilliant, athletic, and "heavy." We no longer want to feel the need to perform sexually, socially, or in any way to live up to an imposed male role, from a traditional American society or a "counterculture."

We want to love ourselves. We want to feel good about and experience our sensuality, emotions, intellect, and daily lives in an integrated way. We want to express our feelings completely and not bottle them up or repress them in order to be "controlled" or "respected." We believe it requires strength to let go and be "weak." We want to enjoy masturbating without feeling guilty or that masturbation is a poor substitute for interpersonal sex. We want to make love with those who share our love, male or female, and feel it should not be a revolutionary demand to be either gay, heterosexual, or bisexual. We want to relate to our own personal changes, motivated not by a guilt reaction to women, but by our growth as men.

We want to relate to both women and men in more human ways—with warmth, sensitivity, emotion, and honesty. We want to share our feelings with one another to break down the walls and grow closer. We want to be equal with women and end destructive competitive relationships between men. We don't want to engage in ego battles with anyone.

We are oppressed by conditioning which makes us only half-human. This conditioning serves to create a mutual dependence of male (abstract, aggressive, strong, unemotional) and female (nurturing, passive, weak, emotional) roles. We are oppressed by this dependence on women for support, nurturing, love, and warm feelings. We want to love, nurture, and support ourselves and other men, as well as women. We want to affirm our strengths as men and at the same time encourage the creation of new space for men in areas such as childcare, cooking, sewing, and other "feminine" aspects of life.

We believe that this half-humanization will only change when our competitive, male-dominated, individualistic society becomes cooperative, based on sharing of resources and skills. We are oppressed by working in alienating jobs, as "breadwinners." We want to use our creative energy to serve our common needs and not to make profits for our employers.

We believe that Human Liberation does not stem from individual or social needs alone, but that these needs are part of the same process. We feel that all liberation movements are equally important; there is no hierarchy of oppression. Every group must speak its own language, assume its own form, take its own action; and when each of these groups learns to express itself in harmony with the rest, this will create the basis for an all embracing social change.

As we put our ideas into practice, we will work to form a more concrete analysis of our oppression as men, and clarify what needs to be done in a socially and personally political way to free ourselves. We want men to share their lives and experiences with each other in order to understand who we are, how we got this way, and what we must do to be free.

This is a classical statement for the emergence of Men's Studies as a legitimate academic area, and its significance is unquestionable. The statement appeared in *Liberation* in 1970—a time when the male led Black movement was peaking and the women's movement was beginning to hit its stride. During this period, and immediately afterwards, worthwhile books and articles about men and masculinity began to appear in increasing numbers—for example, Jack Balswick's *Types of Inexpressive Male Roles* (1969); Lionel Tiger's *Men in Groups* (1969); Sidney Jourard's *Some Lethal Aspects of the Male Role* (1971); Joseph Pleck's *Psychological Frontiers for Men* (1973); Joseph Pleck and Jack Sawyer's *Men and Masculinity* (1974); Marc Fasteau's *The Male Machine* (1974); Jack Nichol's *Men's Liberation* (1974); Warren Farrell's *The Liberated Man* (1974); and Peter Filene's *Him/Her/Self: Sex Roles in Modern America* (1976).

The proliferation of books and articles about men and masculinity during the early and middle 1970s did not mark the first time men had been major subjects of interest; it did, however, signal a new era in examining and analyzing men's issues. Prior to this time, the traditional male role was in most cases approached from a perspective that extolled male privilege and male benefits. The male who internalized society's definition of masculinity and whose behaviors followed the same line was rewarded with high esteem—and rightly so, many felt. After all, males who assumed a traditional male role were thought to be benefitting not only themselves but also the entire society. Balswick's contention that men did not feel "free" to be expressive without having their masculinity questioned, and Jourard's informed remarks about the lethal nature of the male role, caused a number of social scientists to question their own acceptance of this role as positive. Following closely were works by such scholars as Joseph Pleck, Marc Fasteau, Warren Farrell, Peter Filene, and others which began to examine even more critically both functional and dysfunctional aspects of the traditional male sex role for men, women, children and, in fact, the whole society. This remains a major focus of the study of men today, although there are additional ones considered in a later section in this chapter. For now, let us turn our attention to some basic concepts which will be useful as we examine more closely men in the United States.

Basic Concepts Related to the Male Sex Role

A minimal number of concepts should be at one's fingertips if the nature of the male sex role is to be understood. Being able to distinguish clearly between sex, gender, gender identity, gender roles, sex roles, male dominance, and sexism is essential to understanding males and masculinity.

Sex

Labeling a person at birth who possesses an XY chromosome pattern, a penis, testicles, seminal vesicles, prostate glands, male and female hormones as *male* is appropriate according to the term, *sex*. It is also appropriate based on the term *sex* to label a person *female* who possesses at birth an XX chromosome pattern and female internal and external sex organs. The assignment of these persons to the male and female categories, respectively, is based on the biological characteristics of chromosomes, hormones, anatomy, and physiology.

While assigning persons at birth to male or female sex categories is important, the biological characteristics on which the assignment is made may not play the critical role in producing behavioral differences between the two sexes, as some people believe. While males and females have different compositions of hormones, these differences alone may *not* cause differences in male and female behaviors. They may only *predispose* the sexes to behave in different ways. If these differences are shaped and nurtured by environmental factors, then they quite likely will be manifested in different behaviors for males and females. On the other hand, if such differences are not shaped and nurtured by the environment, male and female behaviors may be strikingly similar. The greatest support for this position comes from the work of John Money and Anke Ehrhardt (1972), John Money and P. Tucker (1975), Maggie Scarf (1976), and Imperata-McGinley et al. (1979). Succinctly put, *sex* is a biological concept, not a social/cultural concept.

Gender

If many male and female behaviors are not the result of biology, then what does cause male and female behaviors? The answer to this question lies in the concept of *gender,* an achieved status that is a function of socialization and has social, cultural, and psychological components (Franklin 1984, p. 2). Gender refers to *social conceptions of what it is to be masculine and what it is to be feminine.* In our society, most people seem to feel that it is not masculine for males to assume secretarial positions nor feminine for women to play football. These are social expectations for behaviors of males and females. Males rather than females are expected to play football, because playing football in American society is a set of behaviors associated with the male sex (although occasionally females have broken the sex barrier and played football). In the same vein, females rather than males still are expected to perform secretarial behaviors (despite the growing number of males entering the profession) because such ''support'' roles are associated with the female sex. While *sex refers to the biological, gender refers to the social.* More and more we have discovered that many of the behavioral differences between males and females in our society have much more to do with social and psychological traits linked with males and females (gender) than with biological traits (sex) differentiating between males and females.

Gender Identity

Besides sex and gender, *our conceptions of ourselves as males and females—a very subjective view of self—*also is critical in the area of gender. This concept is referred to as *gender identity.* An interesting thing about gender identity is that it is analytically distinct from sex, gender, sex role, and sexual preference. A biological male, for example, may possess numerous social and psychological traits associated with masculinity, perform sex roles associated with males, and yet consider himself a member of the female sex category. Many biological males have found themselves in this precise position; the result in modern times has been an increased number of transsexuals. Through surgery and hormones, these males' physical appearance has been altered to conform to their *gender identity—their own conception of themselves as a member of a gender category.*

From the above discussion, we see then that persons are not born with gender identities, and many certainly deviate from the two-category gender system found in most cultures throughout the world. The deviation from a biopolar gender system typically occurs in at least one or more of several dimensions. For instance, some persons deviate biologically in that they are born with either ambiguous genitalia or both female and male genitalia, or they manifest ambiguous hormonal patterns during adolescence. Still others deviate from the two category gender system on a psychological level, exhibited by their preferences for activities primarily associated with the gender other than the one to which they were originally assigned.

It is true that some support can be found among contemporary researchers for moving beyond biopolar gender identities (Pleck 1975; Rebecca et al. 1976; Freimuth and Hornstein 1982; Pleck 1981) and toward integrating female and male characteristics. Such departures, however, often seem to be stigmatizing and confusing to many in American culture. This leads to a critical question: Is it possible in America for one to have a gender identity other than feminine or masculine?

At present the answer to this question seems to be no, despite the proliferation of research on androgyny within the last decade. While non-sex-typed orientations seem to be exciting academically, they remain puzzling to most people in America. To say that some persons consider themselves to be neither masculine nor feminine, but rather some combination of both is enigmatic for many in our society. Even when some men's scores on sex role tests allow them to be defined as androgynous, many of them are no less concerned about traditional sex role distinctions than men whose scores define them as masculine (Heilburn 1986).

Certainly, the fact that men appear to be equally sensitive to sex role stereotypes regardless of gender must be related to gender socialization. Phyllis Katz (1986) has implied that part of the confusion surrounding non-sex-typed orientation may stem from conceptualizing androgyny for socialization practices and implications of androgyny for gender identity. How does one teach a child to be androgynous? Are children to be taught that gender is irrelevant? On the other hand, should children learn content specific information about the two genders and then combine them? Katz alludes to Sandra Bem's article (1983), which stresses the need to develop gender aschematic children. Bem feels that numerous cognitive processes including perception, memory, and learning processes are affected by gender scheme socialization. She suggests numerous methods of innoculation against gender scheme socialization, such as the provision of androgynous models, the inhibition of cultural messages about gender, and a general provision of information on individual variability, cultural relativism, and lethal aspects of sexism. Along with Bem's ideas on gender identity, Katz's conclusions are instructive: "Instead of exaggerating sex differences in children, we might do better to consider the enormous overlap and not define maleness or femaleness as antithetical. Instead of 'Vive la difference,' we might more seriously consider 'Vive la similitude' " (1986, p. 59).

Gender Roles

The concept *gender role* is used in this volume to refer to those behaviors defined by society as appropriately masculine and/or feminine. In a sense, gender role refers to a process of "becoming." One is not born masculine or feminine—rather, through a long period of socialization one becomes masculine, feminine, or some combination of the two. While our society generally socializes young males to perform masculine behaviors and young females to perform feminine behaviors, in recent times some parents have tended toward androgynous socialization of their children (teaching the assumption of a kind of gender role that may be highly masculine and highly feminine, depending on the situation; or teaching the blending of masculine and feminine roles within a situation).

Graham Staines and Pam Libby (1986) recognize two approaches to the conceptualization of gender roles: a traditional (global) approach and a revised (role-specific) approach. A traditional approach to gender roles assumes that they are a subset of social roles consisting of a female role and a male role. Scholars using a traditional approach to gender in research generally have been concerned with how people *believe* men and women *should* behave; how people *believe* men and women *do* behave; and how men and women *actually do* behave. Thus, prescriptive expectations, predictive expectations, and actual behaviors are critical components of gender from a traditional perspective.

According to Helena Lopato and Barrie Thorne (1978), a revised perspective of gender role analyzes social roles enacted by both men and women and seeks to discover what difference gender of the role incumbent makes: How does gender affect the experiences of performing various social roles? (Staines and Libby, p. 215). The revised approach to gender roles also encourages thinking about gender roles as those social roles affected by the gender of the role occupant. In a nutshell, the revised approach to gender is situation specific, examines specific types of behaviors (e.g., nurturance of friends, crying behavior), and assesses the relative experiences of females and males assuming specific social roles.

Sex Roles

All cultures seem to define some behaviors as feminine and some as masculine. For example, worldliness, dominance, aggressiveness, and nonemotionalism are considered to be components of masculinity in America, while talkativeness, gentleness, dependence, and expressiveness are perceived by many as feminine traits. Because American culture establishes sets of cultural expectations for members of each sex based on culturally shared conceptions of what it means to be masculine and feminine, another concept emerges as important: *sex roles*.

Sex roles refer to *combinations and clusters of gender roles deemed permissible for members of a particular sex category to assume.* Sex roles define boundaries in a culture. In America, for example, while a given male may not be expected to display only those traits associated with masculinity (male gender), he is expected to engage in behaviors overall which are sufficiently distant from the female sex role. If he does so, he is playing out the male sex role in America. While gender roles have changed from time to time, sex roles are relatively constant. For instance, it is still considered, by many societies, feminine to nurture children, but today the male sex role in America allows men to play out this ''feminine'' gender role. The same can be said for crying behavior. Men today remain within the boundaries of the male sex role even if they cry. In short, the concept ''sex roles'' is a more encompassing concept than ''gender roles.'' Pleck's observation (1976) that the modern *male sex role* emphasizes the feminine gender roles of emotional intimacy, interpersonal skills, and heterosexual tenderness is a case in point.

Defining androgyny can be a risky business despite the proliferation of studies in the past ten years using the concept. Initial theoretical works by several scholars (Carlson 1971; Block 1973; Constantinople 1973, and others), followed by the development of measures of gender by Sandra Bem (1974) and Spencer, Helmreich, and Stapp (1974), actually led to a conceptualization of androgyny based on the notion that femininity and masculinity are separate poles and are to be measured separately. It was this line of demarcation and the discovery that large numbers of college students describe themselves using both masculine and feminine associated traits which led to the conceptualization of androgyny in terms of high masculinity and high femininity manifested by sex role variability/flexibility from social situation to social situation.

In contrast to this view is another which suggests that androgyny describes behavior within a situation which integrates or blends masculine and feminine behaviors into a distinct and/or unique type (Kelly and Worell 1977; LaFrance and Carmen 1980). While the idea of androgyny as blended masculine and feminine behaviors within a particular situation is a well-known view, relatively little research has been directed to the phenomenon or a comparison of the two conceptualizations. Preliminary efforts indicate, however, that males appear more likely to display discrete masculine or feminine behaviors across situations whereas females are more likely to display blended sex role behaviors (Heilbrun 1981; Heilbrun and Han 1985; Schwartz 1982). More recently, Heilbrun and Bailey (1986) have found little support for the prevailing assumption that masculinity and femininity develop independently. Instead, they found a positive relationship between the presence of masculine and feminine traits within the same person regardless of sex.

Straines and Libby, in defining the traditional approach to gender, provide us with critical aspects of a proposed distinction between gender roles and sex roles. They state, following points made by Lopato and Thorne, that the traditional approach to gender roles seeks to uncover highly general gender-linked behavioral characteristics—global personality traits prescribed for each of the sexes.

The concept of sex roles, as used in this volume, will refer to those widely held and shared prescriptive and proscriptive expectations associated with the sexes. We should keep in mind that a particular member of a sex category may perform masculine, feminine, and androgynous gender roles. At a higher level of aggregation, though, assessments will be made of that individual's sex role performance or the extent to which combinations and clusters of specific gender roles approximate society's definitions of appropriate sex-gender linkage. In other words, is an individual's behavior overall sufficiently sex-typed or sufficiently cross-sex-typed from a societal point of view?

Male Dominance

It does not seem possible to discuss adequately the male sex role in the United States without mentioning male dominance. Male dominance is a belief, usually reflected in the ethos of a society, that males are more worthy than females and should have more power and prestige than females. An essential ingredient of male dominance is its institutionalization in a culture. This means that male dominance is built into the basic institutions of a society such as the economic, political, religious, and educational institutions. Due to its generic nature and the subtleties in the way it is reflected, male dominance becomes as much a part of individual lives and everyday social interactions as living itself, leading directly to societal sexism.

Sexism

Perhaps because male dominance is so much a part of American society, it has been axiomatic that an ideology would develop to support it and the ensuing sex and gender inequality. Many who support such an ideology justify their position by referring to biological differences between the sexes which make men superior to women. Never mind the fact that little evidence exists to support such a pernicious ideology. Male sexism has three major aspects: a belief that males are superior to females; an ideology that supports relegating females to a lower position than males; and behaviors by males and females based on the beliefs and ideology. The latter frequently entails sexism being a part of the norms and standards of the society.

Men's Studies as an Emerging Discipline in American Academia

In March 1983, Armando Smith, in an editorial in the *Chicago Men's Gathering Newsletter,* noted that the men's movement and men's movement issues were beginning to receive serious scholarly attention. Citing Joseph H. Pleck's *The Myth of Masculinity* (1981) and Dennis Altman's *Homosexual Oppression and Liberation* (1971) as examples of such scholarly work, Smith hailed these and others as contributing to the growth of a men's movement.

By January 1984, the Men's Studies Task Group of the National Organization for Men (now known as the National Organization for Changing Men) had organized itself to the point where an inaugural issue of the *Men's Studies Newsletter* could be published. Edited by Harry Brod, who was assisted by the Program for the Study of Women and Men in Society at the University of Southern California, the inaugural issue was seen as an important stage in the evolution of Men's Studies as an academic discipline.

Harry Brod, in an introductory editorial statement to the first *Men's Studies Newsletter,* observed that the field was being "increasingly recognized and institutionalized" (p. 1). As examples of the proliferation of Men's Studies, Brod referred to the Men's Studies courses beginning to appear in college catalogues as standard offerings and the number of Men's Studies articles beginning to appear in academic journals.

In addition to a "national announcement" for the development of a Men's Studies discipline, the first edition of the *Men's Studies Newsletter* provided something else. It served to *inform* those interested in men's issues that there could be a solid base from which to work toward making Men's Studies legitimate. It may seem odd that this would be necessary, given early writings by psychologist Joseph H. Pleck (who can be legitimately referred to as the father of Men's Studies),[1] Robert Brannon, Jack Balswick, Sidney Jourard, Robert Staples, and others. Yet, despite a considerable amount of work relevant to Men's Studies produced by academicians from the mid-1960s on, Men's Studies did not gain legitimacy prior to the 1980s. Consider the following statement published in the inaugural (October 1982) issue of the *Men's Studies Newsletter,* excerpted from an article entitled "Modern Men or Men's Studies" by Eugene R. August:

> Because masculinity is now described as an historical construct imposed upon a biological given, critics cannot discuss knowledgeably the concept of a male hero in a literary text without some understanding of the definition of masculinity in its culture. . . . Moreover, it would be rash for the literary critic to attempt to describe a male's development in a work of fiction or biography written in our own culture without some knowledge of the underlying rhythms of American men's lives described by social scientists. . . . Such an examination will require scholars to reopen the question of just how much we really know about men and to introduce into the curriculum new or revised knowledge about men's history, men's psychology, men's images in literature and the arts—in short, an array of new or modified men's studies.

The early 1980s were pivotal years for the emergence of Men's Studies as a legitimate academic discipline. The early work of members of the Men's Studies task group seem to be bearing fruit. These laborers include Martin Acker, Shepherd Bliss, Robert Brannon, Harry Brod, Samuel Femiano, Martin Fiebert, Sam Gange, Alan Gross, Michael Kimmel, Leonard Levy, Mike Messner, Joseph H. Pleck, Steve Trudel, Billy Worters, Michael Whitty, and others.

Immediately after the first and second editions of the *Men's Studies Newsletter* (January 1984 and May 1984), the *Chronicle of Higher Education* (June 20, 1984) carried an announcement that the University of

---

1. Brod (1987, p.53) has referred to Pleck as the leading scholar in Men's Studies as an academic field. Michael Kimmel's profile of Joseph Pleck in *Psychology Today* (July 1987) underscores the fact that Pleck "has helped reshape our ideas of the male sex role" (p. 49).

Southern California had added a men's curriculum, offering a Program for the Study of Women and Men in Society (formerly known as the Women's Studies Program). Also carried with the announcement were interviews with several women professors and Professor Harry Brod, who was with the USC program at the time, as well as interviews with Professor Ruth Bleier and Professor Verta Taylor (of the University of Wisconsin, Madison, and The Ohio State University, Columbus, respectively).

The *Chronicle* article suggested that there would be considerable debate over the step that USC had taken. The debate would stem from what was perceived as a lack of maturity of research and theory on women as well as the political problem of "fear" that Men's Studies would co-opt Women's Studies, based on the interviews conducted with women professors. More important than the cautious approach to Men's Studies reported in this article, however, was the publicity given the fledgling concept. Men's Studies was becoming recognized at least as a potential discipline.

Despite continuing controversy, Men's Studies courses, academic articles, and textbooks on men and men's groups of various kinds have continued to increase in number. As Brod often suggests, the field of Men's Studies "is at the point where Women's Studies was two decades ago. It's just beginning" (p. 8). Since 1984, the beginning has been somewhat phenomenal. For example, it is estimated that in 1984, courses on men were offered in only thirty colleges. By 1986, nearly two hundred campuses offered such courses (Petzke, 1986). Men's Studies continued to receive publicity as evidenced by the February 11, 1986, and April 28, 1986, articles in the *Wall Street Journal* and *Newsweek*. As the publicity and interest in Men's Studies continue, so does the controversy. In the next section, I examine this controversy more closely, relying heavily on the work of Harry Brod, James Doyle, Michael Kimmel, Martin Acker, and Robert Brannon, as well as on my own reflections.

Men's Studies Defined

It should not be surprising to find controversy surrounding the emergence of Men's Studies as an academic discipline. After all, two decades ago when Women's Studies challenged traditional gender knowledge with a feminist reconstruction of knowledge (Brod 1986) that discipline, too, was steeped in controversy. Out of that controversy, however, an invigorating, creative, legitimate, and highly respected discipline has emerged. But, as Brod states, "the rationale for Women's Studies rests on the proposition that traditional scholarship reflects a male oriented or androcentric bias . . . distortions resulting from which have resulted in women's experiences and perspectives being systematically written out of what has been taught as 'knowledge.' '' What all of this means is that Women's Studies finds as the rationale for its existence reconstituting knowledge to include modification of traditional disciplines by systematically ''bringing women in.''

Men's Studies, on the other hand, has no such rationale—or does it? Brod thinks it does. He finds that the new Men's Studies does have a legitimate rationale for existence, because it is not the old scholarship with an androcentric bias; it, too, ''attempts to emasculate patriarchial ideology's masquerade as knowledge.'' Brod states further:

> Androcentric scholarship is only seemingly about men. In reality, it is at best only negatively about men, i.e., it is about men only by virtue of not being about women. In a more important positive sense, its consideration of generic man as the human norm functions to exclude from consideration what is distinctive of *men qua men*. (Emphasis added)

One sees from Brod's analysis that traditional male-biased scholarship really has told us little about men by constructing a ''universal paradigm for human experience.'' On the other hand, the new Men's Studies complementary to Women's Studies has as its subject matter ''*the study of masculinities and male experiences as specific and varying social-historical-cultural formations.* . . . [Moreover,] men's studies situate masculinities as objects of study on a par with femininities, instead of elevating them to universal norms'' (Brod 1987, p. 40, emphasis added).

Brod contends that the new Men's Studies raises new questions while simultaneously showing how established frameworks are inadequate in explaining old ones. In the areas of work and the family, for example, Brod says that established frameworks frequently conceptualize women as working mothers while statistics on working fathers generally remain unavailable, not even collected by the Census Bureau. A question also is raised about the usage of concepts on fathering that speak more to female than to male life cycles and thus fail to delineate critical dimensions of male parenting. As an example, Brod points to dual labor market analyses which denote the working-mother concept as not only that some women have children but also that the work women do in the paid labor force is a ''mothering'' kind of work. Analogous concepts for men would be working father and "fathering" work, though such concepts presently are nonexistent.

Other issues and questions raised by the new Men's Studies are lodged in such areas as violence, health, sexuality, culture, and the list goes on. Following Brod's lead, for example, one can ask, What concepts of men as citizen-warriors have shaped our tradition of political theory and practice? How much more would we know about health sciences if gender bias had not prevented us from looking for DES sons and miscarriages and birth defects among their offspring? Is pornography constitutive, expressive, or distortive of male sexuality? How have concepts of the "hero" been shaped by rhythms of male life cycles? Furthermore, according to Brod, and I concur, these few questions by no means constitute even a major portion of those to be asked and simply are intended to be illustrative of ones to be asked and those that are just now beginning to be asked in the new Men's Studies.

Controversies in Men's Studies

What Perspectives Should Characterize Men's Studies?

A most controversial issue in Men's Studies is what gender related perspective(s) should be taken into account in studying masculinities and male experience. Is it possible for a Men's Studies discipline to endorse feminist arguments such as the one that posits the notion that men's interests actually are advanced by societal social structure? Important are the diverse social and political bases for Women's Studies and Men's Studies. For example, the social and political bases of Women's Studies in America lie quite comfortably within the realm of feminism which stresses teaching women that while they may have been taught to believe their interests are maintained and perpetuated by society, clearly this is not the case. On the other hand, according to the feminist perspective, men's interests *are* constructed and supported by patriarchy—and patriarchy characterizes American society. Men's Studies as a discipline has no analogous political and social bases. Still, this does not mean that there is *no need for Men's Studies*. As Brod suggests, "the claim must rather be not that men's interests are not being advanced by society, but that the sort of men's interests being advanced are interests men would be better off without." As the parent organization of the new Men's Studies suggests, this means assuming a *profeminist* perspective on masculinity and the male experience.

If profeminism, as opposed to feminism, in Men's Studies were the only problem related to perspectives in the area, this controversy could be easily ended. Unfortunately, this is not the case. For some scholars, related controversy relevant for perspectives in Men's Studies centers not on profeminism vs. feminism but on profeminism versus anti-feminism. Profeminists in Men's Studies recognize that women have been oppressed by men; that men have gained privilege from this oppression; that men have reaped numerous disadvantages from patriarchy; and that society as a whole has suffered greatly from sex and gender inequality. On the other hand, scholars who embrace an antifeminist perspective use as a point of departure the beliefs that: (1) women benefit greatly from men's enactments of the traditional male sex role; (2) the consumer-oriented female sex role exploits men; and, (3) the dysfunctional consequences of the male sex role place men at a disadvantage in American society. This is the same potentially explosive controversy challenging the men's movement in America and undoubtedly will require a cautious search for a solution in the years to come.

The Threat to Women's Studies

Is the movement toward gender studies a neoconservative attempt to co-opt Women's Studies by men? In the May/June 1986 issue of the *Men's Studies Newsletter,* published by the National Organization for Changing Men, Sam Femiano, cochair of the Men's Studies task group for the organization, penned his thoughts on Diane Petzke's article ''Men's Studies Catches On at Colleges, Setting Off Controversy and Infighting'' (Feb. 1986). Lamenting Petzke's focus on conflict and controversy within Men's Studies, Femiano suggested that reporters might even be reluctant to write a story on the subject unless it had the same focus as hers. Recounting that two other reporters, Anne Smith of the *Wall Street Journal* and Jane Rosenthal, a free-lance writer, also seemed to have the same focus, Femiano called for Men's Studies task group members ''to be sensitive not to further this type of media attention since it is not accurate regarding our goals and philosophy'' (p. 7).

Femiano's comments are well taken, and I think he is correct to express concern over the focus of publicity. Dwelling only on conflict and controversy directs attention away from critical issues, for example, How are men's lives affected by, and how do they in turn affect, social forms of masculinity? Do various forms of violence and destructive aggression, which damage many people physically and psychologically, relate directly to deliberate and vicarious male-sex-role socialization?

On the other hand, it cannot be denied that many Women's Studies academicians fear cooptation of Women's Studies by men or Men's Studies. However, some of the arguments in opposition to Men's Studies, such as "most college classes are Men's Studies classes" and "only the female sex should be given special attention to correct standard discipline" are unacceptable for reasons earlier stated. Perhaps as more Men's Studies courses are added to college curricula, more students are exposed to Men's Studies courses, and more gender programs follow the lead of the University of Southern California's Program for the Study of Women and Men in Society, it will become apparent that the threat of men coopting Women's Studies is much more imagined than real and certainly not even a latent goal of Men's Studies.

The Dynamics of Sexual Preference in Men's Studies

Within Men's Studies are two issues, sexual preference and race, which have the potential to present problems of monumental proportions. These are two issues which also have confronted Women's Studies. Women's Studies has been relatively successful in meeting the challenges posed by the sexual preference issue but not nearly as successful in meeting the challenges posed by the race issue. This may be due to a variety of reasons which include *less homophobia* among women, since women are less constrained by the homophobia norm than men. On the other hand, because the minority group issue is seen by many minority group women as a delicate one which pits minority women against minority men, Women's Studies' solutions to this issue are yet to be found.

Already the parent organization of Men's Studies, the National Organization for Changing Men (N.O.C.M.), is presented with the same two problems from time to time. For instance, the issue of sexual preference is of paramount concern to N.O.C.M., which describes itself in its Statement of Principles as *gay affirmative* among other characteristics. In fact, the task forces on Gay Rights and the one on Homophobia have had high interest and member participation in the past. From time to time, however, heterosexual men who are attracted to N.O.C.M. decry the organization's pro-gay stance and/or emphasis. As a result, some even question their own position in the organization and others simply drop out of the organization.

Men's Studies, however, stands to benefit from N.O.C.M.'s interest in homophobia as a dysfunctional consequence of male sex role socialization. Because the parent organization of Men's Studies stresses the fact that society teaches men a homophobic orientation for purposes of maintaining male power, male privilege, and male domination (this is discussed in chapter 4), potential challenges to Men's Studies sexual preference positions undoubtedly will be successfully met in a way similar to the way Women's Studies has met the challenges—in a nonhomophobic manner.

A fear that some who are interested in Men's Studies could have is that Men's Studies could become an academic gay male ghetto because it deals both objectively and compassionately with gay issues, among others. The obvious implication is that the discipline will attract numerous gay male academicians. Aside from the irrelevance of such fears, there is no reason to expect this to be the career path of Men's Studies. Men's Studies is devoted to the multifaceted nature of men, including the lives of gay men as men and straight men as men.

The Dynamics of Race in Men's Studies

A potentially perplexing issue for Men's Studies, which may not be as easily solved, is the *integration* of the issues of minority group men and mainstream men. Women's Studies has faced the same issue and has yet to come up with a satisfactory solution. For both Men's and Women's Studies the problem is that an academic discipline is attempting to grow from a social movement or social movement organization in which relatively few minority group people participate. For example, while N.O.C.M. avows to be antiracist, an occurrence at its January 1986 midyear council meeting threatens to push its antiracist stance into the background. A resolution was passed by council members, the guardians of N.O.C.M., to terminate the organization's Task Group on Racism and Sex Roles due to lack of member interest and/or participation. While six other task groups were terminated for the same reasons, the visibility of N.O.C.M.'s antiracist posture may very well be affected. Obviously, lack of interest in racism by N.O.C.M. does not bode well for integrating minority group men into Men's Studies.

Part of the problem is confusion over which academic discipline should have primary responsibility for race issues. Is ''minority group men'' a topic for race relations, ethnic relations, or Men's Studies? It cannot be denied that presently Men's Studies primarily is a white male enterprise. Is it reasonable to think that middle-class white men will want to devote a large portion of Men's Studies to minority group men's issues?

As a case in point, while preparing this chapter I received the following correspondence from a N.O.C.M. member (his racial classification is "white") who was somewhat chagrined about what he perceived as N.O.C.M.'s lack of interest in race. As a response to this, the N.O.C.M. member constructed the following proposal for possible inclusion in N.O.C.M.'s statement of principles:

> We acknowledge that racism, although a problem throughout our society, must be addressed as an issue for men. For men of color, combatting the oppression of racism is an obvious priority. White men have been the greatest perpetrators of and reaped the most benefits from racism throughout history. N.O.C.M. is committed to dismantling the institutions and practices of racism in our society. In this struggle we need be forever vigilant in confronting the racism which carries over from the society at large to our organization. We are also committed to exploring the differences of male experiences of men of diverse racial, ethnic, and national cultures. (Easton 1986)

I believe the point is made. Men's Studies will be faced with such problems, and what will this mean for the emerging discipline? On the other hand, can the discipline retain its legitimacy if it is concerned only with mainstream men's issues? To be sure, this issue will have to be seriously addressed by Men's Studies scholars.

Three Theoretical Perspectives
Used to Study Men and Masculinities

Today, the study of men and masculinities is emerging as an important component of gender studies. While the discipline remains to be well defined, it is beginning to take shape. Major aspects of Men's Studies must be devoted to men's relationship to society, men's relationships with each other, and men's relationships with others. This means that our assumptions about the social order, social interaction, and social behavior are important considerations. Is society orderly and is social change something that disrupts its tranquil nature? Or, in contrast, is society always characterized by conflict because social change occurs only via social conflict? In the same vein, regarding social interaction and social behavior, do persons interact and behave instinctively or as the result of learning? Such issues will be debated for some time to come and cannot be settled in this volume. Nevertheless, as we study men and masculinities, accompanying us will be assumptions and images about the nature of society, social behavior, and social interaction. Three such sets of assumptions are used in this volume. They are the *structural-functional* perspective; the *conflict* perspective; and the *symbolic interaction* perspective. Each is discussed briefly below.

Structural-Functionalism

From a structural-functionalist perspective, the ways men interact with others (other men, women, and children) in American society contribute to the maintenance of American society. This means, for example, that men's aggressiveness, competitiveness, and homophobia (traits commonly associated with American men) all have helped maintain society. Also contributing are men's dominance over women in most areas of society, and male behaviors manifesting toughness, stoicism, violence, and so on. Such patterns of behavior, to follow further the structural-functionalist point of view, must contribute to American society's maintenance because American society has survived for many years during which time American men exhibited these traits. Now this is not to say that all traits exhibited by American men are functional for American society's maintenance. Some appear clearly dysfunctional. Cases in point are the discriminatory behaviors toward women and toward ethnic and racial minority group men exhibited by many white men in powerful positions. There is little doubt that such behaviors (especially within educational, economic, and political institutions) thwart the discovery of potential talent and hinder individual contributions and creativity.

How, then, is it possible to say that powerful white men's discriminatory behaviors, as components of American society, contribute to the maintenance of American society and are therefore functional? This point is possible to make because not only are parts of the system (i.e., relationships among parts and between parts and the whole) the foci of the functionalist perspective, included also are some specifications of the *for whom and/or for what* of social consequences. Men's dominance in American economic and political institutions may be very functional for men (producing power, prestige, esteem) even though it is debilitating and thus dysfunctional for most women (many of whom experience pay inequity, hold low-level jobs, and have little prestige).

Also critical from a functionalist perspective is the distinction between manifest functions and latent functions. Sociologist Robert Merton (1968) defines manifest functions as those that are intended, open, or anticipated, while latent functions are unexpected, unintended, or unanticipated. For example, the fact that husbands' family participation is positively related to husbands' well-being and to family satisfaction may argue well for future enlargement of husbands' family role. Yet, it must be remembered that these are manifest functions of husbands' family role enlargement. Another function of husbands' family role enlargement is less productivity and ambitiousness for men in their paid work, which is costly for men and probably unintended (Pleck 1985).

One of the more appealing things about functionalism for the study of men and masculinities is its emphasis on functional alternatives. Functional alternatives is a concept which recognizes the fact that a particular function can be fulfilled by several structures (Merton 1968, p. 878). Many Americans believe fervently that male youth membership in the Boy Scouts of America, attendance at one of the military academies, and participation in competitive sports (e.g., Little League baseball, football, basketball, soccer) all contribute variously to male youth instruction in masculinity. Such societal agencies are seen as helping young males become ''productive'' men in American society by facilitating their assumptions of societally sanctioned male sex roles. If the assumption of a ''productive'' sex role by a given male youth is based, in part, on internalizing role expectations for self and other males while emphasizing militarism, competitiveness, and aggressiveness, among other attitudes and behaviors, then these agencies undoubtedly are instructive. On the other hand, more and more people in American society have begun to see other structures as possibly contributing to the sex role socialization of young males. Increasingly, socialization structures stressing *less* militarism, *less* competitiveness, and *less* aggressiveness in men and *more* cooperative, *more* sensitive, and *more* nurturing male behaviors are seen as *functional alternative structures*. Such structures include various men's organizations, men's support groups, and male youth auxiliaries where cooperation, nonviolence, and nurturing are seen as appropriate components of the male sex role. As the definition of the male sex role expands, we can expect an increase in the number of functional alternative structures that teach males to be men. In the same vein, as the definition of masculinity broadens, the number of roles men can ''safely'' assume will increase.

Conflict Theory

In contrast to structural-functionalism, the conflict perspective argues that social conflict, social strife, dissent, and the like are normal functions of a society. While there is much diversity of belief among conflict theorists (e.g., Karl Marx, Ralf Dahrendorf, Gerhard Lenski, Lewis Coser, and Randall Collins), they agree that social conflict is normal. Because of the tendency for individuals as groups to husband some resource(s), both material and nonmaterial, clashes between those with abundant amounts and those with little are inevitable. The clashes can occur between individuals, groups, and even societies.

From a gender studies perspective, conflict theory can be related to social interaction between men and men, men and women, and men and children. The relationships are direct and based on the social resource "masculinity," with all its accoutrements. For example, wealth, power, prestige, and influence, together with independence, aggressiveness, competitiveness, and success are seen as accompaniments of male dominance, and social dominance in males *is* masculinity. In fact, social dominance in people generally is defined as masculine (e.g., society defines adult maturity as endorsing masculine qualities). The point here, however, is that much conflict in American society exists because of the struggles between groups of men, between groups of men and groups of women, and between groups of men and children for the unequal resource "masculinity." While "masculinity" as a resource appears on the surface to be ascribed, much of it is socially constructed and achieved. Americans value and give power to those things, social and material, which are possessed in great amounts by some men. Social behavior and interactions become, then, characterized by struggles for desired social resources.

What the above paragraph means is that in American society white males have an edge on societally valued social resources, followed by males of various racial and ethnic groups, followed by women of various racial and ethnic groups. Actually, this is the theme of Margaret Polatnick's (1978) work entitled "Why Men Don't Rear Children." In this article Polatnick step by step shows how males maintain a power advantage over females by not engaging in parenting behavior. When child rearing is defined by men as women's domain, men are freed to achieve, pursue responsible positions, and maintain authority and power. Polatnick states further that men reap the advantages associated with *avoiding* child rearing and do not experience the disadvantages *associated with* child rearing, such as subordinating one's personal goals and putting others ahead of oneself. The conclusion is obvious: *child rearing in our society places one in a powerless position, while avoiding child rearing results in power and prestige.*

Symbolic Interactionism

Something so special goes on in social interaction that it remains uncaptured by those who use perspectives other than symbolic interactionism to examine the process. Most social scientists credit early scholars such as Charles Pierce, William James, John Dewey, James Baldwin, Charles H. Cooley, and most notably George H. Mead with emphasizing the distinctive features of this process. The features include group living and/or negotiations between people; shared meanings (creating and using shared symbols); and the social construction of behavior. From a symbolic interactionist perspective, "society is symbolic interaction in process" (Franklin 1982, p. 84).

It is through the use of symbols and/or shared meaning that we are able to engage in the empathic understanding with others which allows us to have the same experiences. In other words, from a symbolic interaction perspective, the self is reflexive—the individual can become an object unto self. This is done via adopting the positions of others and viewing oneself from these positions. Because such a process makes us distinctively human, it is also the process which makes studying social interaction particularly unique. I do not respond directly to another's act; rather, I respond to my interpretation of another's act. If my interpretation is similar to other interpretations, I can engage in concerted action. Because each of us is capable of responding to our actions from the other's point of view, shared meaning can occur, and new realities can be constructed through the use of symbols and shared meanings.

While the male sex role has existed for decades in the United States, only within the last two decades or so have the realities of misogyny and/or sexist practices emerged. Why? Because what occurs between the sexes has been "constructed," "interpreted," and "shared" as sexist and misogynistic by an increasing number of people. As sociologist Herbert Blumer (1969) said, persons act toward objects on the basis of the meanings objects have for them; the meanings of objects for persons arise out of the social interaction that one has with one's fellows; and these meanings are handled in, and modified through, an interpretative process used by the person in dealing with the things encountered. Vander Zanden (1986, p. 51) believes that this means that "reality does not exist out there in the world but is manufactured by people as they intervene in the world and interpret what is occurring there." Obviously, interpreting the male sex role from a symbolic interaction perspective is somewhat different from an interpretation using structural-functionalism or conflict models because of its emphasis on the special character of social interaction. Nevertheless, in this volume we will integrate knowledge about men from all three perspectives. At the macro level, we will employ both structural-functionalism and conflict approaches in examining men and masculinities while micro-level analyses will frequently draw on symbolic interactions.

Researching Men and Masculinity

How is research best conducted in studying men and masculinity? In order to respond appropriately to this question, it is necessary to recognize theory as the first essential stage in the research process. There is no substitute for theoretical insight, because theory guides the research endeavor. This is just as true for the study of men and masculinity as it is for other studies in the social and natural sciences. We are just beginning to construct theoretical knowledge about men and masculinity that can be subjected to empirical testing. Theoretical works by Joseph Pleck, Robert Brannon, Jack Balswick, Gregory Lehne, Alan Gross, and others are brilliant steps in this direction.

While most social and behavioral scientists will agree that theory is essential in social research, there may be much less agreement about the type of research deemed most appropriate to use in studying men and masculinity. On a general level, research about men involves choosing and conceptualizing a research problem; deciding upon appropriate methodology and the production of data; data analysis; and dissemination of findings and conclusions. Most social research about men also is more acceptable if the standards of objectivity, precision, and disclosure are met, meaning that certain conventional canons of the scientific process are followed.

As the study of men and masculinity has evolved, two general research approaches have been followed: qualitative research and quantitative research. The qualitative research has included personal accounts of aspects of men's lives, such as those in Pleck and Sawyer's (1974) *Men and Masculinity.* An example of quantitative research is Pleck's *Working Wives/Working Husbands* (1985).

Because Men's Studies is an emerging discipline, the debate over the "scientific" appropriateness of qualitative versus quantitative methods has not yet surfaced. It is important to note, however, that debates of this kind have frequently occurred within other disciplines in the social sciences. Within these disciplines—sociology, psychology, anthropology—social research on men is most likely to be conceptualized, formulated, and conducted. Thus, as Men's Studies assumes its place as an academic discipline, a debate over qualitative versus quantitative methods is likely to develop. On the other hand, it is entirely possible that the very nature of the ''new'' study of men and masculinity will mitigate such a debate, since both approaches will be recognized as legitimate. Let us briefly consider the roles of qualitative and quantitative research methods in the study of men and masculinity.

Qualitative Methods

During the early years of Men's Studies, qualitative research methods played crucial roles in the discipline's development, especially in the theoretical realm. Sociologist Herbert Blumer (1969, p. 143) has said that ''theory is of value in empirical science only to the extent to which it connects fruitfully with the empirical world.'' For Blumer, this meant concept clarification: concepts are the only means of establishing such connections because they point directly to empirical instances. Concept clarification also enables one to get a general sense of reference, relevance, and guidance in approaching empirical instances. Raw material may be produced by qualitative methods involving data production and analyses—for example, participant observation, case history examination, and content analysis of letters, diaries, and other historical records. Empirical instances can not only provide conceptual clarity but test existing theoretical formulations and proposals for new theories. The emerging status of Men's Studies dictates the use of qualitative methods that allow *concept formation, concept clarification,* and *concept refinements*—all absolutely essential if the study of men and masculinity is not to remain vague and undefined.

Brian Miller's ''Adult Sexual Resocialization'' (1978), described in greater depth in chapter 6 of this book, is a methodologically qualitative study of married men who have various degrees of sexual and social involvement in the gay world.

Miller's findings were based on two-to-four-hour-long, in-depth, audio-recorded interviews with thirty men who identified themselves as presently homosexual according to sexual scales used and who had been or were heterosexually married. Most of the interviews were held in the respondents' residences. Miller's subjects were part of a larger study on gay fathers, and his semistructured interview technique allowed probing for information concerning the subjects' children and relationships with mates, lovers, gay friends, and straight friends. Whenever possible, detailed interviews were conducted with the men's children, wives, and lovers. Additionally, in-depth details about the men's lives as men were learned via pictures, hobbies, and mementos.

Given the lack of knowledge about gay husbands, Miller's qualitative study provided valuable information about the intimate lives of an aggregate of people not easily visible to the public. The fact that the sample of gay husbands was small and nonrepresentative does not diminish the value of the study. Processes related to adult sexual resocialization were uncovered, and such processes may have universal application. These processes could only have been obtained by means of the qualitative methods used. Thus, Miller's intensive examination of the lives of thirty gay husbands is an excellent example of what some believe is the only valid way of understanding in rich detail processes not easily observable by the social scientist.

Quantitative Methods

Survey research, experimental studies, and secondary analyses, among other methods, frequently use numerical techniques in classifying and analyzing data. As theoretical formulations are constructed, undoubtedly research in the area of men and masculinity will take on a more quantitative flavor. This will occur because of the need to progress from constructing theories to testing them.

Frequently, going beyond theory construction to theory testing involves converting data into some form appropriate to analyses of numbers. When large amounts of data can be manipulated, numerous cases can be used in tests of theoretical formulations. In addition, many feel that quantification enables the researcher to follow more closely the canons of science; it facilitates observation that is systematic in attempting to avoid biases when evaluating hypotheses.

Sociologist Kriss Drass' study, "The Effect of Gender Identity on Conversation" (1986), is a quantitative study of gender differences in conversation. Drass sought to examine the relationship between gender identity and verbal behavior in same-sex interactions. Defining gender identity as the set of meanings persons use to refer to themselves as male or female, Drass hypothesized that gender identity was a better predictor of variation in people's verbal behaviors in conversations than their gender position. In other words, when Zimmerman and West (1975) concluded that in cross-sex interactions males *overlap* (begin speaking a little early or before the final words of a speaker are spoken but yet somewhat appropriate) and *interrupt* (intrude on the speaking rights of another person before there is a possible speaker-turn transition point), further clarification of the roles of sex and gender was needed.

Using a technique developed by Peter Burke and Judy Tully that measures role identity, Drass assessed gender identities of ninety-one college undergraduates. Differences in verbal behavior were assessed by recording and analyzing the conversations of fifteen female dyads and thirteen male dyads.

Hypothesizing that "regardless of a person's gender, the higher his/her gender identity score (that is, the more malelike its meaning), the more likely the person is to overlap and interrupt," Drass' hypothesis was not falsified. Drass found (using t-tests) that the more malelike the person, regardless of sex, the greater the tendency of that person to overlap and interrupt in conversations.

It should not be necessary for those doing research on men and masculinity to choose between qualitative methods and quantitative methods. Both can generally be used for different purposes, with no *one* method assuming a superior role. Presently, however, we do not need to be overly concerned with this issue in Men's Studies, since much qualitative *and* quantitative work remains to be done.

2

Men and Culture

Men in America have a distinctive design for living. The design centers around men constructing ways to survive as individuals and as members of a group. The ways men construct to survive as individuals are much more apparent than their strategies constructed for group survival. For instance, most of us probably are very much aware of the strategies individual men in our lives use to survive (e.g., our fathers, sons, friends, brothers, husbands, lovers, etc.). But, we may not be aware of the fact that men as a group also share strategies for their survival. Such strategies, nevertheless, are developed by men, do exist, and are reflected in society's basic values, ideas, and standards.

Survival of men is a part of the basic ethos of American society. From 1630 to the present, basic American values have favored male survival as a group over female survival as a group. Survival of men emphases have ranged from the *physical* to the *psychological* beginning with what Pleck and Pleck (1980) refer to as the agrarian patriarchal period of men's history (1630–1820). Of this period, Pleck and Pleck write:

> It might be justly claimed that the dominance of husbands over wives and that of fathers over sons were the twin cornerstones of colonial social relations. Fathers wanted sons to bear their name, to help in working the land, and to attend to them in old age. Despite the fact that mothers and older children were expected to care for infants, ministers beamed their advice to fathers, not mothers, in supplying the discipline and education necessary for a son's fa-

ther's direction. . . . In all the colonies, transmission of property defined the rights and obligations between father and son. (Pp. 10–11)

Discussing further the practice of property transmission between fathers and sons, Elizabeth Pleck and Joseph Pleck point out that only very poor white men and male slaves were excluded from the patriarchal system (adult male slaves were not considered men). The authors suggest that approximately 90 percent of white male society participated in the patriarchal system described above. Surely participation in the patriarchal system existed primarily *to insure the survival of sons in order to secure farm labor and caretaking of aged males*.

With physical survival of men basically secured through the transmission of property from father(s) to son(s), early subsistence problems were solved in favor of males. Early survival of men did, however, involve more than finding solutions to subsistence problems. Men also had to construct solutions to problems of group task accomplishment, maintaining order, reproducing new members, and socializing new members.

Today, solutions constructed for societal survival often involve social construction efforts shared by women as well as men. This kind of intersex cultural sharing was not characteristic of early America. Not only were men in charge of all basic societal institutions during the agrarian patriarchial period (e.g., the family and economic, political, religious, and educational institutions), but even the one function over which women seemingly would have had control was decidedly male dominated—reproduction of new members.

It is important to realize that during this early period in American history females were greatly outnumbered by males. As a result, wives were purchased by propertied men and in many instances even female *children* were made brides. It is said that the competition for wives was a fierce one, with women being pawns in games played by men. While men's games with women as pawns are more sophisticated today, they are by no means a cultural item of the distant past, as recent scandals in politics and religion show.

Men, Culture, and Biology

Certain basic biological needs must be met by all men if they are to survive—eating, sleeping, protection from the environment, reproduction, and nurturance of offspring. In infrahumans, innate patterns determine how these needs are to be met. For a given species this means that survival is insured since all members meet these needs in more or less identical ways, because they inherit specific patterns with little variation. For example, some species of birds inherit specific patterns for building nests which protect their young from the environment.

Humans, on the other hand, vary considerably in the behaviors they construct to meet their basic biological needs as well as their secondary social needs. They do so, according to many social scientists, because humans do not inherit constant instinctual patterns of behavior. Human behaviors are highly variable and changeable, both individually and culturally (Tischler, Whitten, and Hunter 1986, p. 66). *Through instincts, infrahumans meet their needs and through culture, humans meet their needs (both biological and social)*. This is especially important when one considers that men frequently are thought to exhibit certain kinds of behavior precisely because they are *men*. "It's just a part of men's nature," "All men act that way because they are just born like that," or some variant statement signifying innate traits in men frequently can be heard as explanations of a specific man's behavior. The perspective taken here, in contrast, assumes that men's behaviors, beliefs, and attitudes are learned. Moreover, while some behaviors, beliefs, and attitudes may seem to be similar among large numbers of men in America, the similarity is a function of cultural norms and sanctions, not innate instincts. Let us consider a rather common trait which can be found in a great many American men—*dominance*. Quite frequently some persons feel this trait is innate in men, but, as is shown below, this trait has a social genesis.

Dominance

Because male dominance is so universal, many people believe that it is an innate male personality trait. A person espousing this point of view is likely to think that it is quite natural for husbands to assume the role of major family decision-maker; for boys in mixed sex play situations to take over playground equipment whenever they want and for girls to submissively leave the playground equipment until the boys no longer want to play (Phillips, 1982); for men to harass women on jobs (MacKinnon, 1979); and even for male college students to interact in aggressive ways with female professors. Male dominance, then, seems ubiquitous. In fact, what Deborah David and Robert Brannon (1976) defined as the dimensions of masculinity in America (and masculinity is always a cultural definition) are direct derivations of male dominance. Not only do some believe that male dominance is innate, but they also believe that Brannon's dimensions of masculinity (''No Sissy Stuff,'' ''The Big Wheel,'' ''The Sturdy Oak,'' and ''Give 'em Hell'') are innate. This will be discussed later, but first let us examine more carefully a central thesis: that *men's dominance and other aspects of ''the way men are'' are not innate in men.*

Jean Stockard and Miriam Johnson (1979) make a convincing psychological argument for the point of view that males' motives for dominating women derive from two major sources: ''the fear and envy hypothesis'' and ''the tenuous masculine identity hypothesis.'' It is important to point out that both hypotheses are based on a gynocentric explanation of male dominance which suggests that men have a psychological need to dominate women. Furthermore, this need is thought to emerge as a direct result of males' early contact with and dependence on females.

The gynocentric explanation also focuses on the ''primacy'' of a feminine orientation in both sexes, noting that ''phallic pride in boys is a secondary manifestation developed as a reaction to and defense against aspects of the mother relationship'' (Stockard and Johnson 1979, p. 200). The phallocentric explanation, as reflected in the work of psychologist Sigmund Freud, focuses on the Oedipal period in child development and ''the child's relation to the father in creating and affirming sexual identity'' (Stockard and Johnson 1979, p. 200). According to the phallocentric perspective, male dominance is a function of the fact that the male penis is superior to the female clitoris.

Because Stockard and Johnson's argument is consistent with a profeminist thought, as is the gynocentric perspective, their contribution— two hypotheses in gynocentric thought—is presented.

The Fear and Envy Hypothesis

Based in large part on the works of scholars such as Ernest Jones (1948; 1957; 1966), Melanie Klein (1960), Karen Horney (1967a; 1967b), and Hoffmann Reynolds Hays (1972), Stockard and Johnson point out that the ''males' fear and envy of women hypothesis'' has been quite apparent in literature focusing on the gynocentric perspective. The position assumes that ''male fear and envy of women derive in one way or another from the fact that women bear children and are the primary caretakers of children'' (p. 204). It is because of this fear and envy, in part, that male dominance is constructed via defining and redefining the male role.

But, male fear and envy of women is only part of the source of male dominance. A second part relates to sex role identities of males.

The Tenuous Masculine Identity Hypothesis

Recognizing the primacy of the feminine orientation for both sexes, the "tenuous masculine identity hypothesis" argues that males have a rather fragile male self-concept because masculinity can be constructed by males only after they separate themselves from femininity, which is derived from their mothers. Stockard and Johnson rely heavily on the work of Stoller, who writes that masculinity is not "a core identity" and that "every male must overcome and resist the excessive merging with the mother that actually happens with the male transsexual" (Stockard and Johnson 1979, p. 206).

From a "tenuous masculine identity hypothesis" perspective, there are other indications that males are challenged in their efforts to develop masculine identities. For example, for some time compulsive masculinity has been said to be one outcome when a male fails to make the shift properly from a feminine identity to a masculine one. Compulsive masculinity is thought to occur especially in males who do not enjoy positive relationships with male role models from whom they learn masculinity. Walter Miller (1958) contends that compulsive masculinity is a response some boys reared in predominantly female homes make (reaction formation) to being surrounded by females. Acts of delinquency and toughness are, for Miller, efforts to prove masculinity and are more prevalent among father-deprived males.

It is when Stockard and Johnson discuss the link between male sex role identity and male dominance that their contribution becomes especially significant for the concern here—male dominance as a socially derived cultural trait. Recognizing Chodorow's (1974) contention that masculinity is defined largely in terms of that which is not feminine or women-involved, Stockard and Johnson also quote Chodorow's notion that the male child learns to deny attachment and deep personal identification with his mother (p. 209). He does so by denigrating and devaluing femininity. In addition, as Chodorow emphasizes, socially the male child "also appropriates to himself and defines as superior" certain social activities and aspects of male culture.

Going a step further, Stockard and Johnson feel that society gives prestige and authority to males, thus providing the most effective and concrete support for masculine identity (p. 209). Not only are men different, but men are better, is what society says. It is these greater rewards, according to the authors, that cause men to construct a male sex role identity which emphasizes separating self from femininity—thus, we have the other part of the picture of the social basis of male dominance. Because male dominance can be discussed not only, as it is here, from a social psychological perspective, but also from a systems perspective, the relationship between male dominance and social institutions is a critical one and deserves mention. Stockard and Johnson also comment on this aspect of social support for male dominance which is covered in a later section.

A discussion in the early 1980s by psychologist Joseph H. Pleck (1981) presents a parallel, through strikingly different, view of the social/cultural construction of masculinity and its traits, such as aggression, dominance, and the like. From Pleck's perspective, not only is it implausible that male dominance is innate, but it is also highly unlikely that male dominance develops from "within" as the preceding arguments would suggest. It is only fair to point out that Stockard and Johnson's discussion of male dominance does emphasize the role of institutional support in the development of male dominance. Still, their overriding concern is with "what causes men to construct a male sex role identity." Does this mean that there is an innate, psychological need in men to develop their sex role identities—elements of male nonmaterial culture? Joseph Pleck thinks not and has critically analyzed what he has termed the "male sex role identity paradigm."

The Male Sex Role Identity (MSRI) paradigm, according to Pleck, is a set of ideas about sex roles, especially the male role, that has dominated the academic social sciences since the 1930s and more generally has shaped our culture's view of the male role (1981, p. 1). Specific features and assumptions of the paradigm include the notions that (1) the fundamental problem of individual psychological development is establishing a sex role identity; (2) sex role identity is the extremely fragile outcome of a highly risky developmental process, especially so for the male; (3) the failure of some men to achieve a masculine sex role identity as reflected by homosexuality is a major societal problem; (4) men's insecurities in their sex role identities result in delinquency, violence, and hostility toward women; and (5) there is an innate psychological need in males to develop a male sex role identity (pp. 3–4).

The MSRI paradigm can be formulated more systematically in eleven propositions, each of which represents a particular line of research on sex roles conducted by social scientists, particularly personality and social psychologists.

1. Sex role identity is operationally defined by measures of psychological sex typing, conceptualized in terms of psychological masculinity and/or feminity dimensions.

2. Sex role identity derives from identification-modeling and, to a lesser extent, reinforcement and cognitive learning of sex-typed traits, especially among males.

3. The development of appropriate sex role identity is a risky, failure prone process, especially for males.

4. Homosexuality reflects a disturbance of sex role identity.

5. Appropriate sex role identity is necessary for good psychological adjustment because of an inner psychological need for it.

6. Hypermasculinity in males (exaggerated masculinity, often with negative social consequences) indicates insecurity in their sex role identities.

7. Problems of sex role identity account for men's negative attitudes and behaviors toward women.

8. Problems of sex role identity account for boys' difficulties in school performance and adjustment.

9. Black males are particularly vulnerable to sex role identity problems.

10. Male adolescent initiation rites are a response to problems of sex role identity.

11. Historical changes in the character of work and the organization of the family have made it more difficult for men to develop and maintain their sex role identities. (Pleck 1981, p. 9)

Rejecting critically the basic tenets of the MSRI paradigm, Pleck sets forth an alternative paradigm he calls the Sex Role Strain paradigm. An underlying assumption of the SRS paradigm is that there is not an innate pyschological need for sex-typed traits in males; rather, social approval and situational adaptation often result in males' exhibitions of sex-typed traits. Because of sex roles, individuals are socialized to have personality characteristics that are dysfunctional; for men this means aggression and constriction (pp. 134–35). The Sex Role Strain paradigm propositions constructed by Pleck (1981) are as follows:

1. Sex roles are operationally defined by sex role stereotypes and norms.

2. Sex roles are contradictory and inconsistent.

3. The proportion of individuals who violate sex roles is high.

4. Violating sex roles leads to social condemnation.

5. Violating sex roles leads to negative psychological consequences.

6. Actual or imagined violation of sex roles leads individuals to overconform to them.

7. Violating sex roles has more severe consequences for males than females.

8. Certain characteristics prescribed by sex roles are psychologically dysfunctional.

9. Each sex experiences sex role strain in its paid work and family roles.

10. Historical change causes sex role strain. (P. 9)

Ethnocentrism, Sexism, and Sex Role Relativism

It may be difficult for some people to believe that men as a social group are being viewed in this volume as having a culture—a way of seeing things, of doing things, of making things—in short, a design for living. Now this does not mean that all men do things exactly alike. It does mean, however, that within certain boundaries, most men in America do many things in strikingly similar ways despite variations in income, race, ethnicity, political beliefs, educational levels, and so on. American men's penchants for violence, competitive sports, high status, viewing women as sex objects, and self-reliance, coupled with their disdain for identifying self with anything vaguely feminine, indicating physical or mental weaknesses, and passivity all are examples of perceptions, attitudes, and the like shared by most men in America.

Recognizing that some men in America vary from the above, I still believe that most American men probably would experience cultural shock if suddenly they were placed in an environment which did not support the above mentioned penchants and disdains.

Speaking of cultural shock, most women probably would have that experience if they could spend some time unobtrusively in a men's barbershop, a men's sports locker room, an adult bookstore (most adult bookstores have clientele that is primarily male), and, of course, any number of bars, clubs, lounges, and other facilities catering to men. In these men's environments, entirely different behaviors, roles, norms, and values exist; in short, the fact that the woman has entered a new culture quickly becomes apparent to her.

Important to mention here is the fact that not only do men *expect to find* such behaviors, roles, and values in their environments, but they *like* having them as parts of their environments. For many men, male social- ization has taught them that these aspects of their environments are not only appropriate but are much better than other "wimpy" or "sissified" ones which stress things like cooperation, sensitivity, helping behavior, and so on. It is not necessarily coincidental that frequently women's envi- ronments consist of just such characteristics.

Sidney Jourard's "Some Lethal Aspects of the Male Role" (1969) points out numerous decidedly deadly and personally dysfunctional con- sequences men experience when they embrace the traditional male sex role in America. When such a role is uncritically accepted and internal- ized by men to the exclusion of those behaviors more beneficial to them, negative results for men occur; Jourard states:

> Men die sooner than women, and so health scientists and public health officials have become justly concerned about the sex differ- ence in death age. Biology provides no convincing evidence to prove that female organisms are intrinsically more durable than males, or that tissues or cells taken from males are less viable than those taken from females. A promising place to look for an expla- nation of the perplexing sex-differential in mortality is the transac- tion between men and their environments, especially their inter- personal environments. In principle, there must be ways of behaving among people which prolong a man's life and insure his fuller functioning, and ways of behaving which speed a man's progress toward death. (P. 21)

For men to experience these unfortunate consequences because they come to believe that their ways of doing things are the only right and good ways and for them to judge others by those yardsticks reflect "gender ethnocentrism" at its worst. The point has even greater significance given the number of men who extend aspects of their gender (masculin- ity) in competitive, violent, and aggressive ways that hurt others as well as themselves.

Jourard's revealing account of how men hurt themselves and others by clinging to their gender enthoncentric views long after their useful- ness is over is instructive here. Commenting on how men achieve mean- ing and value in life, Jourard implies that aging presents problems for many men precisely because of their gender ethnocentric view that mean- ing and value in life can be achieved only via gainful employment, social status, and sexual potency. Women, Jourard says, continue to find mean-

ing in life and reasons for living long after men feel useless and un-
needed.

It seems clear that the male role provides many opportunities
for dispiritation to arise. The best example is provided by the data
on aging. It is a well-documented observation that men in our society, following retirement, will frequently disintegrate and die not
long after they assume their new life of leisure. It would appear that
masculine identity and self-esteem—factors in inspiration for
men—are predicated on a narrow base. If men can see themselves
as manly, and life as worthwhile, only so long as they are engaged
in gainful employ, or are sexually potent, or have enviable social
status, then clearly these are tenuous bases upon which to ground
one's existence.

Thus, if man's sense of masculine identity, as presently culturally defined, is a condition for continued existence and if this is
easily undermined by vicissitudes of aging or the vicissitudes of a
changing social system, then indeed, the male role has an added
lethal component. (Pp. 27–28)

While Jourard makes no such explicit claim, I suggest that many
men's senses of masculine identity involve ethnocentric views of how
meaning and value in life are achieved and maintained. When these men
are no longer physically able to exhibit behaviors which support their
rigid masculine identities, instead of altering and/or modifying their
views, they stubbornly hold on to them. The result is predictable—they
become dispirited and fall victim to some infectious disease, heart failure, or other malady.

Gender ethnocentrism can surely lead to the above negative consequences for males, alone and in social interaction with others, such as
family violence, dysfunctionally aggressive behavior toward extrafamil-
ial persons, and unnecessary competitiveness. But perhaps one of the
most societally dysfunctional consequences is *sexism. Gender ethnocentrism directly leads to sexism.*

John Brigham (1986, p. 319) defines sexism as "any attitude,
action, or institutional structure that subordinates a person because of his
or her sex." He states further that sexism is caused by cultural, historical, and economic factors. Agreeing with Blumberg (1977), Brigham
feels that this can include the way that a society divides its tasks, which is
dependent upon (1) the type of society involved, (2) the labor supply
available, and (3) the congruence between needed tasks and childbearing. Describing *hunting and gathering societies* as those where women

enjoy relatively *high status* because often they gather food and *horticultural societies* as *egalitarian* because of congruence between hoe cultivation and child care, Brigham goes on to expand his "causes of sexism thesis." Borrowing further from Kolata (1974), Brigham notes that *agricultural societies* involve land ownership and animal domestication; property must be defended and inherited. Brigham points out that men tend to dominate the division of labor in most agrarian societies and that plow activities generally are not compatible with child care. In such societies, Brigham concludes, women's status is *low* because of male concerns with division of labor and inheritance (p. 321). Obviously, Brigham's argument here is woefully inadequate! It is doubtful if sexism in agricultural societies is in part due to *male concerns with inheritance and the division of labor*. That women in these societies are not involved in deciding the division of labor and inheritance exemplifies exclusionary sexist practices which favor men.

Finally, Brigham notes, the emergence of an industrial society beginning in the nineteenth century led to a further decline in the status of women in America. He believes, like Basow (1980), that industrialized society's low view of women's productivity may be a carryover from its agrarian heritage.

It should be obvious to most people that the causes of sexism are numerous and complex, involving sex-role socialization, political power, aspects of men's culture, and so on. No explanation of sexism which involves a simplistic description of societal types is appropriate for a phenomenon which has widespread consequences for both its victims and its perpetrators. While Brigham's definition of sexism is quite appropriate for our purposes here, his account of its causes is not acceptable. Reasons for its unacceptability should become apparent in the following chapters. Nevertheless, the relationship between gender ethnocentrism and sexism should be fairly explicit at this point. Manifestations of this relationship are reflected throughout society. One specific manifestation to be dealt with in a later section is sexism in language. For example, language used to describe women's social interaction is permeated with both gender ethnocentrism and sexism. Lastly, while sexism can be directed toward persons of either sex, personal and group directed sexism in America appears to be toward females.

That sex roles in the United States are in states of transition and that this is perceived as highly desirable by many persons make objective observations and/or understanding of the male sex role difficult. Yet, there is a great deal of merit in approaching the male sex role from a gender relativism perspective. Such a perspective is qualitatively different from the somewhat masculinist perspective taken by Goldberg (1976; 1979; 1983), or the feminist perspective of James Doyle's *The Male Experience* (1983), or even my own profeminist perspective in *The Changing Definition of Masculinity* (1984). The gender relativism perspective requires that the male sex role is approached from a point of view that explores (1) why the role exists, (2) how it is maintained, and (3) what purposes it serves men—all as seen from the male point of view. Initially, this means that no judgments are made regarding the "goodness" or "badness" of aspects of the male role. Rather, the objective of male sex role analyses is to understand how men construct social patterns which enable them to survive as men, however unappealing these social patterns may be to feminist-oriented persons (Hess, Markson, and Stein 1985, p. 67).

Gender relativism in academic writing, which embodies all of the above features, may be more informative for persons interested in sex-role equality than even feminist or profeminist approaches. I contend that this is so because the former can serve to draw sharp lines of demarcation between myths and facts about the male sex role. Once such distinctions are made, overgeneralizations and inaccurate generalizations can be minimized. This would allow those interested in sex-role equality to pinpoint more precisely those aspects of male sex-role construction which are inimical to males' functioning on a sex-role equality level. An example of a gender relativism approach to the male sex role is presented below.

Carole Tavris, in an article for *Cosmopolitan* (1986, pp. 229–31) examined ten generalizations commonly made about the male sex role and concluded that nine were "myths" and one was "truth." They are:

1. Men are not romantic. [myth]
2. Men are more independent than women. [myth]
3. Men handle being rejected better than women. [myth]
4. Men are sexual predators. [myth]
5. Men are always ready for sex. [myth]
6. Men don't have close friends. [myth]
7. Marriage is for women, not men. [myth]
8. Men are more assertive than women. [myth]
9. Men don't feel emotions as strongly as women do. [myth]
10. Men and women do speak two different emotional languages. [truth]

Tavris' construction of myths about men is based on selected findings from psychotherapists, health scientists, and social scientists like Carin Rubenstein, Phillip Shaver, Zick Rubin, George Goethals, Jessie Bernard, Sharon Brehm, Susie Orbach, and Louise Eichenbaum and her own research published in *Anger: The Misunderstood Emotion* (1986). In some ways Tavris' myths may constitute a construction of myths quite similar to the ones she "debunks" by documenting selective findings from the aforementioned scholars. Yet, Tavris' perspective in this construction is congruent with gender relativism. For example, she states, "Just because male friendships aren't like female friendships certainly does not mean that most men don't have close friends or that their friendships aren't as good as those between women (if it works for them?)" and men "may not talk about their hurt, but silence does not signify lack of feeling. Quite the contrary, evidence suggests that their grief may run deeper and be harder to repair than women's" (p. 30). It would seem that discovering subtle and not so subtle differences between men and women on certain social attributes would be far more effective in the determination of pathways to sex-role equality than reliance on worn and archaic stereotypes which may actually impede such a determination. The one truth that Tavris found speaks definitively to this issue: men and women speak two different emotional languages. I will add to this that a *gender relativism perspective* is necessary to understand the emotional language men speak and women speak.

Components of Men's Culture

A basic theme in this chapter is that men in America share values, meanings, and material items—in essence, a culture, a separate world. This culture may be remnants from an earlier period of society in America referred to by Elizabeth Pleck and Joseph Pleck (1980) as the "Strenuous Life Period" (1861–1919). This time, which is discussed in greater detail in the next chapter, is described as one characterized by a separate flourishing men's world of men's clubs, saloons, cults of body building, and the like. Pleck and Pleck state: "The form and content of this men's separate world varied between social groups, but flourished everywhere in male-only institutions, which made these years the heyday of men's public culture" (p. 28).

Today, laws exist to prevent the establishment of male-only institutions and organizations. Yet, few can quarrel with the fact that sex segregation remains a prominent feature of American life. I contend that the result is a separate men's culture with both nonmaterial and material aspects. Moreover, men's culture is maintained and supported by society as a whole—men, women, and children. Let us consider, first of all, symbols, meanings, values, norms, and sanctions as elements of men's nonmaterial culture.

Symbols

David Popenoe (1986, p. 55) writes that culture depends on people's ability to create and use symbols, which are any items that meaningfully represent something else. A circle with an arrow stands for a human with a penis (♂); a circle with a cross represents a human with a vagina (♀). So do the words *male* and *female*, respectively. By using drawings, words, numbers, gestures, and the like, we make sense of our worlds, communicate with each other, and store knowledge.

There is some debate over the arbitrariness of symbols. Popenoe (p. 55) contends that symbols often resemble the ideas they represent and implies that some symbols have *not* been chosen arbitrarily. Tischler, Whitten, and Hunter (1986, pp. 81–82), in contrast, state that symbols unlike signs, need *not* share any quality at all with what they represent; they are entirely arbitrary. It is the latter conceptualization of symbols that is used in this chapter, along with the understanding that men's symbols (1) affect men's perceptions, (2) are separate from the things they symbolize in socially significant ways, (3) predefine things, and (4) shape men's culture.

The color blue, for example, symbolizes "appropriate" coloring of clothing for infant males. Certainly, it is difficult to form perceptions of very young infants, yet clothing cues us to the kinds of behaviors many persons deem appropriate to direct toward infant males. For example, following genital inspection, newborn males are described by physicians and nurses as robust and strapping, while newborn females are seen as petite and adorable (Doyle 1983, p. 91). Parents' descriptions of newborn infants differ by sex. Daughters are seen as softer, prettier, more delicate, and smaller, while sons are thought to be more alert, stronger, more coordinated, and firmer. Actually, male and female infants, in a study conducted by Rubin, Provenzano, and Luria (1976), did not differ appreciably in weight, height, and Apgar scores, including ratings of color, reflex irritability, muscle tonicity, etc. If the color of clothing signifies to us that an infant is male or female, undoubtedly our perceptions of him/her will be affected, as will the behaviors we direct toward the little male or female. Later, the initial color distinction will mesh with other symbolic differences for the male sex to form a part of men's nonmaterial culture.

Language

An assumption underlying this chapter and, in fact, the entire volume is that young males gradually become men by coming to share ideas, meanings, values, and norms considered appropriate for men in society. Since time began and in all cultures, the chief vehicle by which young boys have come to share masculinity is through the shared symbol system of men's language. Before discussing men's language specifically, let us consider the gender issue in language in America generally. This is important because men's language is not entirely separate from the general culture's basic language. Stockard and Johnson (1979) believe that in most societies, language embodies male dominance. Certainly, our society is no different. They write: "What is male in a language is generally basic; what is female is usually subsidiary and/or deprecated . . . the language that males use is always seen as the language of the society; the female version is called 'women's' language" (p. 5).

Examples of a portion of what Stockard and Johnson are referring to include basic concepts in American language, such as the word *mankind* used to refer to "humanity," common sayings like "that's women's work" as opposed to "that's men's work," and the use of the pronoun *he* when the sex of the person is unspecified (Eitzen 1986, p. 252).

In addition to our culture's language having a definite general male orientation, men as a group create and use esoteric systems of shared symbols which may not be completely understood by women. Often such systems of symbols are created within the confines of men's culture in places like men's clubs, men's and boy's locker rooms, men's bars, men's stores and barbershops. Much of the language created, like the language of the larger society, devalues women and expresses dominance over them. Unlike the language of the larger society, however, men's language is more likely to denigrate women, support sexual exploitation of women, and encourage violence toward them.

That young boys are instructed in men's language quickly becomes apparent when one visits sports locker rooms, boy's camps, barbershops, and the like. Boys who do not wish to be aggressive, daring, or brave in such settings may be referred to as "wimps," "girls," "sissies," or "women." Implicit in these labels is the idea that femininity is an undesirable quality. Barrie Thorne's findings suggesting that boys on a school playground who are referred to as "sissies" suffer low status, while girls who are referred to as "tomboys" actually experience an increase in social status, provides support for the early devaluing of femininity by young members of society—especially young males.

It really is no wonder that young males learn to devalue and denigrate women and femininity. There is more than ample opportunity available for boys to learn sex-role stereotypes, homophobic values, and the denigration/devaluation of women. A relatively recent study of a Black male urban barbershop is a case in point and revealed the following:

> (1) Approximately three-fourths of the conversations were devoted to sex roles (e.g., attitudes toward househusbands, working mothers, fathering, the nature of homophobia); (2) adult male customers pay lip service to sex-role equality (numerous men made the comment or a variant that "women should receive pay equal to men for the same work, but you know women can't do men's work like men"); and (3) stereotypes about males and females were perpetuated in barbershop conversations (e.g., "by nature" a man is polygamous, or "a woman always takes care of her child"). . . .
>
> Women in Bob's barbershop frequently are referred to as "bitches," "whores," "hammers," "cunts," and the like. . . .
>
> If the sexual epithets are not enough to teach young males "manly" attitudes toward women, language used in Bob's barbershop to describe sexual encounters certainly picks up the slack. Stockard and Johnson (1980) have observed that "many slang words used to describe sexual intercourse also connote dominance and aggression. To get "fucked," "screwed," "reamed," or "had" implies that one has been victimized. (Franklin 1985, pp. 972–74)

Men's language in the United States is replete with sexist epithets, and if the Edward Sapir and Benjamin Whorf thesis is correct when it hypothesizes that *language structures perception*, then our view of women is appalling. Consider the idea that "bitch," "whore," "cunt," and "slut" are a part of the screen through which men (women and children also can be included) *see, interpret,* and *understand* women. Is there any wonder why women and the closely associated gender, femininity, are assigned low status in American society? Sapir (1949) writes:

> Human beings do not live in an objective world alone . . . but are very much at the mercy of the particular language which has become a medium of expression for their society. The "real

world'' is to a large extent unconsciously built up on the language habits of the group. No two languages are ever sufficiently similar to be considered as representing the same social reality. The worlds in which different societies live are distinct worlds, not merely the same world with different labels attached. (P. 162)

Values

Values are defined generally as shared assumptions about what is right and wrong in a society. They do not tell us explicitly which behaviors are appropriate and which ones are not appropriate. Values do, however, "provide us with criteria and conceptions by which we evaluate people, objects, and events as to their relative worth, merit, beauty, or morality" (Vander Zanden 1986, p. 31).

In America, main values and value configurations are reflected in books, magazines, art, movies, folklore, and numerous other media. Values also are highly interrelated and often emotionally charged. Perhaps it is this last quality which accounts for the great difficulty faced when attempts are made to alter values. After all, most people's individual values are derived in part from general cultural values and are used to justify their own behavior. Men's values are cases in point.

While men in America are quite diverse, radical feminists may have a point when they minimize the tendency to draw vast distinctions between men in America—e.g., poor white men, Hispanic men, Black men, middle-class white men, Native American men. Generally, values in American culture favor men, and these values are passed on through the culture's symbol system from adults to children and from adult to adult (Popenoe 1986, p. 57). Men, especially, are likely to deeply internalize these values, especially those which allow them to evaluate the appropriateness and inappropriateness of their own behavior. Komarovsky (1973) and Deutsch and Gilbert (1976) have alluded to the concern which males often express over the appropriateness of their behavior from a masculinity perspective. Many males seem to feel that they do not quite live up to some nebulous masculine ideal. One reason for this may be that the male sex role is a complex one to fulfill. It is fraught with contradictions which often lead to debilitating sex-role strain for American men. While some changes in American conceptions of masculinity have occurred in recent years, many of the stereotypic male-valued traits cited by Rosenberg nearly two decades ago remain ones highly endorsed by society for males. Traits such as aggressiveness, competitiveness, independence, logical thinking, decisiveness, violence, worldliness, stoicism, self-confidence, ambitiousness, and dominance, among others, form a value system internalized by males and by others which guide males' thinking and behaviors with self and with others.

John E. Williams et al. (1982) in a cross-cultural study of gender stereotypes among university students in twenty-five countries, found that, aside from minor variations between countries, there was general similarity in cultural sex trait characteristics across countries. Williams et al. conclude that the cross-cultural agreement on gender stereotypes stems from the interaction of biological factors, social functions, and sex-role ascription expectations and justifications. Because of biological differences between men and women, societies found it socially efficient to assign women domestic duties and men duties external to the home. Once differential sex roles were made, men and women were empowered with differential "natural" traits, such as, men are innately more "active," "autocratic," and "daring," while women are more "affected," "affectionate," and "mild." The establishment of these beliefs has been tantamount to the development of an international value system which favors men. What we think of as stereotypes associated with masculinity have been the central principles of men's culture in America (and, obviously, elsewhere). These principles, in turn, constitute an evaluative standard for men's folkways and men's mores. Those values associated with men and those associated with women are shown in table 2.1.

Norms

For some time now there has been some debate over whether the male sex role is more restrictive than the female sex role. Seyfriend and Hendrick (1973) and Feinman (1974) contend that men experience greater negative sanctions than women do when they violate sex-role norms. The literature on gay men and women also would tend to support the greater restrictiveness of the male sex role. Yet, a great proportion of violence men direct toward women stems from the perpetrator's perception of the woman as being "out of place," "not submissive enough," "too aggressive," or "too competitive." Regardless of which sex role is more restrictive or the quality of the restrictiveness, in the United States there are rules of conduct for men which specify acceptable behaviors (prescriptions) and those which specify unacceptable behaviors (proscriptions). Moreover, some of the rules of behavior are more important than others. Let us consider social norms for men according to a rather common classification scheme: folkways, mores, and laws.

Table 2.1
Core Values Underlying the Beliefs and Behaviors
of Men and Women in America

Values Associated with Men*	Values Associated with Women*
active	affected
adventurous	affectionate
aggressive	anxious
autocratic	attractive
coarse	complaining
courageous	curious
daring	dependent
dominant	dreamy
enterprising	emotional
forceful	fearful
independent	feminine
inventive	gentle
masculine	mild
progressive	prudish
robust	self-pitying
rude	sensitive
severe	sentimental
stern	sexy
strong	soft-hearted
tough	submissive
	superstitious
	weak
	whiny

* In 23 or more of the 25 countries.
Source: Adapted from J. E. Williams, *Adult Sex Stereotypes*.

Folkways. How American men behave in ordinary day-to-day activities is governed generally by customary ''ways of doing things'' passed from one generation of men to another. As a rule, these ''ways of doing things'' relate to men's behaviors that are not essential for the survival of society or for the survival of men as a group. Neither society nor men as a group is threatened if a man does needlework on a public park bench while watching his baby play in a baby carriage. Just as nonthreatening to society and men as a group are folkway violations which occur when avant garde men in East and West Coast cities wear long dresses and carry purses on city streets during daylight hours. While individual violators generally are not punished severely, there may be some informal reaction to folkway violations. Our man on the public park bench is sure to cause a few raised eyebrows, and, our men in dresses are likely to evoke comments, laughter, and even ridicule, all signaling to the men that they are not following folkways for men closely enough.

Presently, folkways for American men are undergoing transition. It is frequently said that the informal rules for men's behaviors are unclear or at best confusing. One even hears political figures, religious leaders, and others in the public eye lamenting the blurring of sex-role distinctions in society. Occasionally, efforts are made to attach moral significance to men's folkways. This has been apparent especially since the early 1980s with the resurgence of political and social conservatism. Despite some rather concerted efforts, few have been successful. The primary reason is because many of the folkway violations have accompanied societal movement, however slight, toward sex-role equality. Thus, while many of the folkways for men that are in transition reflect some involvement with societal values for men, many of the folkway violations reflect a growing societal valuation of sex-role equality as a norm. Obviously, the growth is not rapid enough.

Mores. Of much greater significance for men's behavior are those norms that are considered essential for society's survival and for men's survival as a group. These are norms that are strictly enforced, and while some violators may be negatively sanctioned informally, the sanctions are still powerful because they have the full force of the community. Hess, Markson, and Stein (1985) state the following about mores:

> Those who violate the mores are therefore subject to stronger sanctions than those who fail to observe the folkways. Whereas folkways depend on people's willingness to follow custom, mores are stricter standards. Group reaction such as scorn and isolation replace the more personal reactions to violators of folkways. (P. 72)

Mores also tend to be more closely tied to values in the sense that mores generally reflect values—the basic beliefs of a society or culture. There are numerous specific mores related to the American man's role in society, a role which is demanding, complex, and not very specific. The generality of the role results in numerous variations of "men" in America—all of whom fulfill some "minimum demands of the role" (Brannon 1976, p. 11). Variables including age, class, ethnicity, race, physique, and personal talent all contribute to the diversity of men in America and to heterogeneity within men's cultures. Despite the permutations, however, Brannon feels, and I agree, that "there are a small number of basic themes which pervade and ultimately define the male role" (Brannon 1976, p. 12). Actually, these "dimensions of the male role" can be thought of as prescriptions and proscriptions for males that society deems critical for its survival and men deem essential for the survival of men as a group.

Generally, men are expected to establish sufficient distance from femininity. The distance is necessary to avoid the stigma of the stereotyped feminine characteristics and qualities. Since the early 1970s, some redefining of characteristics and qualities associated "solely with femininity" has occurred. Increased sensitivity, self-disclosure, and expressiveness often are allowed for some men in some situations, especially after they have established firmly their masculinity. The sports figure who cries after a losing effort in a close game, a powerful male society leader who sheds a tear when commenting on a national tragedy, and a television evangelist who begs forgiveness for his "sins" are examples of males who may be allowed a bit of expressiveness if they have secured their "masculinity" earlier by establishing sufficient distance from femininity.

Men also are expected to attain power, prestige, high status—in sum, *success*. Those who do not become successful by societal standards or by some subgroup's standards can expect to receive the scorn of society or of members of their subgroups. Violating this mos (singular form of *mores*) affects not only an individual male but also those with whom he is close, for example, wife, children, siblings, parents, etc. Aside from assaults on a man's self-concept, failure to succeed results in men and those close to them experiencing numerous kinds of subsistence deprivation, including poor health care, inadequate or no food, substandard or no housing, and the like. To be sure, this is frequently society's response to a man not behaving as he "ought to."

Men in America are also supposed to be "tough," "confident," and behave in a self-reliant manner. Violations of the constellation of behaviors surrounding these mores can contribute to a man's violation of the success ethic for men; and it also can result in a loss of status or prestige apart from success. A critical ingredient for a president of the United States seems to be that the candidate should be male, white, *tough*, confident, and self-reliant. (No one should run the country but him. God forbid that his wife, who may be expertly qualified, should help him make decisions!)

Perhaps in order to be tough, confident, and self-reliant, another set of prescriptions for men says that men should behave aggressively, violently, and in a daring manner. Despite all of the public discussion about how changes in men are desirable and about how men have changed, it is interesting to note that not only have drastic increases in male violence occurred in society within the past decade, but seemingly it has been supported, if not condoned. Vigilante killings, vigilante movies, federal aggression, ''Rambo-like'' tactics indicate that Brannon's ''Give 'em Hell'' prescription for American men is alive and well as we move forward into the late 1980s and 1990s.

Gradually women have made inroads into some domains of men. What will this mean? Will women, in addition to affecting more significantly general American culture, have a greater effect on men's culture? Will men's culture simply cease to exist as sex-role distinctions decline? Will, in effect, a new sex-integrated culture emerge, stressing sex-role equality to such an extent that sex stratification becomes antiquated? If so, then the real basis of men's culture in America will no longer exist. Given the often disastrous results for society, a decline or change in male culture may be desirable.

Laws. In general, norms that have been enacted by federal, state, and local governments to regulate human behavior apply not only to men but all persons within the society. Occasionally, however, there are exceptions, that is, laws which apply only or primarily to men. An example would be the selective service law which requires eighteen-year-old males to register for possible duty in the nation's armed services should the need arise. Also applying primarily to men are child support regulations which require men to pay child support to mothers when they do not reside in the home with mother and child(ren).

It can be said that on an even broader level many other laws regulate primarily the human conduct of men, since women constitute such a small minority of the violators. Spouse abuse, spouse rape, and non-spousal rape are examples of such violations. Many persons probably would argue that it is precisely because of the sex specificity of such laws that they have proven to be so difficult to enforce. Only recently have rape laws become adequately enforced in many areas of the country. One glaring exception has been when the accused was Black and the victim, white. All other combinations of perpetrator-victim rape historically have been, and many would say still are, handled less than adequately.

Because men regulate women's and children's conduct, there is little need for laws to regulate the behavior of women and children. Therefore, it is axiomatic that most laws really exist to regulate the behavior of men. In fact, this may be quite logically linked to the state of the judicial system in America today. Basically, in America, men make the laws, men break the laws, and men sidestep the laws—it is all a part of men's culture. This idea is expanded in the chapters to follow. Let us conclude with a discussion of men's culture and changing American values.

Changing American Values

Traditional American values stressing personal achievement, work, moral concern, humanitarianism, efficiency, progress, material advancement, freedom, and patriotism surely have always been linked intimately with values related to masculinity. Many aspects of Brannon's prescriptions and proscriptions for men discussed earlier are strikingly similar to the traditional American values listed above. This is to be expected, since men historically have been in charge of society's basic institutions responsible for maintaining both the nonmaterial and material culture. But, American values for some time now have been in states of conflict and change. Both Daniel Bell (1976) and Christopher Lasch (1979) have spoken speculatively about conflict and change in societal values. Very broad trends point to conflicts between older capitalistic values, such as frugality, thrift, achievement, and hard work, and personal pleasures, expressiveness, self-fulfillment, and the like. Simultaneously men as a group have been exhorted by sociologists, psychologists, historians, activists, and others to pursue life styles which can bring greater personal fulfillment, emotional expressiveness, and satisfaction (often referred to as a greater development of feminine aspects of self). It is not coincidental that many of the changes proposed for men in society also are touted as needed changes in societal values (Yankelovich 1981). Quests for self-fulfillment, emotional expressiveness, and personal pleasures can be legitimate values for men to pursue only if they are seen as legitimate values for all members of society to pursue.

Despite frequent calls for changes in American values that would promote increased gains for women and support and respect for the civil rights (and, therefore, humanity) of all people, cultural hegemony remains a prominent feature of American society. Men in powerful positions still create and enforce rules of conduct often inimical to the lives of women, children, other men, and themselves. The 1980s, for example, has brought with it much opposition to the ideals of the 1960s. Hess et al.

(1988) allude to the strong public support for the military and increasing opposition to the rights of women, gays, and minorities. They conclude that there is a value split in our society that reflects a basic dualism in the culture. Which values will dominate in the decades to come, according to Hess et al., depend on the choices of the younger generation today.

3

Social Structure

Chapter 2 argues that a men's culture exists within the United States. Such a culture is supported by norms, statuses, roles, interaction, and groups in American society. In other words, the nature of America's social structure facilitates the development and maintenance of a men's culture. The ways that various parts of society are structured and interrelated influence men's everyday behavior. For example, an individual man who displays aggressive and competitive behavior does so not simply because he is "that type of person" or has "that type of personality." He does so, in part, because of his position within the social structure, a position which may be determined by race, sex, ethnicity, family background, and the like. In short, the society's social structure influences the individual man's behavior.

Social structure, Hess, Markson and Stein (1988, p. 76) have said, describes "the ordering of everyday behavior and social relationships in a relatively predictable way." It is no accident that men assume dominant positions in all of society's basic institutions on both a macro-system level and a micro-system level. Indeed, organization, consistency, and stability are the purposes of social structure. As Vander Zanden (1986) notes, "social structure gives us the feeling that life is characterized by organization and stability" (p. 40). Certainly, it is unfair to women that American society has been formed or shaped in a sexist manner from this country's inception, but it is a social fact that this sexist social structure exists external to individual men themselves. This does not mean that individual men who engage in sexist behavior are to be held blameless.

52

They are not, and should be taken to task on appropriate occasions. At the same time, it is also necessary to recognize those components of the social structure which may be constraining men's behavior and fostering their sexist actions.

Recognition of the social ordering constraining men's behaviors does not mean support for male sexist behavior nor does it mean that sexism is an inevitable feature of American society. Certainly, America's present-day social structure favors male privilege. However, this does not mean that the social structure is a fixed entity. As Vander Zanden points out, the social structure has to be "continually created and re-created through the interweaving and stabilizing of social relationships" (1986, p. 40). In America, male privilege and dominance have been created and re-created through numerous epochs and/or periods as described by Elizabeth Pleck and Joseph Pleck (1980).

The social structure that has evolved in our society can give us a glimpse of the way men's behaviors are patterned. It is obvious that the patterning of men's behavior is based on male dominance and this is reflected throughout the social structure (e.g., the family institution, the economic system, the polity, the educational system, the religious and belief system). In order to understand a group of men's behaviors, it is necessary to go beyond men's unique individual characteristics. One has to refer to male dominance qualities of America's social structure rather than individual men's sexist qualities. Referring to social structure in this manner means elaborating on what is really a complicated set of relationships specifying how men are affected by types of patterned interaction. Benokraitis and Feagin's (1986) discussion of organizational, institutional, and cultural discrimination speaks precisely to this point. Going beyond individual discrimination, which is unequal behavior on a one-to-one basis, Benokraitis and Feagin state:

> At level two—organizational discrimination—the unequal behavior occurs because of practices, rules and policies that are different for each sex. For example, women's athletics programs have very low budgets and few resources, while men's athletics programs garner budgets, facilities and support.
>
> At level three—institutional discrimination—the unequal behavior is established and deeply internalized by participants who share expectations across family, political, economic, educational, military, and religious institutions.
>
> At level four—cultural discrimination—sex inequality is built into our literature, art, music, language, morals, custom, beliefs

and ideology. In art, we see women as seductives (Bellini, Titian), as sex objects (Ruben, Renoir), as masses of distorted sex organs (Picasso), and as grotesque molls (Lindner). (Pp. 36–37)

From a social structure perspective, sex discrimination, where males are dominant and females are subordinate, is an integral feature of the organization and stability of American men's and women's daily lives. For example, regardless of a woman's professional status, in America she is likely to feel the sting of sex stratification. Many women in top professional positions experience in their work what is called "dumping"—"getting" someone else (i.e., a woman) to do a job you don't want to do and then taking credit for the results (Benokraitis and Feagin 1986, p. 86). One form of dumping which many top professional women experience is segregating top workers by sex. The women's job is to get the work done, while the men's job entails merely critiquing the work and implementing the results in highly visible and prestigious ways (Benokraitis and Feagin 1986, p. 86). These and numerous other patterned interactions describe the interweaving and stabilizing of social behavior between American men and women. In order to explore further the nature of such a social structure, let us examine more closely some key components. Though of a different nature, patterned interactions also characterize relationships between American men as well as between American men and children. What are these patterned interactions? Essentially, they are societal properties, such as statuses and roles, which have emerged to stabilize social relationships among men and between men and others.

Every male who becomes an adult member of American society must come to realize that his behavior has to fit into an American mold for men. If a particular man does not come to this realization, it is very likely that he will experience social dysfunctioning. What does an American mold for males consist of? Well, it is made up of various social roles and social statuses, with accompanying obligations as well as rights and privileges. Of course, these obligations, rights, and privileges may be modified somewhat by such factors as ethnicity, race, and age, which are discussed elsewhere in this volume. Nevertheless, generally the statuses and roles constrain all men's behaviors.

Another feature of the societal properties describing the relationship between men and the social structure is that the properties lie outside of individual men. While the individual male has to internalize societal statuses and roles for men, it must be remembered that these are societal statuses and roles and not the individual male's statuses and roles. Such societal properties and how they relate to each other and to other aspects of society such as social institutions constitute the social structure.

Properties of Social Structure

David Popenoe (1986) points out that the complexity of society has rendered sociologists incapable of reaching a consensus on a set of concepts for describing social structure. Because of this lack of agreement, Popenoe devised what he termed "a simplified conceptual map based on ideas from the work of many sociologists" (p. 77). Popenoe's lead will be followed in this volume as our discussion turns to men's relationship to properties of social structure.

Beginning with micro properties of social structure, including status and role, the discussion of men and properties of social structure proceeds to men in social groups and organizations. A final section of this chapter relates men to the macro social groupings of institutions, communities, and societies.

Men and Micro Social Groupings

In some ways it is easy to overlook the influences of micro units of social structure in daily social interaction. We hear so much about how social structural properties like the economy and the political system affect our likes, our dislikes, our participation in societal activities—in fact, all aspects of our daily lives (including cognitions, affects, and behaviors). Perhaps it is because of the relatively fixed quality of certain macro aspects of social structure that we attribute much individual behavior to macro groupings like educational, political, and religious institutions—and even to societies.

Macro groupings play important roles in our daily lives; however, those "very simple and elementary forms of social interaction" also are critical ingredients. The fact that American society espouses significant enough features of democracy in its political institutions to allow criticism of President Ronald Reagan's April 15, 1986, decision to bomb Libya is not sufficient to explain individual decisions to support or not to support the bombing. While some portion of a social structural explanation can be used to explain individual decisions, a full explanation must also include more immediate circumstances and situations. This dictates including those simple and elementary forms of social interactions, in other words, micro units of social structure.

Simple and elementary forms of social interaction such as a group of men who work together in a coal mine, a man and a woman in a romantic relationship, or a man who rears four children single-handedly are all examples of micro grouping. In each case, specific people are involved (sociologists call them status incumbents), but it is not these people who are the important properties of micro-level social structure. Instead, it is the patterned regularities of the status incumbents.

Statuses and roles are micro-level properties of social structure which round out explanations of aspects of our daily lives. For example, in our society, meaning emerges for us regarding positions in micro social systems when persons are male mine workers in coal mines, male partners in heterosexual romantic relationships, and male single heads of household in households with children. In fact, for many people, the meanings which emerge regarding these male positions (statuses) are privileges, competition, dominance, and aggressiveness.

Ascribed and Achieved Statuses

Undoubtedly, the fact that some people are born male in American society defines their social positions in micro social systems in particular ways. Of critical importance is that the biological fact of being male is very difficult to change. Yet, this fact alone, and not being born male, greatly affects the social lives of males and females in America. Like race, age, and ethnicity, maleness require no effort on the part of a person. Yet sex determines greatly where one stands in micro systems and macro systems. Being a male in American society, like most other societies throughout the world, is an ascribed status which most often positively affects one's life chances. On the other hand, being a female in America is a social position based on the ascribed characteristics of sex which negatively affects life opportunities.

Much is made of the so-called gains that American women have made since the early 1970s. Regarding this issue, Benokraitis and Feagin (1986) point to what they call "a disturbing trend in the thinking of many Americans over the last decade." The "thinking" relates to a growing feeling among many people that sex discrimination is no longer an issue in the United States. Benokraitis and Feagin reject this thesis and systematically examine women's positions in society, in organizations, and in micro systems. They uncover much evidence that women still are being assigned to inferior social positions on the basis of their sex, which is still regarded by many as inferior to the male sex.

In contrast to such a discriminating way of assigning persons to social positions in society, is it possible in America to assign persons to social positions solely on the basis of merit, choice, desire, and effort? In other words, is it possible to assign men and women to social positions on the basis of achievement rather than ascription? On the surface, it seems that achieved statuses characterize the social position of many people in America. College professor, engineer, factory worker, and physician are often classified by social scientists as achieved statuses. They are thought to be social positions which are filled through training, hard work, merit, and the like. We will explore later whether many of such statuses disproportionately held by men are in actuality achieved ones. Presently, let us examine a concept which is inextricably interwoven with social position: social role.

Social Role

Behavioral specifications for persons occupying social statuses refer to the rights, duties, and obligations associated with social positions. Referred to as social roles by social scientists, these expected patterns of behavior are both prescriptive and proscriptive. Each social status has associated norms which specify appropriate and permissible behaviors (role prescriptions) and norms which indicate inappropriate and nonpermissible behaviors (role proscriptions). Hess et al. (1985) point out that statuses and roles tend to occur in organized sets and are generally complementary. They also refer to early statements by Robin Williams (1970) which suggested that "everyone is either male or female and of a certain age, and thus every other status is influenced by age and gender statuses" (Hess et al. 1985, p. 89). Precisely how the status male affects males' other statuses and other social roles, and the relationship between male as a social position and expected behaviors for males are all central issues in this section.

A basic thesis here is that, in America, sex refers to ascribed characteristics which can ultimately determine one's social position in the social structure. In our society, if a person is born male he automatically enjoys a higher social position relative to a person who is born female. The moral rightness and the social desirability of the superior social status of males are not issues here. The point to be made is that sex is a critical variable determining ones' overall social status in the social structure. In actuality, sex may be thought of as a master status. Vander Zanden defines a master status as "a key or core status that carries primary weight in a person's interactions and relationships with others." In the United

States, aside from the sex variable, race and age perhaps are the two other statuses which for men carry the most weight.

Because male status carries with it rather strenuous and often conflicting rights and duties defining appropriate behaviors (social roles), whether or not a particular male can adequately perform his role frequently is related to his age. For example, males are expected, if necessary, to defend themselves and their loved ones physically against physical aggression from other males. Because the ability to physically defend certainly is related to age, a substantial number of men find themselves occupying an ascribed status as they age, which defines their rights and duties in ways that are particularly stressful.

In American society, maleness is valued, but old age is a devalued status. Both expected rights and expected duties are truncated as men age. What this means for most aging men in our society is that their rights and duties as males decrease rapidly as they grow older; gradually they become persons with no useful place in society. It should be apparent that this is an extremely traumatic experience for persons who have experienced expanded rights and duties. It seems that society "enjoys" the benefits of males conforming to such expansive expectations and then offers few benefits to them when they are no longer physically able to perform according to male sex role prescriptions and proscriptions. For men in America, the master status, sex, initially offers rich privileges and prerogatives, but ultimately most men must face "psychological death"—old age.

Another core status for men in America, also ascriptive, is race. Quite generally this means that maleness as a master status combines with still another master status, race, to produce a set of rights and duties for men which may or may not be logically consistent. For white males, the combined statuses of sex and race may produce a set of stressful roles (see the next section of this chapter), but at least the rights and duties exist within a supportive societal framework. Even as the status of women has undergone some minor modifications dictating changes in women's roles, society still supports those males who cling to traditional male sex roles (especially white male sex role expectations like aggressiveness, independence, dominance, protectiveness, decisiveness, etc.) in their relationships with women.

Maleness as an ascribed status for minority males is much more complex. For Black males, Native American males, Hispanic American males, Asian American males, and other minority group males, ascribed statuses based on race often combine with maleness to produce roles practically impossible to perform.

Consider the case of the 1984 and 1988 presidential candidate, the Reverend Jesse Jackson, whom some feel was the choice candidate of the lot—except for his ascribed status, "race," and his tendency to eschew some traditional American male characteristics like "toughness," a "give the Communists hell" attitude, aggressiveness, and dominance. While the Reverend Jackson may have been able to silence critics about his male perspective, which modifies traditional male sex role stereotypes, he could not overcome the negative influence of his ascribed status, race. It was virtually impossible for many American voters to perceive the Reverend Jackson beyond his "Blackness." For these persons, Jackson's race was a master status, which did not interact with Jackson's other statuses in ways sufficient to make him a viable presidential candidate. In fact, the statuses combined to produce role expectations that were impossible for him to fulfill. *USA Today* editor Barbara Reynolds describes what can be referred to as conflicting role expectations for Jackson stemming from incongruent master statuses in her book entitled *Jesse Jackson: America's David* (1985). Though much less visible, literally millions of minority group men are assigned incongruent ascribed master statuses daily which produce unrealistic role expectations for them.

From our earlier discussion of the linkage between status and role, it is probably quite easy to understand that the set of social roles associated with sex is deemed extremely important by society in general. The importance of sex roles is manifested in numerous ways throughout the social structure. Socialization institutions, political, economic, religious, and governmental institutions, and numerous other agencies and organizations in society all prescribe and proscribe behaviors for males and females. In the great majority of instances, the prescriptions and proscriptions favor male social superiority and/or female social inferiority.

In addition to sexist role expectations for men supported by our society, other aspects of the male sex role frequently render men incapable of participating fully and safely in the human experience. As discussed in chapter 2, Sidney Jourard (1971) calls these components of the male sex role lethal ones for men. For example, he refers to a link between societal conceptions of manliness and men's self-disclosure. The male sex role prescribes low self-disclosure for masculine men, suggesting that it is manly to be somewhat closed about oneself. At the same time, this lack of openness, says Jourard, creates undue stress and a special proneness to illness and even death at an early age (1971, p. 36).

Critical also, from Jourard's perspective on the male sex role, is that men in America traditionally have been socialized to assume an instrumental role, which means relating impersonally to others. Men relating to others without insight and nonempathically may also mean, according to this line of thought, men learning to ignore their own feelings and self-signals that all may not be well with them. Jourard states:

> Manly men, unaccustomed to self-disclosure and characterized by lesser insight and lesser empathy than women, do violence to their own unique needs and persist in modes of behavior which, to be sure, are effective at changing the world, but no less effective in modifying their "essence" from the healthy to the moribund range. (P. 38)

Lethal aspects of the male sex role also include "incompetence at loving" and "dispiritation." Because the male sex role traditionally has de-emphasized knowing the unique needs of others via the capacity to "imagine the real" and the ability to "let be," maleness often has meant awkwardness and crudeness in loving others as well as in being loved by others. On this latter point, Jourard feels that being loved by others requires, on some occasions, being "psychologically naked," and being "psychologically naked" is diametrically opposed to being masculine. This means that quite a few men in America are difficult to love just as they find it difficult to love others.

Finally, the male sex role is said to result in dispiritation for many men. Jourard points out that self-esteem and masculine identity are critical for men to manifest. However, these aspects of the male sex role also may be quite difficult for large numbers of men to achieve. Race, age, ethnicity, economic status, and the like are capable of interfering with the attainment of male self-esteem and/or masculine identity as defined by society at large. One example of this difficulty occurs often as men age. Because male perception of self is based on tenuous factors, like social status, physical strength and sexual potency, it is inevitable that dispiritation occurs for many men and that often this results in their subsequent disintegration. Jourard states:

> It is as if the body, when a man is dispirited, suddenly becomes an immensely fertile "garden" in which viruses and germs proliferate like jungle vegetation. In inspirited states, viruses and germs find a man's body a very uncongenial milieu for unbridled growth and multiplication. (P. 41)

Role Performance

How men's behaviors in their social statuses are viewed and evaluated depends on the particular theoretical perspective used to understand the male sex role. Generically, according to sociologist James W. Vander Zanden, "in real life a gap often exists between what people should do and what they actually do" (1986, p. 42). Why this gap between social role and role performance exists for some men probably is apparent from the previous discussion of multiple statuses men occupy. Before examining male role performances in terms of specific behaviors, let us return to an earlier discussion of two paradigms related to the male sex role which also may shed light on male role/male role performance discrepancies: the Male Sex Role Identity (MSRI) paradigm and the Sex Role Strain (SRS) paradigm.

Depending on the paradigm endorsed, a particular man's sex role performance is viewed either as a function of his internal psychological development or as a function of societal expectations external to the individual male. If the male sex role identity paradigm is reflected in evaluations of a male's sex role performance, then those evaluating the sex role performance assume that his sex role has developed from within (Pleck 1981, p. 4). This means, for example, that the man is innately programmed to develop a traditional male sex role identity and thus give traditional male sex role performances. These developments and performances by men in America, according to Pleck, are supported and encouraged by societal processes and institutions, such as the socialization process, the family, religious institutions, and so on. Now, this does not mean that all runs smoothly for men in American society. As the propositions in chapter 2 indicate, quite a few men experience difficulties performing their sex roles. The difficulties for men, as viewed from the MSRI perspective, are due to factors within the men rather than from factors external to them. More pointedly, inadequate male sex role performance is due to inadequate male sex role identity development caused by such forces as paternal absence, maternal overprotectiveness, the feminizing influence of schools, and the general blurring of societal gender roles for males and females. Manifestations of inadequate male sex role performances, following the MSRI paradigm rationale, include homosexuality, violence, hostility toward women, juvenile delinquency, and other similar social pathologies, all of which characterize many men's behaviors in our society.

In contrast to the MSRI paradigm, the implications of the Sex Role

Strain paradigm for evaluating men's sex role performances are much more in line with current social scientific thinking regarding social status and social roles. Contemporary views on social roles suggest that persons occupy numerous statuses and that single statuses frequently have multiple social roles. Thus, role conflict, which occurs when persons experience conflicting expectations because they occupy several statuses, is a common occurrence. A male high school swimming coach whose son swims for a rival team is likely to experience role conflict when his team and his son's team compete against each other. As a father, he may be expected to support his son in the competition, but as the coach of his team, he is expected to support his student swimmers. Black judges may experience similar role conflict stemming from general societal expectations that they will be totally objective in administering justice and a Black community's expectations that the Black judge will make decisions from a Black perspective.

In addition to role conflict, role strain is commonplace in our society. Role strain occurs because a single status frequently has multiple roles, and often these roles are incompatible. Occupying the status of man in America axiomatically results in role strain for most men. In heterosexual romantic relationships, men often are expected to exhibit "manly" qualities like confidence, protectiveness, toughness, and so on. Simultaneously, many women feel that men also should be more open, exhibit some vulnerability, and show tenderness.

While role strain is experienced by most, if not all, men in the United States, it is particularly acute for minority group men and poor white men. Not only do these men experience role strain stemming from incompatible expectations for the status "man," but they also experience role expectations for the status "minority group member," which often conflict with the role expectations for "man." Consider the following dilemma experienced by many Black males in American society:

> Black males are expected (both by society and the Black subculture) to exhibit dominance, competitiveness, aggressiveness, and so on. They also are expected to display submissiveness, passivity, cooperativeness, and the like. The larger society expects Black males to exhibit their "feminine" traits in social interaction outside of the Black subculture but expects (and to some extent encourages) the exhibition of their masculine traits within the Black subculture. The Black subculture (especially peer Black women) expects Black males to exhibit androgynous traits within the Black

subculture and masculine traits outside of the Black subculture. Yet, the Black subculture's socializing institutions teach Black men to inhibit their "masculine" traits outside of the Black subculture and to exhibit them within the Black subculture. If you are confused by this, imagine how Black male youth must feel. (Franklin 1984, p. 60)

Dimensions of the Male Role

As a general rule, it can be argued, males in the United States are expected to behave in ways opposed to societal harmony and integration. Moreover, the male role also dictates that males behave in ways antithetical to themselves. "Wounds are wounds," according to David and Brannon, and millions of "human beings who are male have been wounded— are wounding themselves" with the crude demands of the male sex role (David and Brannon 1976, p. 5). These demands, Brannon goes on to say, wound virtually anyone and everyone who lives in a male-dominated society.

Referring to "social role" as "any pattern of behaviors which a given individual in a specified (set of) situation(s) is both: (1) expected and (2) encouraged and/or trained to perform" (p.10), David and Brannon's point of departure is to discuss sex as a learned social role. Contending that "much of what we associate with being male or female is actually a learned social role," and recognizing that biology may interact with social learning in certain ways, Brannon goes on to discuss, generally, the male sex role.

A core requirement of the male sex role is the establishment of sufficient distance from femininity. Beginning in childhood, males are constantly reminded that they must avoid being associated with stereotyped feminine characteristics and qualities—they must not be like girls, not like women. Boys learn quite early that one of the greatest insults which can be hurled at them is to be called "a girl" or "a woman." Therefore, to be thought of as "manly," boys learn that they must avoid the stereotypical feminine things.

This socialized avoidance of anything feminine during boyhood (Brannon says that this is a part of the definition of masculinity) bleeds over into male adulthood. It is manifested in men's conversations, food, leisure time activities, and work. Because openness and vulnerability are so closely associated with "the way women are," displaying certain emotions like fear, tenderness, trust, love, and weakness are discouraged in men. It is not that men do not feel these things, it is that they are discouraged from expressing them. The first dimension of the male role which is capsulized in the foregoing discussion is called "No Sissy Stuff: The Stigma of Anything Vaguely Feminine."

A second dimension of the male sex role is "The Big Wheel: Success, Status, and the Need to Be Looked Up To." Becoming a "big wheel" is a sure way to the pinnacle of masculinity in American society. Wealth, fame, or at least some of the symbols of success can practically assure most males of being perceived as masculine. This is especially the case if the male happens to be white, Anglo-Saxon, and Protestant. (Of course this is a figure of speech, since we would extend "Anglo-Saxon" to include all northern European or white males, and "Protestant" as used here is not limited to non-Roman Catholic Christians.) But, what if the male is Hispanic, Native American, Asian American, or white but poor? Does a male from these groups or like ones have to fulfill the "Big Wheel" dimension of the male role in the same way as the middle class white male? No! There are other routes to status for men in America. Societal standards for success and "making it" in general can be rigid and exclusive. Yet, ethnic group males, racial group males, and lower socioeconomic group males can "make it" by subcultural group standards, which may depart significantly from societal status rankings. Status rankings for many subcultural group males in America are based on varied qualities such as physical aggressiveness (Brannon calls it the major currency on which status is based in some subcultures while recognizing that it plays some role in the general cultural male role), daring behavior, "rapping," and "cool pose."[1]

A third dimension of the male sex role is "The Sturdy Oak: A Manly Air of Toughness, Confidence, and Self-Reliance." Strikingly similar to the "cool pose" mentioned above as a substitute route to manhood for Black males especially, this dimension of masculinity emphasizes style rather than substance or tangible achievement. When interacting with a "manly male," one should get the feeling of some combination of strength, determination, confidence, self-reliance, courage, toughness, and stability.

While it is easy for a particular male to carry off the tough guy-sturdy oak image if he is physically large, an imposing physical stature is

1. According to psychologist Richard Majors (1986), "cool pose" is a term representing a variety of attitudes and actions that serve the Black man as mechanisms for survival, defense, and social competence. Such attitudes and actions are performed using characterizations and roles as facades and shields.

not absolutely necessary. The average male of slight stature can earn the same reputation simply by displaying an air of toughness and confidence. David and Brannon (1976) state:

> *The Sturdy Oak and the Average Guy.* The need to be seen as a tough customer operates on Park Avenue as well as the gridiron. In executive jobs in which effectiveness can't be gauged directly, promotions often go to a man who has built the best reputation for toughness. In one company it's fairly common practice for a new regional manager to fire 15 of his 60 branch managers, without regard to competence, just to show his superiors he's tough enough to handle the new job. (Pp. 26–27)

A final dimension of the male sex role to be discussed is "Give 'Em Hell: The Aura of Aggression, Violence, and Daring." In America, it seems that this last dimension firmly establishes a male's manhood even if he fails on all other dimensions. Aggression and violence must be aspects of our culture's ethos because they are omnipresent in American society.

Societal condemnation of extreme male aggressiveness and violence certainly exists in America. Yet, societal support for male aggressiveness and male violence are integral features of male socialization and many male's everyday lives. Men in executive positions in business, in sports competition, and in politics are very visible examples of men who are both expected and encouraged to be aggressive. Predictions are often made that a given male will be successful in business, sports, and politics precisely because he has developed a personal norm of extreme aggressiveness.

Probably only a few men's socialization experiences include parental encouragement of unprovoked violent behaviors toward others, although many more men have been given parental encouragement and approval for using violence to defend self against the aggressive acts of others. But, as Brannon points out, "the line between self-defense and violence for the sheer fun of it is narrow in theory and often ignored in practice, especially among adolescent boys out of sight of adults" (p. 29). Moreover, aggression and violence in male sports beginning with Little League and extending through high school and into professional leagues is unabashedly supported, encouraged, and often demanded by parents, coaches, and spectators.

Even so-called "average" males do not escape role expectations that they become aggressive and violent on certain occasions. For example, we all are socialized to expect men to be aggressive in heterosexual

sexual matters. Despite some minor changes in American men's and women's sexualities, the male-dominated sexual script has not been rewritten in contemporary times. Men still are expected to aggress sexually and women are expected to submit sexually.

In another area of social life, men frequently are expected to become violent—that is, if they are "real" men. Men are expected to internalize a norm of territoriality. If another male infringes on our personal space, we are not supposed to accept this. We are to defend, sometimes violently, that space. This can mean becoming violent with a drunken male who blocks our path and demands spare change or becoming violent with a construction worker who shouts an obscene remark at our date (Brannon 1967, p. 33).

David and Brannon's description of the male role, as they admit, summarizes the total male role in pure form. This means that we are dealing with an ideal type and should not expect to find one man fulfilling all of the demands. This is the nature of sex roles as David and Brannon see them. The only problem is that many outside of gender studies do not make this distinction between "actual" male roles and "ideal types." David and Brannon conclude, "Real people do not and cannot fulfill the idealized cultural prescriptions in every respect, and are not expected to" (p. 36). Still, others within gender studies have questioned the utility of conceptualizations like sex roles and gender categories. In the next section, some of these questions are explored as a perspective on masculinity is presented which goes beyond traditional emphases on sex roles and gender categories.

Beyond "Sex Roles" and "Gender Categories": A Social Practice Approach to Masculinity

That men typically are found in superordinate positions and women in subordinate ones is the touchstone of what Tim Carrigan, Bob Connell, and John Lee (1987) call "a new sociology of masculinity." According to these theorists, there are three sources of this new sociology of masculinity. They include: (1) a focus on sexual power and its pursuit between and within sex categories; (2) an emphasis on currents of feminism that focus on the sexual division of labor, occupational sexual politics, and the interplay of gender relations with social class dynamics; and (3) a divergence from past theoretical paradigms which stress the dichotomies of structure versus individual and society versus the person (p. 65).

With respect to the first source of this new perspective on masculinity, an accurate account of masculinity must not only face the issue of social power as it relates to the sexes but also explore the question of sexual power inside sex categories. This means, for example, that relationships between heterosexual and homosexual men must be looked at. This pursuit should be seen as possibly resulting in a conception of masculinity as a political construction. Important here is that masculinity as a political order means that certain of its forms can be explored as socially dominant or hegemonic.

The second source of Carrigan, Connell, and Lee's new sociology of masculinity is the analysis of masculinity as related to the currents of feminism that focus on such issues as the social definition of occupations as "men's work," "women's work," or "less manly work," the latter being seen in interpretations of manual labor as "more masculine" than professional or white collar work.

The final source of the new perspective on studying masculinity is a focus on theory development which emphasizes the historical production of social categories. Also critical in this new theoretical approach is an emphasis on power as the ability to control the production of people biologically and psychologically and an emphasis on large-scale components of social structure as both objects and effects of collective practice.

The point of departure for Carrigan, Connell, and Lee is discounting the gender and sex role frameworks as well as functionalist sex role theory often used in theoretical and research discourses. They argue that Talcott Parsons, a key proponent of functionalist sex role theory, ignored power relations between men and women, took "sex roles" themselves for granted in most of his arguments, and when sex role differentiation was the basic problem to be explained, rejected biological explanations and derived social patterns of sex roles from a general sociological principle of structural requirements of any social order. Critical in Parson's analysis, they point out, was the distinction between instrumental and expressive roles within the conjugal family (thought of as a small group and as a necessary agency of society responsible for socializing the young). Carrigan et al. quote from Parsons and Bales (1953):

> Relative to the total culture as a whole the masculine personality tends more to the predominance of instrumental interests, needs, and functions, presumably in whatever social system both sexes are involved, while the feminine personality tends more to the primacy of expressive interests, needs and functions. We would expect, by and large, that other things being equal, men would assume technical, executive, and 'judicial' roles, women more supportive, integrative, and 'tension-managing' roles. (P. 101)

According to Carrigan et al., little attention is given to how many men and women actually assume such roles. Additionally, Parsons paid scant attention to the issue of homosexuality, indicating only that it is universally prohibited, serving to support sex role differentiation. This is quickly dismissed by Carrigan et al. as false, since homosexuality was and is institutionalized in some societies. They also pointed out a tendency for such theoretical discussions (1) to ignore tension and power processes within gender relations; (2) to imply that gender analysis is always differentiation and not relation; and by logical derivation, (3) to assume that the link between female and male sex roles is one of complementarity rather than power.

Carrigan et al. consider other issues related to masculinity, including a sociology of masculinity which appeared before the advent of the sex role paradigm. This "old sociology," appearing in the 1950s and 1960s, was devoted to understanding those males found to be "social problems"—juvenile delinquents, street-corner men, beatnicks, and the like. A popular explanation emerging from such analyses was "father absence." Just as salient in the old sociology of masculinity was Ruth Hartley's (1959) idea of an overwhelming presence of mothers in boys' lives and the contribution of this presence to anxiety in boys. Such anxiety was seen as expressing itself in "overstraining to be masculine," eschewing anything feminine, and misogynous attitudes and behavior.

Perhaps one of the most important contributions to an understanding of masculinity, according to Carrigan et al., is the notion that sex role literature (1) does not distinguish adequately between expectations of behavior and actual behavior, (2) sees variation from male norms as deviance, and (3) frequently views this deviance as unexplained, residual, and essentially in a nonsocial category. Carrigan et al. recognize the contributions of Brannon and Pleck discussed earlier. However, they feel that the work is static, concentrates on change as something that happens to sex roles, and fails to capture change as a dialectic arising within gender relations.

The new analysis of masculinity recognizes the sources discussed earlier and focuses on the historical production of hegemonic patterns of masculinity. Also recognized is the fact that masculinity is a social practice and a property of human sociality; it transcends biology. Biology does not present society with clear-cut categories of people (Carrigan et al. 1987, p. 95). Historical conditions, on the other hand, do facilitate the formations of gender groupings. Such historical conditions where power is won and maintained (hegemony) involve persuasion, including commercial mass media which construct images of masculinity; socially de-

fined divisions of labor; and state (government) negotiations and en-
forcements of incentives to conform to hegemonic masculinity patterns.
A statement by Carrigan et al. may be instructive as we attempt to capture
the essence of the new sociology of masculinity:

> Masculinities are constituted, we argued above, within a
> structure of gender relations that has a historical dynamic as a
> whole. This is not to say it is a neatly defined and closely integrated
> system—the false assumption made by Parson, Chodorow, and a
> good many others. This would take for granted what is currently
> being fought for. The dominion of men over women, and the su-
> premacy of particular groups of men over others, is sought by con-
> stantly reconstituting gender relations as a system within which
> that dominance is generated. Hegemonic masculinity might be
> seen as what would function automatically if the strategy were en-
> tirely successful. But it never does function automatically. The
> project is contradictory, the conditions for its realization are con-
> stantly changing, and, most important, there is resistance from the
> groups being subordinated. The violence in gender relations is not
> part of the essence of masculinity (as Fasteau, Nichols, and Rey-
> naud, as well as many radical feminists, present it) as much as a
> measure of the bitterness of this struggle.'' (Pp. 98-99)

Social Groups

Discussions of social structure typically include analyses of social
groups, which are social units characterized by shared feelings of unity
among members involved together in patterned social interaction and
constrained by social norms. Given such a definition of social group, is it
possible, then, to discuss a collection of males in America at any point in
time as a group? Perhaps not, but I contend that, at the very least, men in
America constitute a social category—a set of people all sharing a social
status or, in some instances, several social statuses.

Certainly, it is impossible to say that all men in America interact or
conceive of themselves as a social unit. Yet, social norms do exist which
constrain their behaviors. Moreover, for significant numbers of men, a
''we-feeling'' does exist. Frequently, however, this ''we-feeling'' is
mitigated by class, race, ethnicity, and the like. I have been struck by the
observation that men of diverse social characteristics frequently bond, at
least on the surface, in opposition to threats to male dominance and/or
privilege. It seems that one by-product of the modern-day women's

movement has been to raise men's consciousness regarding their social commonalities. An example of this would include the emergence in recent times of a continuum of men's organizations ranging from those that are politically conservative on gender issues to those that are politically liberal on these issues. One of these organizations, the National Organization for Changing Men (N.O.C.M.), is a liberal group of men who define themselves as being supportive of such men's issues as improved fathering, lessening homophobia, improved men's mental health, and gay rights, and of women's and men's issues, like ending violence toward women, ending sexual harassment, improving equity in the workplace, and so forth. National task groups formed by the N.O.C.M. membership are listed below, followed by the organization's statement of principles explicating N.O.C.M.'s philosophy.

Ending Men's Violence	Men and Mental Health
Fathering	Men's Culture
Gay Rights	Men's Studies
Homophobia	Pornography
Male-Female Relationships	

N.O.C.M. Statement of Principles

The National Organization for Changing Men is an activist organization supporting positive changes for men today. N.O.C.M. advocates a male-positive, pro-feminist, and gay-affirmative perspective. Open to men and women, it is committed to a broad goal of personal and social change.

We believe that the new opportunities becoming available to women and men will be beneficial to both. Men can live as happier and more fulfilled human beings by challenging the old-fashioned rules of masculinity that embody the assumption of male superiority.

Traditional masculinity includes many positive characteristics in which we take pride and find strength, but it also contains qualities that have limited and harmed us. Our love of men and our joy in being men move us to protest the ways men are wounded and alienated in this society. Our understanding of how each man is damaged enables us to understand how others are damaged.

As an organization for changing men, we strongly support the continuing struggle of women for full equality. We applaud and support the insights and positive social changes that feminism has stimulated for both women and men. We oppose such domestic violence, sexual harassment, and many others. Women and men can and do work together as allies to change the injustices that have so often made them see one another as enemies.

One of the strongest and deepest anxieties of most American men is their fear of homosexuality. This homophobia contributes directly to the many injustices experienced by gay, lesbian, and bisexual persons, and is a debilitating restriction for heterosexual men. We call for an end to all forms of discrimination based on sexual-affectional orientation, and for the creation of a gay-affirmative society.

We acknowledge, too, that many people are oppressed today because of their race, class, age, religion, and physical condition. We believe that such injustices are vitally connected to sexism, with its fundamental premise of unequal distribution of power.

Our goal is to change not just ourselves and other men but also the institutions that create inequality. We welcome any person who agrees in substance with these principles to membership in the NA-TIONAL ORGANIZATION FOR CHANGING MEN. (*Brother* 1987)

In contrast to the left end of the continuum is the right end, which includes men's organizations that are politically conservative on gender issues. Two such organizations are Men's Rights, Inc., and the National Congress for Men, both of which claim that men's rights often are neglected in the clamor over women's rights. Men's Rights, Inc. is concerned, like N.O.C.M., with sexism and men's problems. I hasten to add, however, that the similarity between the two organizations seems to begin and end with those avowed concerns.[2]

Men's Rights, Inc. states its philosophy as fostering the understanding that the provider and protector roles have dehumanized, damaged, and limited men in ways as serious and pervasive as the reproducer (sex object) and child socializer (housewife) roles have done to women. Just

---

2. This was never more evident than during the 12th National Conference on Men and Masculinity in Hartford, Connecticut, June 25-27, 1987. While one of the goals for the conference was to open dialogue with other men's organizations with whom N.O.C.M. had experienced past conflict, in some ways the goal was an aborted effort. Frederick Hayward, the founder and director of Men's Rights, Inc. met with N.O.C.M. council members, outlined goals of the organization and suggested ways in which MR, Inc.'s goals may dovetail with N.O.C.M.'s goals. Also during this meeting several N.O.C.M. council members voiced some concern that the goals of the two organizations were solipsistic and different rather than shared. A major roadblock seems to have hinged on the profeminist philosophy of N.O.C.M. which many N.O.C.M. members feel sets it apart from less profeminist organizations, including MR, Inc. The MR group meeting scheduled for an hour and a half the last day of the conference seems to have caused quite a stir resulting in some N.O.C.M. members scheduling a type of protest meeting during the scheduled period. At any rate, the hoped for realization of common ground between the two organizations awaits development.

as the idea that "women are on a pedestal" clouds women's problems, saying that "it's a man's world" obscures men's problems.

Men's Rights, Inc., is perhaps best known for its Men's Rights Media Watch compiling what it terms the best and worst in advertising, evaluated in terms of the protrayal of males. Additionally, MR Media Watch also judged 1986 books and news stories, awarding Warren Farrell's *Why Men Are the Way They Are* best book and ATCOM's "Marriage and Divorce Today" and "Sexuality Today" best in news. The following excerpt from a press release summarizes Men's Rights, Inc.'s philosophy.

> MR, Inc. is dedicated to ending sexism in a way that recognizes the social, psychological, physical, legal, and economic problems of men. It seeks to make available to men the wide range of options that are now available to women; to insure men the right to nurture and the power to raise children; to correct the social and economic pressures and the legal inconsistencies which fill our prisons and cemeteries with men; to correct the low standards of male self-image, health, and safety; to educate women as to their own continuing roles in perpetuating sexism; and to eliminate the dictum that the worst failure a male can commit is the failure to live up to his self-destructive male role. (Men's Rights, Inc. 1987)

Another organization politically conservative on gender issues is the Washington-based National Congress for Men. Very similar to MR, Inc. a founder member of NCM, the organization devotes its attention to correcting what it calls the callous and unfair treatment of men. John Rossler, its president, devotes his energies to opposing what he terms are efforts to devastate and denigrate fatherhood and supporting efforts to revitalize fatherhood to be all it can be. Lamenting the treatment of women as a favored group by the government, Rossler feels that the government may be wise to institute programs for women which help them appreciate the nonmonetary importance of fathers to their children. Perhaps then, he believes, fewer fathers and their wallets would disappear (Rossler 1987).

In general, right-wing men's organizations, perspectives, and/or views express responses to what many perceive as reductions of "men's patriarchal privileges." These responses constitute what Lance Egley (1985) calls "anger at the inequities between static men's roles and changing women's roles" (p. 6). On right-wing gender perspectives and men's groups, Egley says further:

When masculinist men are aware of being angry, they are willing to state openly what changing men want. Angry men seek an end to emotional violence (threats, labeling, name-calling, put-downs) used by women. Masculinist men recognize that expectations and statements indicating men are nonemotional, nonintuitive, or violent make it more difficult for men to change these attributes. Masculinists specify legal issues of equitable child custody and support awards and the military draft and begin by recognizing that both the masculinist and feminist men's movements [support] men's health issues. [See, for example, Sam Julty 1980.] Masculinist men support feminist men in the belief that sharing personal experiences and emotional awareness are keys to change. The function of men's anger is to guide identification of personal needs, leading to assertion of boundaries. Anger can be a tremendous source of energy. (P. 6)

A critical difference between men's perspectives and groups on the Left and those on the Right appears to be in the area of profeminism. Men's responses to changing women's roles generally have been one of the following: promen, with little or no interest in women's issues and/or rights, or promen/profeminist, with emphasis on gender eglitarianism. Both responses, I contend, have resulted in increased interaction and recognition of men's common interest for many with an accompanying awareness of differences in men's groups and their perspectives.

Men and Social Institutions:
A Case of Domination and Power

A cursory examination of American society reveals that intimate relationships exist between men and the various social institutions. Social institutions are enduring sets of cultural values, norms, and social relationships centered around critical societal functions. Critical societal functions are those activities which must be carried out if a society is to survive. For example, every society must find solutions to the problems of reproduction of new members, socialization of new members, economic maintenance of societal members, and protection of societal members from each other and from external threats. Generally, in America, social institutions have emerged which are primarily concerned with single functions, although there can be overlap. The family as an institution has tended to focus on reproduction, although at times it also has focused on the distribution of goods and services, the socialization of the young, instilling a sense of purpose, and protection of its members from internal and external threats.

The roles of sex and gender are important considerations when discussing American social institutions. The importance of these variables stems from the enormous influence and power of males and masculinity on and over American institutions and the relative lack of influence and power of females and femininity on and over the same. What all of this means is that solutions to society's survival problems are decidedly male oriented and masculine. Furthermore, the values and norms which influence American societal role expectations for members usually are biased in favor of males and supportive of masculinity—all at the expense of females and femininity.

Undoubtedly, enduring patterns of interaction in American society which facilitate finding solutions to our design for living basically are constructed and implemented by men. Vander Zanden (1986, p. 44) has said about institutions that "we are bound within networks of relationships [groups] in which we interact with one another [play our roles] in terms of certain shared understandings [cultural patterns] that define the behavior expected of us as given kinds of people [statuses]." How men and women are located in superordinate and subordinate positions, respectively, within these networks of relationships is discussed extensively in this and other chapters.

Men and American Societies

Social scientists generally define the concept "society" as an aggregate of persons who live together in a common geographical area, share a common culture, identify with each other, and have a feeling of unity. In discussing "society," which can be called the most complex and comprehensive unit of social structure, social scientists have been quite varied in their approaches. Some have classified societies according to modes of subsistence, while others have developed schema of classification based on societal change and/or a kind of communal-associational dichotomy. Our discussion of societies as components of social structure takes a decidedly different direction. First of all, the discussion is limited to America. Secondly, a basic assumption will be that America has been characterized by several societies since its beginning. The basis for each societal type to be discussed is the prevailing conception of masculinity during a particular time period. Pleck and Pleck's seminal work, *The American Man,* is the major source for this discussion. The rationale for discussing "American societies" is that social roles, social statuses, social values, social norms, patterns of social interaction, and social institutions all have changed numerous times during the history of the United States. They have changed so much, I feel, that unique societies emerged from one time period to the next. Thus, in this volume, Elizabeth Pleck and Joseph Pleck's "Four Periods of United States Men's History" are seen as "types of American Societies."

The Agrarian Patriarchial Society (1630–1820)

Elizabeth Pleck and Joseph Pleck describe the American society existing from 1630 to 1820 as being unique in history because of the nature of political, economic, religious, and family life. In American agrarian society, social rank was based on sex, wealth, and age. This meant that older white males typically stood at the apex of the social system and maintained power over adult sons, white women, and "African men and women" (Pleck and Pleck 1980, p. 11). Pleck and Pleck state: "The ideal of a stable social hierarchy ruled by natural male leaders was accepted not only as family practice, but as political doctrine that placed masters above servants, older ahead of younger, and wealthier above poorer" (p. 12). It is said that only very poor white men (the bottom 10 percent of white males) were excluded from this system. Of course, Black men were not even considered for possible inclusion in the system, since they were not thought of as quite human.

Generally, American agrarian society was characterized by men's rule over women; men being favored in all legal and economic matters (husbands owned joint property outright, and they were the only ones who could sign contracts); men being in charge of the religious institutions (only men were allowed to speak in church and to assume leadership positions); and men heading the family institution. Fathers, not mothers, generally were granted custody of children in cases of legal separations (which were few and far between).

In sum, social relations involved the domination of husbands over wives and fathers over sons. Male aggression and competition also were encouraged by agrarian patriarchial society, although the manifestations were in highly patterned cultural events like those among the gentry of eighteenth-century Virginia. Yet, conspicuous features of this society also were manly intimacy and affection between men. Many times this "love" which existed between men did not extend to women. This love between "equals" was acceptable as long as men did not have sexual contact with each other. Succinctly, agrarian society's values, norms, and standards, along with its religious and political institutions, permitted and encouraged male supremacy, patriarchal relations, paternal power in the home and other societal institutions, and the power to define, prescribe, proscribe, and sanction men's behavior.

The Commercial Society (1820–1860)

Distinct features of American commercial society include a social order transformed from an agrarian patriarchy, with a single vertical stratification system where white males occupied the top rungs, to a vertical structure divided into two separate but equal halves by sex. Specifics of the pluralistic social order were that men (husbands) were in control of business and public affairs, and women's (wives') spheres were the home and church. Supposedly, men and women were ideally suited for their separate spheres. Men, because of their practicality and competitive spirit, were quite suited for industry, government, and warfare. On the other hand, because women were thought to be superior in sensibility and piousness, they were deemed most suitable for the home and church. This view of women was quite distinct from the view of women in American agrarian society, which basically characterized women as evil temptresses and given to sexual passion.

Men in American commercial society were viewed as the more passionate sex, and it was the job of good women to help men control their passions and reject the sexual double standard, as well a discourage masturbation tendencies in young males. After all, manliness in commercial society meant piety, self-restraint, discipline, and frugality in sexual matters as well as in business. Excess sex robbed a man of his stamina for work and industry and therefore should be discouraged. The result was predictable. In American commercial society, fertility control (probably coitus interruptus) became the mainstay of the emerging middle class, which set the standard for the social order defining both social conformity and social deviance.

Yet, American commercial society was not as conforming as one may be led to believe. Much deviation occurred. Not all men subscribed to sexual purity, and some Americans rejected the new American Protestantism in favor of Mormonism—the ultimate patriarchal religion. Not only was fertility control not a feature of this new religion, but Joseph Smith's "revelation" also permitted Mormon men to marry several wives while still subscribing to tenets of the Protestant ethic.

Slave men and women also did not conform to the social order's gender prescriptions and proscriptions. While white masters may have wanted to treat these men and women as genderless, they could not anymore than the slaves could view themselves that way (Pleck and Pleck 1980, p. 17). White masters who sought to enhance their images as benevolent patriarchs and profit from their investments encouraged and coerced male slaves to work and assume dominant roles in slave quarters. Preserving the family and male authority among the slaves were considered kindly deeds. Slave men, aside from their masters' goals, recognized value in family decision making and disciplining their children, and this, too, contributed to more deviation from the prescribed social order.

Another form of deviance which occurred in the American commercial society was an organized feminist movement threatening white male power and privilege. The 1848 Seneca Falls Declaration of Principles challenged the separate but equal spheres of the vertical social stratification system. The challenge questioned the idea that men had dominion over women and children and that only men could own property and earnings and, in fact, be in control of public affairs.

Deviance from the commercial society's social norms also entailed a decline in fatherly instruction of boys and the rise of female instruction of young males. Despite these changes in the social order, ''success'' still was a desired goal for white males. In this society, especially near its end (1855), rising above one's humble origins became quite respectable. One did not have to have a genteel background to succeed. The man who made it on his own through hard work and much effort could attain high social status.

Finally, in American commercial society, a separate men's culture emerged involving men meeting at courthouses, churches, city taverns, and blacksmith shops. The proliferation of lodges, debating clubs, militia, and voluntary fire companies attest to the development of this culture. Still, male bonding, older forms of competition, visits to prostitutes, and drinking bouts did not disappear completely. Along with these behaviors, though, were voluntary organizations devoted to sobriety, self-discipline, and temperance. The following captures quite adequately the tenor of American commercial society:

> The commercialism of antebellum society and the effects of the
> Second Great Awakening had taken masculinity out of its older pa-

triarchal mold. Men were no longer the link in the Great Chain of Being just above women; now they played to their own separate but no longer superior sphere. Although this placement was accepted and even espoused by some, it was challenged by feminists, who demanded the right to political power in the men's sphere, and by more tradition-minded women, who sought to reshape and control men's sexuality along purer lines. In a society where fundamental values were being so continually called into question, a range of alternatives, from feminism to the reassertion of religious patriarchy, found adherents. (Pleck and Pleck 1980, p. 20)

The Strenuous Life Society (1860–1920)

The American strenuous life society emerged as a unique response to the threat that American women posed to American men. This society, which existed in America roughly between 1860 and 1920, featured separate spheres for men and women with essentially the same prescriptions and proscriptions for males and females as those in the commercial society. Basically, this meant that women were expected to be and were thought of as morally pure. They also were to provide husbands with refuges from their places of work. Men, too, were expected to be morally beyond reproach, especially middle-class men. Yet, familiar sexual double standards existed. While self-restraint, self-reliance, and anti-intellectualism were associated with masculinity, houses of prostitution still flourished and venereal disease was rampant.

But, it was the movement of women into men's culture and the resulting threat to men which gave this society its unique feature. Women's literature openly attacking men, and women's entrance into previously male-only jobs (e.g., typists, librarians, and sales clerks) actually changed the definition of masculinity. Being masculine became not being feminine and remains so to this day.

As women posed threats to men in America's strenuous life society, Pleck and Pleck (1980) contend that many men developed an almost permanent nostalgia for wartime bonding with other men. In the years between the Civil War and the Armistice after World War I, it seems that quite a few men began a search for a peacetime equivalent to wartime campfires and barracks life. The equivalent that emerged was a ''cult of body building.'' Manifestations of the cult, according to Pleck and Pleck, included the emergence of organized athletics like baseball and boxing; the rise of collegiate athletics; and, the founding by Ernest Seton of the Boy Scouts of America (Seton blamed females for boys' flabby muscles).

An air of comaraderie existed in factories, and separate men's clubs and lodges flourished as men were asked, in the face of women's threats, to forego male competition in favor of male comradeship. Generally, men were admonished to strive for success by making war. However, they were not asked to "make love" as they would be asked to do in the 1960s. Instead, they were asked to "lead the strenuous life." In summary, as relations with women became threatening and fearful and as many men developed a martial spirit, significant societal features emerged. As Pleck and Pleck (1980) state:

> The martial spirit made male friendship into a cult of comradeship whose effects were to be seen in the cult of body building and in the blossoming of paramilitary organizations for boys. The form and content of this men's separate world varied between social groups but flourished everywhere in male-only institutions, which made these years the heyday of men's public culture. (P. 28)

The Companionate Providing Society (1920–1965)

The end of World War I ushered in a new society. In this society men were less interested in warfare and muscular development. They were more interested in romancing women than in cultivating their male friendships. The emergence of coeducational schools facilitated men spending more time with women, resulting in new marriage patterns for men and women. Men began to select marriage partners closer in age. The proliferation of automobiles led to a new phenomenon—dating—which supported even further the demise of male friendships and the increasing companionship between members of the opposite sex.

Strikingly different ideas about sexuality came forth in the companionate providing society. With Freudian ideas about children having sexual urges and fantasies becoming widely known, and a kind of sexual revolution occurring in the 1920s, the stage was set for even more radical ideas about sexuality as well as sexual behavior. Men still were regarded as the sexual aggressors, but women began to be seen as persons who could, and perhaps on occasions even should, arouse their husbands sexually. However, it was the 1948 Kinsey report that defined sexuality in the companionate providing society. Among other findings based on over five thousand case histories, Kinsey et al. (1948) reported that 86 percent of American males had engaged in premarital sex and 40 percent in extramarital sex. Just as shocking to many was the finding that 37 percent of American males had engaged in homosexual sex to the point of orgasm after adolescence on some occasion. With Kinsey's findings, a new conception of sexuality began to emerge. Heterosexual sex began to be perceived as recreational, and homosexual sex among males, while not necessarily acceptable, became recognized as "ordinary."

The companionate providing society also showcased new conceptions of work and leisure as the male work week declined from fifty-nine hours to forty-two hours between 1900 and 1948. Mass consumption became an American family pastime, as the definition of a good male provider began to mean that men could earn enough money to meet their family's rising levels of expectations to make more and more purchases of such items as cars, home appliances, electrical goods, and other modern-day conveniences. "A good provider came to be defined as a husband who paid his bills on time" (Pleck and Pleck 1980, p. 31). Masculinity became connected with a man's purchasing power.

A significant setback to the early stages of the companionate providing period was the Great Depression. However, the end of World War II brought in a new wave of male purchasing power. While the onset of World War II brought vast numbers of women into the labor force, the end of the war resulted in a redistribution of income and benefits—away from women, boys, and older men. On this point, Pleck and Pleck (1980) state:

> More important, a grateful government passed the Servicemen's Readjustment Act in 1944 (the G.I. Bill of Rights), which subsidized college education and home purchases for more than 7.5 million veterans, an unprecedented governmental largesse that transferred 14.5 billion dollars to "G.I. Joes." At least, partially in response to this federal subsidy, men could marry earlier, thereby precipitating the "marriage rush" at the end of World War II, which resulted (permanently) in a falling age at first marriage for American men. (P. 32)

The companionate providing society produced a solution to widespread deficiencies of white males as breadwinners, but it did not end the depression for great numbers of Black men. In fact, Black male unemployment (twice that of white males) and the gap between white male and Black male earnings (Black males earn about 60 percent of what white males earn) have remained constant since the end of World War II. This society, it seems, created a permanent underclass—the Black race.

Another feature of the companionate providing society was increased male competition and a de-emphasis on male camaraderie. This feature was encouraged by the emergence of the corporation, with its emphasis on business sensibility, efficiency, rationality, coolness, suppression of affect, and the like. After all, this modern-day male had to be the mainstay of a new class characterized by mass consumption. While intimate male-male friendships existed to some extent among adolescents, the separate male culture appeared to decline dramatically in the companionate providing society. Moreover, this society was vastly more ethnically and racially heterogeneous than past ones, which undoubtedly mitigated maintenance of the male culture. It may even be possible to say that with male competition in the business world, ethnicity and race combined to create antagonism between large numbers of males in the companionate providing society. One final effect on the tenor of this society is the entrenchment of women in the home. Because many men had little time for child-rearing activities or home management activities, women became the sole child-rearers and home managers. Yet, separate spheres for men and women were not entirely maintained. Men provided, women and children consumed; men were companions to women and skilled lovers, and assumed breadwinner roles. Still, men ruled in all spheres in the companionate providing society, and as we see later, challenges to that rule would soon come.

Contemporary Society (1965–present)

Contemporary society and the various roles of men in it are major topics considered in the chapters to follow. What should be apparent at this juncture, however, is that men's roles and/or masculinity have undergone changes since the beginning of an American society. To quickly review, masculinity initially (in the agrarian patriarchal society) was defined as heading agencies within the key social institutions of the family (the home), legal and economic units, and the religious institutions (churches). Great spiritual capacity also was an ingredient of masculinity. With the commercial age society came an alteration in masculinity and, thus, social relations between the sexes. Masculinity still meant being in control of business, legal, and economic institutions, but a separate sphere had emerged where women were in control of the home and church because of their perceived piousness. Masculinity now meant also practicality, competitiveness, and sexual passion. Further changes in masculinity accompanied the strenuous life society as masculinity became equated with muscular development, physical aggressiveness, and anti-intellectualism—in fact, the opposite of femininity. The companionate providing society altered masculinity further in that being a skillful lover and a provider were added to the definition of masculinity. Physical aggression and prowess gave way to interpersonal skills, rationality, and efficiency.

But, what has masculinity been since 1965? For one thing, contrary to popular opinion, it has not remained static. It is confusing at best to understand what is meant when someone says that he/she longs for the days when "men were men." What kind of man? One who writes to another man "my dear" and "I love you"? On the other hand, could this nostalgic person desire a society where men were in control of the family and granted custody of children in divorce cases? Still yet, could our sentimental yearner be a person who would like to see a proliferation of male-only lodges, clubs, and taverns?

In a very real sense, contemporary society, with its complexity, heterogeneity, and rapid change, has responded to the challenge of living by devising social procedures, establishing social relations, and devising social institutions in adaptive ways heretofore unseen. The need for such unique adaptations surely exists because contemporary society contains in abundance all the basic features of past American societies. In addition, changes in Black males' masculinity along with changes in the masculinities of Hispanic males, Native American males, and Asian-American males, and others have affected contemporary society. Certainly, the modern-day Black male-led movement in the late sixties and early seventies, the gay liberation movement, the modern-day women's movement, and the emerging men's movement (however fragmented)—all contribute to unique features in contemporary society—a society that constantly develops advanced technology, complex organizations, and relationships to meet the needs of its members.

Yet, contemporary society is also an American society that today is beset with social problems: hunger, destructive competition between its members, violent aggression between racial and ethnic groups, sexual exploitation of women, intergroup prejudice and discrimination, child abuse, wife abuse, and in general, dysfunctional living patterns basically promulgated by men.

As we proceed in the following chapters, the nature of this fifth society should become clear. However, we must keep in mind that contemporary society will change—in fact it is entirely possible that a new society will emerge.

4

Becoming "Boys," "Men," "Guys," and "Dudes"

Persons born possessing XY chromosome patterns, male and female hormones, a penis, testicles, seminal vesicles, and prostate glands generally are identified as biological males. These biological males, however, are *not born* "boys," "men," "guys," or "dudes." In order for one of these social beings to come about, a kind of transformation process must occur. Involved in the transformation most generally is a socialization process whereby biological males learn attitudes, motives, values, skills, feelings, knowledge, and behaviors associated with being boys, men, guys, and dudes. The critical point here is that biological males *must learn* to be one of the above social beings; they are *not born* these social beings. Stated differently, a given biological male youth becomes a boy not simply because he has "male biological equipment" but because he learns to feel, think, and act like a boy. While Zane Grey's reputed comment that "every boy likes baseball, and if he doesn't he isn't a boy" might have been insensitive to differences among male youth, it was definitely on target with respect to the social determination of "boyhood" in America during the times of Zane Grey.

To illustrate further the social nature of being a particular type of male, let us consider the term "dude," most commonly used today among certain minority groups males in urban inner-city areas. In such areas, it is a term used frequently by some males to refer somewhat affectionately to a fellow male who is perceived as "cool," who has the "right" attitudes and values (ones similar to the male who is labeling), and who displays behaviors deemed acceptable by the "dude" peer group. Obviously, not all biological males are seen by those minority group males as falling within the "dude" category despite the fact that they have male biological characteristics. For instance, older males, much younger males, those males who are not seen as "cool," and those who do not behave in ways deemed acceptable by in-group males are not perceived as "dudes." This means that being a "dude," just as being a boy, a man, or a guy, involves much that is "socially constructed" and "socially determined." Yet, to be a boy, man, guy, or dude is not divorced totally from biology. When these social beings are compared with female social beings, girls and women, biological differences are apparent. As stated in chapter 1, males and females both possess estrogen, progesterone, androgen, and testosterone. In males, however, the dominant hormones are androgen and testosterone, while the dominant ones in females are estrogen and progesterone. Other biological differences between males and females relate to the different biological equipment the two sexes bring to the reproduction arena and the different roles assumed by males and females in the reproduction process.

Additional biological differences between the sexes which are proposed relate to physical strength, mental abilities, sexual drive, physical appearance, and bonding behavior. Because males have greater upper-body muscular development than females, they also typically develop greater physical strength related to lifting and throwing. Females, on the other hand, develop greater physical endurance. Males and females also seem to develop differently with respect to mental abilities, with females being superior in verbal development during a particular period of the life course and males in general being superior at tasks requiring spatial perception and mathematical skills. This is discussed in more detail below in a brief review of the now classic Maccoby and Jacklin study (1974).

Males and females generally are also different in physical appearance. Such differences usually are apparent at birth. Newborn males on an average are longer and weigh more than newborn females (at birth, American males average 19.8 inches and 8.4 pounds, while American females average 19.3 inches and 7.5 pounds). Average height and weight differences between males and females continue into adulthood as secondary sex characteristics become apparent (e.g., hip contours, muscular development, body hair, shoulder width, voice tone, etc.).

Lionel Tiger and Robin Fox (1971) offer still another biologically based difference between the sexes. They contend that males and females bond differently. Females are said to bond almost instinctively with their newborn babies, while males are said to be biologically programmed to bond with other males similar to themselves. Rooted in evolutionary prehistory, according to this line of thought, male bonding behavior occurs because the behavior has been selected and has survived in the course of evolution.

One of the most comprehensive studies related to psychological sex differences and one which has been widely cited was published by Eleanor Maccoby and Carol Jacklin in 1974. The meta-analysis was based on an examination and interpretation of findings from over sixteen hundred studies in the gender literature related to psychological sex differences between males and females. Despite some arguments to the contrary (e.g., Block 1976), Maccoby and Jacklin's conclusions generally are accepted in the field with minor modifications. They found strong support for greater verbal and physical aggression in males than females; greater visual-spatial ability in males than females; greater mathematical skills in males than females beginning around age twelve; and greater verbal ability in females than males between the ages of eleven and eighteen years. Mixed findings were reported by Maccoby and Jacklin on the issues of sex differences with respect to activism in social play, competitive behavior, intersex dominance efforts, and passive behavior. Since sex differences refer to biological differences between males and females, contemporary evidence seemingly offers little support for a biological explanation of the vast behavioral and psychological differences between males and females. Instead, such differences seem to have a sociocultural basis; biology does seem to play some role in psychological sex differences, but the precise nature of this role remains to be determined.

In Samuel Osherson's *Finding Our Fathers* (1986), one easily can get the impression that masculinity in its various forms is innate in persons born male. When Osherson suggests that boys in early childhood (around age three) begin a search for a masculine model on which to build a sense of self, while simultaneously withdrawing from women and femininity, the die is cast. One senses that for Osherson a kind of masculinity with stereotyped and dichotomized thinking is lurking inside of the boy pressing him to identify with his father or a father figure. This rudimentary bit of masculinity which presses the boy to identify with his father or some father figure is seen as crucial for the development of full masculinity as an adult male. Generally this means that boys have to give up "mother" for "father," but who is "father"? Osherson says that "father" often is a shadowy figure at best, difficult to understand. The result is that boys rarely experience fathers as sources of warm, soft nurtur-

ance, and what actually happens is that mother or some other female provider picks up the slack. Discussing the implications of this for young
males, Osherson states:

> If father is not there to provide a confident, rich model of man-
> hood, then the boy is left in a vulnerable position: having to dis-
> tance himself from mother without a clear and understanding
> model of male gender upon which to base his emerging identity.
> This situation places great pressure on the growing son, as well as
> the father. We often misidentify with our fathers, crippling our
> identities as men. Distortions and myths shape normal men's pic-
> tures of their fathers, based on the uneasy peripheral place fathers
> occupied in their own homes. Boys grow into men with a wounded
> father within, a conflicted inner sense of masculinity rooted in
> men's experience of their fathers as rejecting, incompetent, or ab-
> sent. (P. 4)

Osherson's ideas about how boys become men seem to be firmly en-
sconced within what psychologist Joseph Pleck calls the Male Sex Role
Identity paradigm discussed in chapter 2.

Despite Osherson's acknowledgement of Pleck's *Myth of Masculinity* (1981), he forges ahead and presents an analysis which, in part, is
based on a male sex-role identity paradigm. The assumptions underlying
this paradigm have been outlined earlier and will not be repeated here.
One assumption, however, related directly to a biological determinism
view of masculinity should be mentioned. The MSRI paradigm, as outlined and explicated by Pleck, presumes *an innate psychological need in
males to develop a male sex role identity* (pp. 3–4). This feature of the
MSRI paradigm is an implicit part of Osherson's conception of male psychological and social psychological development. Therefore, it is possible to interpret Osherson's perspective as saying that males become
boys, men, guys, and dudes because of their innate need to do so. In this
chapter, however, a different position is taken. Males become different
kinds of social beings because of a socialization process which is some
function of biology and environment.

What Is Male Socialization?

By now it should be fairly clear that becoming a boy, man, and so on
from our perspective primarily involves a learning process. The newborn male, for example, typically has transmitted to him all of the man-

ners of a boy and simultaneously learns, through interactions with others, that he is a boy or at least not a girl. We will return to this point a little later. The critical idea is that newborn males become socially defined males and labeled accordingly through a process of learning which involves the inculcation of a culture's definition of masculinity and the development of the male self. This means that male socialization is *a dual process of becoming a male social being which involves (1) the development and awareness of the male self and (2) learning societal prescriptions and proscriptions for males*. Several theoretical approaches have been developed within the social sciences to understand how persons acquire a sense of self and how they learn the ways of a given society. Essentially this is what this chapter is all about. While our concern is restricted to male socialization and only tangentially relates to female socialization, with one or two exceptions, the materials presented easily can be modified to include female socialization.

Approaches to Male Socialization

Before exploring male socialization in more detail, it should be pointed out that there is not complete agreement in the gender literature over how we are transformed from biological newborn males and females into boys and girls and men and women. Some feel, for example, that the transformation process occurs primarily via social learning involving reinforcement and modeling, while others contend that cognitive development is the essential ingredient in the process. Beginning with Lawrence Kohlberg's cognitive developmental analysis, four approaches to male socialization as related to the development of the male self are presented below. While the approaches will vary considerably, one thread of continuity will run throughout the perspectives, and that is the interaction of biology and environment in producing the social male, whether he is a boy, a man, a guy, or a dude.

Becoming a Boy:
Lawrence Kohlberg's Cognitive Developmental Analysis

Julius Lester (1973) gives a classic account of numerous incidents throughout his childhood, adolescence, and young adulthood related to his process of male association. Consider the following excerpts:

As boys go, I wasn't much. I mean, I tried to be a boy and spent many childhood hours pummeling my hardly formed ego with failure at cowboys and Indians, baseball, football, lying, and sneaking out of the house. . . . I tried to believe my parents when they told me I was boy, but I could find no objective proof for such an assertion. . . . Through no fault of my own I reached adolescence. While the pressure to prove myself on the athletic field lessened, the overall situation got worse—because now I had to prove myself with girls. Just how I was supposed to do that was beyond me, especially because, at the age of fourteen, I was four foot nine and weighed 78 pounds. . . . I tried, but I wasn't good at being a boy. Now, I'm glad, knowing that a man is nothing but the figment of a penis's imagination, any man should want to be something more than that. (Pp. 112–13)

Lester points out in the above account that he was not especially good at acting out the male sex role societal script. From Lester's perspective, his behavior was not sufficiently masculine to enable him to "earn" the label "boy" or "young man." As he moved from childhood to adolescence to adulthood, Lester, by his own account, moved from one stage of difficulty fulfilling the male sex role to another, realizing finally that male sex role requirements indeed were socially constructed rather than biologically determined.

While Lester was terrorized by the societal sex role script he was supposed to follow, and seemed not to be able to follow it, numerous other people we call "boys" and "men" act out the script with minimum difficulty. How do they accomplish this? For an answer, let us examine several basic ideas underlying the cognitive developmental approach to male socialization. Psychologist Lawrence Kohlberg (1966) is the foremost proponent of the cognitive developmental approach to male socialization. He endorses the notion that *sex role attitudes are patterned directly by the child's cognitive organization of its social world along sex role dimensions*. Many aspects of this patterning of sex role attitudes are seen as universal and involve "natural" components. But it is the nature of the patterning of sex role attitudes that gives cognitive developmental theory its uniqueness among male socialization approaches. The patterning of sex role attitudes is essentially "cognitive" and is embedded in the child's conception of physical things which includes his or her own body as well as the bodies of others. Children's conceptions of their bodies and the bodies of others in turn are related to society's use of sex categories. Societies tend to use sex categories in culturally universal ways which contribute to universality in sex role attitudes. The reason universality in sex role attitudes exists rests on two basic principles:

1. The child cognitively organizes social roles around universal physical dimensions.
2. The child actively organizes his/her perceptions and learnings of social roles around his/her basic conception of his/her own body and the world.

What emerges as important in the development of sex role attitudes from Kohlberg's perspective is the observational learning of social roles rather than learning as some function of reinforcement of one's own responses (p. 83). For Kohlberg, learning is cognitive and includes selection and internal organization by relational schemata. These relational schemata bind concepts of the body, the physical world, the social world, and general categories of causality, quantity, time, space, logical inclusions, and so forth. On cognitive organization, Kohlberg writes that the child's "basic modes of cognitive organization change with age," and this involves changes in the child's conceptions of its physical and social worlds (p. 83). These are "natural" changes resulting from experience—linked changes in the child's modes of cognition. Because the child's sex role concepts are defined in universal physical or body terms (e.g., males are bigger, stronger, etc.), they also undergo universal developmental changes.

When considering the role of socializing agents such as caretakers, parents, etc. in male socialization, attitudes from these sources are seen as differentially stimulating or retarding development of sex role concepts rather than directly teaching them. Male sex role development, for Kohlberg (1966, p. 85), is the result of:

1. The male child actively structuring his own experience.
2. The emergence of basic, normal, adult sexual concepts and attitudes from childish attitudes.

Thus, male sex role development involves restructuring childish sexual concepts and attitudes, which occurs because the child uses the experiences of his body and environment in constructing basic sex role concepts and attitudes.

Basic cognitive categorizing of self (gender identity) and others are critical aspects of male sex role development. The process is initiated when the male child hears and learns the verbal labels "boy" and "girl." A male child learning that he is a boy typically occurs between the ages of two and four, with *most young males learning to correctly label themselves in the second and third year.* During the third year, a boy may begin to generalize sex labels unsystematically to others on the basis of a loose cluster of physical characteristics. He remains, however, uncertain about the constancy of gender and may believe, for instance, that if a boy wears a dress, he changes into a girl, or if a girl wears pants, she changes into a boy. Between the ages of three and five, the boy learns to label others correctly according to conventional cues but still is uncertain about the constancy of gender. *During ages five through seven, the boy comes to realize that gender remains constant,* and this is a part of the general stabilization of constancies of physical objects—the general process of conceptual growth.

Also critical in Kohlberg's analysis of male self development is the boy's development of sex role stereotypes which follows the development of gender-constant categories. Suggesting that culturally universal meanings exist for various objects, including the concepts "man" and "woman," Kohlberg goes on to posit universal meanings of gender roles. He says that boys develop sex role stereotypes not as a direct perception of differences in role models' behaviors but as a consequence of perceived sex differences in bodily structures and capacities together with the general disposition of humans to concrete symbolic thought.

Awareness of generalized genital differences between the sexes and the realization that genitals are the central basis of gender categorization typically occurs between the ages of five and seven. Prior to this, however, there is the development of diffuse masculine-feminine stereotypes based largely on the meanings of nongenital body imagery (Kohlberg 1966, p. 104). By age five or six, males are awarded greater power, strength, competence, and status than females. Females, however, are awarded superior values on nurturance, moral "niceness," and attractiveness. Aside from universal correlations made between bodily structures and symbolic thought, the boy *observes* differences in both familial and extrafamiliar values (e.g., males are more powerful, more competitive, more aggressive, etc.).

The development of these three basic and universal conceptions of gender role in boys between the ages of three and seven are followed by *the development of sex-typed preferences and values.* Before discussing these developments, let us summarize briefly the above three developments (Kohlberg 1966, p.107):

1. During ages three through five, there is the development of diffuse masculine—feminine stereotypes based largely on nongenital body imagery.

2. During ages five and six, there is the development of constant gender categories.

3. During ages five through seven, an awareness of genial differences develops.

If one remembers that the boy's basic sex role concepts develop from his active interpretation of the social order, which defines the sexes in universal ways, Kohlberg's analysis of the development of masculine values easily can be grasped. He feels that the boy's sex role concepts and sex role identity result in masculine or sex-typed values and behaviors. Why should this occur? From Kohlberg's perspective, the boy spontaneously evaluates self and others. Moreover, the boy also has a natural tendency to ascribe worth to himself, to seek worth, to make comparisons between his own worth and that of others, and to evaluate others' worth (Kohlberg 1966, p. 108). Axiomatically, those who are seen as similar to self (other males) will be evaluated more positively than those who are seen as dissimilar (females). This is so because of the boy's tendency toward egocentric evaluation, which also leads the boy to value that which is identified with self and motivates him to enact or conform to whatever role persons like himself perform (regardless of the rewards associated with the role). Conformity to the male role by a male, from the boy's perspective, is seen as morally right, and deviation from the male role by a male is seen as morally wrong. Thus, aside from the "natural" tendency of the boy to identify with similar others (male models), identification with male models is seen by the boy as morally correct.

In summary, Lawrence Kohlberg views male sex role development as being a direct result of sex role identity. After the boy learns to label himself "a boy" and recognizes constancy in gender categories, sex role learning occurs. Typically, the boy acquires those sex role attitudes, values, and behaviors that society deems appropriate for boys to acquire. The following aspects of sex role development define the typical process for boys according to Kohlberg's cognitive developmental perspective:

1. Infancy to age two: The male child hears the label "boy" and sees it being applied to self and some others. He also hears the label "girl" and sees it being applied to some others but not to himself.

2. Somewhere between the ages of two and three, the boy learns his own gender label ("I am a boy").

3. During the age of three the boy comes to know that some others are also called "boys." However, he may not correctly discriminate the sex of others.

4. Between the ages three and five the boy learns to label others correctly according to conventional cues. (He knows that the person is a boy because a boy wears short hair, trousers, and plays with trucks.)
5. Diffuse masculine-feminine stereotypes also develop during the age three to five period (girls play with dolls and always wear dresses).
6. During the ages five and six the development of constancy in gender categories occurs. (Even though a little boy plays with a doll, he is still a boy.)
7. During the ages five through seven the boy develops an awareness of genital differences between the sexes.
8. Following the development of sex role identity, the typical boy expresses a preference for masculine values and behaviors ascribing worth to himself and similar others.

Becoming a Man:
The "Developmental" Work of Daniel Levinson

The biological male develops a male sex role identity and begins to express preferences for masculine values and behaviors. Attention devoted to sex role learning during childhood has given us a pretty good understanding of this formative phase of development, a time during which the individual grows biologically, psychologically, and socially. While there is not complete agreement over the nature and sequence of the periods and transitions in the formative stages, it is generally accepted that "all lives are governed by common developmental principles in childhood and adolescence and go through a common sequence of developmental periods" (Levinson et al. 1978, p. 3). What had been neglected prior to Levinson et al.'s groundbreaking ten-year study was an adequate conception of the life cycle as a whole. In *The Seasons of a Man's Life*, Levinson and colleagues present what they say is a "more detailed picture of development in early and middle adulthood" (p. 4). I would like to add to this that the presentation is a detailed picture of *male* adulthood and therefore is quite appropriate for our concerns here.

To begin with, "becoming a man" from the perspective of Levinson et al., involves qualitatively different periods in male development which follow sequences. The biological male continues to experience growth, development, and character change following the transition from early childhood to adolescence to early adulthood. In other words, the typical male, from birth to death, experiences a *life course*, which may be defined as "the patterning of specific events, relationships, achievements, failures, and aspirations that are the stuff of life" (p. 6). The developmental approach proposed by the authors does not suggest a steady, continuous stream of development. Instead, Levinson et al. view the human male life cycle as following an underlying universal pattern with numerous cultural and individual variations which possibly alter and sometimes even stop the developmental process. Nevertheless, if the process goes on, it is seen as following basic sequences which are discussed below.

Another critical aspect of the Levinson et al. approach is that there are "seasons" within the life cycle, and each period of adult male development has its own distinctive character—"every season is different from those that precede and follow it, though it also has much in common with them" (p. 6). Actually, Levinson et al. feel that seasons are relatively stable, yet dynamic. Change occurs from one season to another and transitions are seen as necessary for these shifts. Let us now turn our attention to the seasons in a typical man's life, keeping in mind that we are referring to qualitatively different periods in a male's development. We begin with the analytical tool used by Levinson et al. to explore the sequence of periods in a male's life—life structure. Life structure is viewed as "the basic pattern or design of a person's life at a given time" (p. 14). It connotes the relationship between the individual and society and involves three elements:

1. The man's sociocultural world, which entails placing him within social contexts such as class, race, family economic system, etc.
2. The man's *self*, including his wishes, feelings, cognitions, behavior, values, and ideals (both conscious and nonconscious)
3. The man's participation in his social world, the various roles assumed by him such as father, husband, friend, lover, and the like

In describing this life structure for a man, Levinson, et al. believe that the most useful components are the choices the man makes and their consequences with respect to the above elements. What does it mean for a man to choose a particular profession? If I choose to become a corporate executive, what implications will this have for aspects of my self and for the way I participate in my social world? Marker events signaling the end of a season and/or the beginning of a season certainly may be influenced by choices in the above areas, but often marker events are not due to a man's voluntary effort or choice. Rather, marker events are involuntary, a result of such circumstances as war, depression, death of others, illness of others, etc. Such events cause the man to be *pushed* into a different period in the life cycle. While the man, in this instance, has no choice but to enter the period, his adaptation to the period will be influenced by how he has developed previously; both will affect his later life. Specifically, the periods in a man's adult development outlined by Levinson et al. are as follows:

1. Early Adulthood—seventeen to forty
   a. Seventeen to twenty-two: Early adult transition (links adolescence to early adulthood)
   b. Twenty-two to twenty-eight: Entering the adult world (creates a first adult-life structure)
   c. Thirty: Transition
   d. Thirty-three to forty: Settling down period (builds second adult structure and reaches end of early adulthood)

2. Middle Adulthood—forty to sixty
   a. Forty to forty-five: The midlife transition (links early and middle adulthood)
   b. Forty-five to fifty: Entering middle adulthood (builds first life structure for middle adulthood)
   c. Fifty to fifty-five: Age fifty transition (works further on tasks of midlife transition)
   d. Fifty-five to sixty: Culmination of middle adulthood (builds second middle adult structure)

3. Late Adulthood—sixty plus
   a. Sixty to sixty-five: Late adult transition (terminates middle adulthood and creates basis for starting late adulthood)

Growing out of an intellectual tradition begun by Sigmund Freud, Carl Jung, Erik Erikson, and others, Levinson et al. set out to gain a deeper understanding of male adulthood through the construction of a systematic conception of the male life cycle. The conception of the male life cycle is facilitated by an intensive exploratory study of the lives of forty men from "diverse sectors of society" (p. 9).

What is the nature of each of the "seasons" of a man's life? The typical male derives much of what he brings to the early-adult-transition period from socialization settings highly supportive of young biological males' assumptions of societally sanctioned male sex roles. In many ways this is quite functional for the first tasks which must be accomplished by the early adult male. For example, traits like "independence" and "decisiveness," which are nurtured especially in young males during childhood, play important roles during the early-adult-transition period. During this period the young male is expected to modify, if not end, his dependent and nurturing relationships with parents and significant others as well as groups and institutions which were supportive during adolescence. He must begin to make choices and preparations for his first adult male life structure. In our society, traditionally this has meant "standing up and being a man."

While the early-adult-transition period may be somewhat unstable for our hypothetical young man, he is expected to resolve all of the anxieties, conflicts, and problems associated with the period and move on to the new period, entering the adult world. During this period, beginning around age twenty-two, the young male is expected to view himself as an adult with all of the traits society ascribes to as "young adult man." Levinson et al. suggest that societal expectations are that the male just entering the adult world should "hang loose," keeping his options open and avoiding strong commitments (p. 79). If explorations were the only societal expectations, a young man entering the adult world easily could resolve conflicts and problems with this period of adult development. However, entering the adult world also means that the young man is expected to create a stable structure. In addition to "explorations," the young adult male is pressured to "grow up," set and define goals, marry, get a job, and, in general, lead a more organized life. Obviously, the crisis that has to be resolved during this period is balancing both exploration and stability in the young adult male's life structure. Traditionally, the conflict has been resolved by young men actually attempting to fulfill the societal expectations of stability as manifested by the proportion of young men who never married.[1] While this cannot be substantiated here, some male instability during the entering-the-adult-world period may be linked to both conflicting societal expectations and early childhood male socialization, stressing male aggression, violence, dominance and so on.

Levinson et al. see the age-thirty-transition period as "a remarkable gift and burden" (p. 84). It is a period for working out plans in the life structure formed during the previous period. Change is characteristic of this period and men are expected to become more serious and stable

---

1. In 1970, only 19.1 percent of men 25 to 29 had never married. By 1985, this proportion had risen to 38.7 percent. The Bureau of the Census reports that young people, in general, are postponing marriage. During the 1960s, the Bureau reports, the median age at first marriage for men and women rose slowly but has increased dramatically since 1970, with the median age of first marriage for men and women in 1985 being 25.5 years and 23.3 years, respectively (Current Population Reports, Oct. 1985, Population Profile of the U.S., 1984/85, Special Studies Series, p. 23; No. 150, p. 22).

with goals set and the means for attaining the goals fully planned. After all, this is the end of the preparatory phase in early adulthood.

The settling-down period (ages thirty-three to forty) supposedly facilitates stability and life satisfaction for males. Change now is seen as creating much strain and many pressures, because men during this period are expected to anchor their lives more firmly in family, occupation, and community (p. 140). Working to advance, including building a better life, becoming more creative, contributing to society, and in a nutshell, fulfilling a dream also are aspects of the settling-down period fashioned for men by the American social order. Again, stressful aspects of the sex role men are expected to assume loom as important. Building family and community ties can create stability for a man, but simultaneous upward strivings in occupation and society in general may mean that stability in his life is threatened. Resolving this conflict certainly is no easy matter and, perhaps, may only occur with a modification in societal expectations for adult males during this period.

The midlife-transition period is one in which the man focuses both on the past and on the future. Because he has begun to recognize his own mortality, our hypothetical man reappraises his past and feels that the time remaining has to be used wisely. Many men during this period begin to question their values and beliefs, recognizing that aspects of their lives have been illusions. Nevertheless, the typical man gradually shifts his focus to the future, making choices that will modify his existing life structure and "provide the central elements for a new one" (p. 194). When the choices and the commitment are made, middle adulthood begins.

The entering-middle-adulthood period is the time when a man must resolve the polarities of young/old, destruction/creation, masculine-/feminine, and attachment/separateness. Levinson et al. say about these concepts that:

> The four polarities whose resolution is the principal task of mid-life individuation are: (1) Young/Old; (2) Destruction/Creation; (3) Masculine/Feminine; and (4) Attachment/Separateness. Each of these pairs forms a polarity in the sense that the two terms represent opposing tendencies or conditions. Superficially, it would appear that a person has to be one or the other and cannot be both. In actuality, however, the paired tendencies are not mutually exclusive. Both sides of each polarity coexist within every self.

Regarding the polarities, the midlife man must confront the young/old polarity within himself, giving up certain youthful qualities and retaining and transforming others; he must also recognize and take responsibility for his destructive actions toward others. Often this is followed by creative impulses to bring something into being; to generate; being confronted with the masculine/feminine polarity, an inheritance from early male socialization, the man must recognize and integrate the masculine and feminine in self. Our man must modify his life structures by forming new relationships with maleness and femaleness. He must come to recognize that while the masculine is reduced in some ways (decline in physical prowess, ambition, achievement, toughness, etc.), it may be enhanced in others because of a lesser need to inhibit the feminine (he can care for a younger man without fearing homosexual meanings—combine work and personal relationships), and our man must also solve the problem of finding a balance between the needs of self and society. Solving this problem means paying more attention to self and becoming less tyranized by ambitions, dependencies, and passions. It also means more involvement with others and performing social roles in more responsible ways such as responding more to the developmental needs of offspring and other young adults. What is occurring here is an integration of the attachment/separateness polarity.

Middle adulthood is followed by the age-fifty-transition period. This period (ages fifty to fifty-five) is a time when the man continues his midlife transition. He can experience crises about the character of his life if this has not been worked out in the midlife-transition period. If our hypothetical man has not altered the nature of his familial relationships or work life, changes in both may be forthcoming during this time. Levinson et al. feel that "it is not possible for the man to get through middle adulthood without having at least a moderate crisis in either the midlife transition or the age fifty transition."

The age-fifty-transition period is followed by the culmination-of-middle adulthood period (ages fifty-five to sixty), a time when the man builds a second middle adult structure which allows him to complete middle adulthood. This is a stabler period and often is characterized by self-rejuvenation and life enrichment. Many men during this time experience great fulfillment, and if a man has survived the crises which can occur in the age-fifty-transition period, he can look forward to this rather pleasant experience.

The late-adult-transition period (ages sixty to sixty-five) comes immediately after the culmination of middle adulthood. During this time a man finishes all the tasks associated with the previous period and creates a basis for starting late adulthood. The major tasks to be accomplished are ending middle adulthood and preparing for late adulthood. Levinson et al. feel that this is a significant time for most men, since it is a major turning point in the life cycle. The man during this period must be prepared to move from center stage and thus receive less recognition because he has assumed less responsibility. This can be a traumatic time if the man does not wisely step aside, allowing his adult offspring and others to assume major responsibility and authority in the family. Obviously, similar steps must be followed in the man's work life lest he becomes "out of phase" with his own generation and in conflict with the new middle-adulthood generation. The man now must find a proper balance between involvement with society and with self.

If our man can concentrate more on self now, becoming wiser and using his own inner resources, this season can be full and rich. This is evidenced by the great works of men like Picasso, Verdi, Freud, and Jung who entered late adulthood and made lasting "wise" contributions to society during this time. Near the end of this period, the polarity *integrity vs. despair* must be reckoned with. A man must appraise his life and if at all possible find meaning and value—gain a sense of integrity. If he does, our man will live his last years without bitterness or despair.

If our man survives various infirmities and chronic illnesses, he will enter late late adulthood. The chief task of this period is to come to terms with the process of dying and prepare for his own death. Peace *must* be made with dying by the man of this period in order for him to get on with his life in late late adulthood, a life where he reaches his ultimate involvement with self—"knowing it and loving it reasonably well, and being ready to give it up" (Levinson et al. 1978, p. 39).

In sum, male socialization, from Levinson et al.'s perspective, involves the development of the self and the acquisition of knowledge, skills, and so on throughout the entire life of a man. Male socialization means that a given biological male develops numerous selves (even core ones) which undergo transitions from one self to another. Male socialization also refers to the fact that the acquisition of skills and knowledge is an ongoing process with various periods in the male life cycle dictating that men acquire certain kinds of skills and knowledge which can be used to construct an appropriate life structure. This process continues until the man reaches the time for which he prepares in late adulthood—death.

Becoming a "Guy":
Albert Bandura's Social Learning Perspective

One of the most important periods in the lives of many males is adolescence. It is a time when most young males experience at least rudimentary development of many "masculine" traits which will undergo refinement later during early adulthood. Traits such as dominance, aggression, competitiveness, and even violence often begin to appear in the behaviors of many male adolescents. While these traits may have been present unsystematically in early and late male childhood behavior, it is in adolescence that they become systematic and purposive. While these qualities may not be readily apparent, frequently they are manifested by adolescent males' overconforming "masculine" behaviors. Why do adolescent males behave in ways which frequently are thought to be dysfunctional for society and for themselves? Why is such destructive behavior so pervasive among male adolescents?

A popular view of adolescence in Western societies is that it is a period of stress and strain, and this is the cause of much inappropriate male adolescent behavior. This may be true; however, the social learning perspective offers us a more systematic way of viewing how males going through adolescence become guys. To begin with, in the view of the chief proponent of social learning theory, Albert Bandura, "except for elementary reflexes, people are not equipped with inborn repertoires of behaviors" (1977, p. 16). Bandura does recognize, however, that the biological is important. He says, "Genetics and hormones affect physical development which in turn can influence behavioral potentialities" (p. 16). Accordingly, while the biological male is born with behavioral potentialities, these alone do not explain behavior. It is through their interaction with experiential influences that male social behavior is determined.

Cognition is a critical element in the determination of behavior. While some approaches to *learning by response consequences* suggest responses are shaped automatically by their consequences (Bijou and Baer 1978; Skinner 1974; Burgess and Akers 1966), Bandura's social learning approach emphasizes cognition as important in most social learning. While it may be possible that some relatively simple actions are modified by their consequences without awareness of the response-stimulus consequences connection, Bandura feels that the cognitive capacities of humans enable them to profit significantly from experience. Because humans are cognitive, response consequences serve two other functions in addition to automatic strengthening of responses: (1) they impart information, and (2) they motivate through incentive.

In learning by response consequences during early childhood, the male child learns to respond in various ways to his environment (which includes others). At the same time he is learning to respond, the male child also becomes aware of the effects his responses produce. When he observes these effects, he then develops hypotheses about the "appropriateness" of his responses which serve as information used to guide his future behavior. If his hypotheses are accurate, this leads to successful performances, but if they are inaccurate, this leads to unsuccessful performances. When the male child's performances are successful, cognitions leading to them are strengthened; when his performances are unsuccessful, his cognitions leading to them are weakened. Thus, our male child learns to be a boy/guy when he behaves as a boy/guy, because he learns that the consequences of behaving as a boy/guy for him are rewarding. This informative function of response consequences operates for the boy when his peer group during adolescence withholds the "regular guy" status from him until his behaviors conform to peer group expectations.

Aside from learning that conforming with American societal sex role expectations leads to positive outcomes (an informative function of response consequences), the typical male child also comes to *expect* certain benefits from behaving in a sex-typed way (a motivation function of response consequences). He foresees the future symbolically by converting future consequences into current motivators of his behavior (Bandura 1977, p. 18). In a given situation, our potential "guy" behaves in a way that he "knows" will bring him rewards. If he is with his friends, this can mean that he lies about his conquest of girls, because he knows the "guys" will hold him in high esteem.

In addition to the automatic strengthening and information functions of response consequences, a third function, reinforcement, also is associated with learning by response consequences. This function is not, however, of the variety that psychologist B. F. Skinner speaks. Reinforcement for Albert Bandura does not mean consequences which increase behaviors automatically without conscious and/or cognitive involvement. Moreover, Bandura feels that the concept "response strengthening" is appropriate to use in describing the effects on a response of reinforcement. Once responses are learned, the likelihood that they will be given in a certain situation can be varied by altering the outcomes they produce. The response itself, however, is not strengthened; rather, the probability of giving the response is altered. This means that the outcome of a response (benefits, rewards, etc.) *regulates some behaviors rather than reinforces these behaviors.* For example, the adolescent boy's peer group *does not strengthen* his hubcap stealing behavior by heaping praise on him, but instead, *regulates his behavior* by increasing the likelihood that he will steal hubcaps.

Learning by response consequences is only one aspect of Bandura's social learning approach to male socialization. A second aspect of social learning theory is *learning through modeling*. Bandura feels that this is the process through which *most* human behavior is learned. By observing others the young male gets ideas about how new behaviors are performed, which later serve to guide his behaviors. The boy is socialized by this process because modeling has a direct influence on learning due to its *information function*. The symbolic representations of the modeled activities acquired by the boy during exposure to the model serve to inform him as to what performances society or significant others deem appropriate. Bandura conceptualizes observational learning as being governed by four processes: attentional processes, retention processes, motor reproduction processes, and motivational processes. It should be pointed out that the processes involved in observational learning are quite complex and involve response information conveyed in a variety of ways. Yet, the basic modeling process is the same regardless of whether behavior is conveyed through words, pictures, or live action.

Bandura's most impressive discussion of the social learning process is learning through modeling. People do not learn only from the consequences of their own behavior. In fact, *most* of our behavior is learned by observing the behaviors of others and the consequences of those behaviors for others. We do not have to make needless error or engage in tremendous amounts of trial-and-error behaviors; instead, we learn observationally via modeling, which is governed by attentional processes, retention processes, motor reproduction processes, and motivational processes.

Following social learning theory, then, young males learn much of their social behavior by paying attention to or observing the behaviors of older male models—thus, *attentional processes*. While much of this observation is casual and direct observation of older males' behaviors in everyday social interaction, symbolic modeling is another source of social learning. Young males acquire many attitudes, emotional responses, and behaviors through television, films, and a variety of visual media.

One does not have to believe that there is a "natural tendency" toward male egocentric (as in cognitive developmental theory) preference in sex role identity to understand why young males learn to engage in sex-typed behavior. From Bandura's social learning perspective, young males come to differentially value older males' behavior primarily because they see male behaviors as engaging, influential, and appropriate. This differential valuation of male and female behavior is both promoted and supported by formal and informal support systems in the society (Block 1983). In addition, young males are instructed both formally and informally that these are the precise behaviors (e.g., behaviors which are independent, self-reliant, strong willed) which society says are appropriate for them to adopt. Given this information, coupled with society's differential valuation of adult male/female behaviors, almost axiomatically young males give greater attention to the behaviors of adult male models—both *direct* behaviors and *symbolic* behaviors.

If the young male is to adequately learn the male sex role, not only must he selectively observe older male models' behaviors, and therefore give them greater attention, but he also must selectively retain the older male models' behaviors. In other words, it is important for the young male not only to pay attention to male behaviors that "guys" engage in, but he must also remember these behaviors—thus, the importance of *retention processes*. This implies that young males in all likelihood develop male-oriented representational systems.

Bandura feels that observational learning relies mainly on imaginal and verbal representational systems related to retention. First of all, imaginal systems emerge because exposure to and emphases on male model behaviors eventually lead to enduring and retrievable images of modeled performances (Bandura 1977, p. 25). The young males' images of certain situations can be mentally called up later, when the situations are not physically present. The second representational system identified by Bandura is *verbal*. According to him, most of the cognitive processes that regulate behavior are primarily verbal rather than visual. Labels are given for behaviors, and this facilitates the retention of behaviors. Moreover, the boy can mentally rehearse adult male behaviors, thus visualizing himself performing the sex role appropriate behavior.

A third component that Bandura feels is critical in social learning through modeling is *motor reproduction processes*. This component recognizes the necessity for the boy to be able to organize his responses spatially and temporarily with the modeled behavior. In addition to cognitively organizing his response, the boy must be able to *physically initiate* the behavior, *monitor it*, and *refine it* from information feedback. If any of these response components are lacking, the boy's behavioral reproduction will be faulty. Such faulty behavioral reproductions are quite frequent, for example, in boys' early efforts to be regular "guys" in boys' peer groups. Through self-correction adjustments from peer group informational feedback, the boy refines his performance of the male/guys role in social interaction. Moreover, he may begin to focus more on the segments of the role that he has learned only partially, which may also enhance his performance. If learning is to occur through modeling it is also important that the modeled behavior is favored over other forms of behavior. People tend to adopt those behaviors which result in outcomes valuable to them. If the outcomes of models' behaviors are valuable to a boy, he will be much more likely to adopt the behaviors than if the outcomes are perceived as unrewarding or punishing. Thus, *motivational processes* are critical components of the social learning process in male socialization. If a male model is seen as repeatedly obtaining desired responses from behaving as a "guy" should, the young male observer is taught to reproduce that behavior. When he tries, he is "prompted when he fails and rewarded when he succeeds." Bandura concludes that all of this quite likely leads observers to match models' responses. Finally, failure to learn by modeling, as manifested by matching behavior, may result from "not observing the relevant activities, inadequately coding modeled events for memory representalism, failing to retain what was learned, physical inability to perform, experiencing insufficient incentives" (Bandura 1977, p. 29).

Becoming a "Dude":
George H. Mead's Symbolic Interaction Perspective

"Mind can never find expression and could never have come into existence at all, except in terms of a social environment" (Mead 1934, p. 223). Symbolic interactionists like George H. Mead, Herbert Blumer, John Hewitt, Gregory Stone, and others feel that there are fundamental socio-physiological impulses or needs basic to social behavior and social organization. Examples, according to Mead (p. 228), include the sex or reproductive and parental impulses. But *the nature and the origin of the self are essentially "social."* On the nature of the self, Mead states:

> Self-consciousness involves the individual becoming an object to himself by taking the attitudes of other individuals toward himself within an organized setting of social relationships, and that unless the individual had thus become an object to himself he would not be self-conscious or have a self at all. Apart from his social interactions with other individuals, he would not relate the private or "subjective" contents of his experience to himself, and he could not become aware of himself as such, that is, as an individual, a person, merely by means or in terms of these contents of his experience. (Pp. 225–26)

With this point of departure, it should be easy to grasp the symbolic interaction perspective's basic dictum that the self is not present at birth, but arises in the process of social experiences and activity, in essence, *social interaction.* Symbolic interactionism suggests, as the perspectives discussed earlier, the social environment plays a critical role in male socialization. What is the nature of male socialization from a symbolic interaction perspective? How do biological males become "dudes"?

The process by which a biological male becomes a dude is no different from the process by which biological males become other social males. To be sure, the outcome of the defining characteristic of a "dude" may describe a male person who behaves in strikingly different ways from many other males, yet the social processes producing the "dude" are the same as the ones producing other social males, for example, the typical traditional middle-class American man. The dude's socially constructed and refined form of self-expression, which may consist of postures manifesting emotionlessness, fearlessness, aloofness, secureness, toughness, and detachment, is built using the same mechanisms as the upper-middle-class corporate executive's, whose behavior follows all of the tenets of the Protestant ethic.[2] Let us consider mechanisms in male socialization designated by the symbolic interaction perspective beginning with an early contribution by sociologist Charles H. Cooley.

Charles H. Cooley (1886–1929) was one of the first scholars to challenge scientific and lay circles on the issue of biological primacy in human nature. Consciousness and self-awareness arise out of social interaction, according to Cooley. Moreover, from this perspective, human nature as manifested in the self develops through social interaction with a primary group. Primary groups such as the family, the play group, and the neighbors are thought to be responsible for the individual's social unity and social nature, both of which are reflected in what Cooley called the "looking-glass self." The looking-glass self consists of the imagined appraisal of others and has three aspects which can be used to describe the male self in the following way:

1. Through imagination a given male perceives how he appears to others (both female and male).
2. The male also imagines how others judge his appearance.
3. The male experiences feelings of pride or mortification depending upon how others judge his appearance.

---

2. This definition of "cool dude" is adapted from Richard Major's paper entitled "Cool Pose as a Cultural Signature."

From Cooley's point of view, the nature of this self consists of feelings toward the self. To be sure, self development is accompanied by reflexive affective experiences (e.g., feelings of pride or mortification), but Mead feels such experiences do not explain the origins of the self (1934, p. 173). Instead, the self is lodged in the cognitive. According to Mead, the self "lies in the internalized conversation of gestures which constitutes thinking, or in terms of which thought or reflection proceeds. And hence the origin and foundation of the self, like those of thinking, are social" (p. 173). The nature of the self from this perspective is explored below, but first let us review a concept developed by sociologist W. I. Thomas which also plays an important role in a symbolic interaction approach to male socialization—"definition of the situation."

W. I. Thomas (1863–1947), another early proponent of symbolic interactionism, felt that the individual and society were in constant conflict because individuals were pleasure-seeking while society constrained the individual. A main goal of the society is to resolve conflicts between it and persons who pursue their own selfish interests. From this perspective, society (consisting of such agencies as the family, the church, the community) exists "to define situations" for individuals. On an individual level, Thomas felt that "definition of the situation" is *a phase of examination and deliberation prior to self-determined acts*. Using subjective facts of experience, the individual arrives at a decision to act or not to act along a given line. Analysis of male behavior from this point of view must take into account the definition of the situation as it exists objectively (in terms of societal constraints regarding male behavior) and as it exists subjectively (as defined by the male involved).

Both Cooley's and Thomas' ideas have contributed much to the symbolic interactionist perspective on socialization and are very much evident in contemporary discussions of the topic. Their contributions as well as those of George H. Mead (1863–1931) will be discussed as a symbolic interaction approach to male socialization.

Because the biological male's self is derived from his interaction with others, it is important to examine precisely how such interaction results in male self-development. To begin with, gaining a sense of male selfhood occurs only when the individual male is capable of *carrying on a conversation of significant gestures with himself using individual others in the beginning, and later, the generalized other.* "Conversation of significant gestures" refers to participation in communication whereby the gestures an individual makes to others are also indicated to himself resulting in the same response being called out in self as is called out in others. For Mead, the ability to carry on this conversation of significant gestures is distinctively human as evidenced by the development of language. Language is felt to constitute significant gestures which have the same effect on those making them as they have on those to whom they are addressed or who respond. For example, in some circles when a young male refers to another young male as a "dude," he experiences the same feelings of coolness, toughness, confidence, and so on that his label brings out in the "dude." On the concept of language, Mead states:

> Language in its significant sense is that vocal gesture which tends to arouse in the individual the attitude which it arouses in others and it is this perfecting of the self by the gestures which mediates the social activities that give rise to the process of taking the role of the other. (Pp. 160–61)

Conceivably, through others' use of the word "boy" to describe a male child, and with the child's gradual ability to use "boy" and words others associate with his being a boy, he begins to describe himself in the same way as others describe him. Because such descriptions have meanings, the young male gradually comes to respond to self just as others respond to self. This response process is aided by the young male's ability to engage in "role taking," which Mead says is refined by the perfecting of the self because gestures arouse in self the attitude which they arouse in others (Mead 1934, p. 161). As the boy gradually begins to use language associated with boys to describe himself that he learns from interacting with caregivers and significant others, his role taking ability allows him to assume the attitudes of others toward himself as well as behave toward himself as he perceives others behave. To be sure, this is a complicated process which involves several phases of development before a full sense of selfhood is attained. The path to full selfhood is described below.

Male socialization is facilitated by a long period of male infant dependence during which his attention is focused on the social environment that provides support, nourishment, warmth, and protection. The infant male quite early begins to seek through gestures, especially vocal ones, those comforts which his environment (usually his family) can provide. Eventually, the child's gestures must call out in him the responses, including corresponding vocal ones, made to him by the caregivers in his environment. Once he has this ability, the male infant stimulates himself to vocalize the sounds the caregivers make. This reaction in a given situation is determined by the social environment, which means that the male infant's social environment determines what responses the infant stimulates in himself and in others. It should be remembered that such responses and stimulations are quite incomplete and immature. Nevertheless, it is this rudimentary process involving interaction with others out of which the child gradually develops a self and thus becomes a social being. In describing much of what goes on during this period, Mead writes:

> Its earliest function, in the instance of the infant, is effective adjustment to the little society upon which it has so long to depend. The child is for a long time dependent upon moods and emotional attitudes. How quickly he adjusts himself to this is a continual surprise. He responds to facial expressions earlier than to most stimuli and answers with appropriate expressions of his own before he makes responses that we consider significant. He comes into the world highly sensitive to this so-called "mimic gesture," and he exercises his earliest intelligence in his adaptation to his social environment. . . . In the normal child, the vocal gesture arouses in himself the responses of his elders through their stimulation of his own parental impulse and later of other impulses, which in their childish form are beginning to ripen in his central nervous system. These impulses find their expression first of all in tones of voice and later in combinations of phonetic elements which become articulate speech as they do in the vocal gesture of the talking birds. The child has become, through his own impulses, a parent to himself. (1934, pp. 368–69)

I and me: Phases of the male self. Once the male child has developed some facility with language, socialization proceeds quite rapidly. As a part of male socialization, male self development is dependent on the young male's ability to carry on a conversation of significant gestures. This ability enables him to become an object unto himself.

Actually, these components are considered to be distinguishable phases of the self as "I" and "me" and are seen as separate but belonging together (Mead 1934, p. 178). The "I" is that with which we identify ourselves. "I" am a man who is attempting to communicate with a reader at this particular time. The "I" is the subject aspect of the self as process, while the "me" is the object aspect of the self. The "I" aspect of self responds to the "me" aspect of self. "I talk to myself, and I remember what I said. . . . The 'I' of this moment is present in the 'me' of the next moment. . . . 'I' becomes a 'me' in so far as I remember what I said . . .'' (p. 174).

According to Mead, the "I" is spontaneous and we are never fully aware of what we are—thus surprising ourselves by our own action. "It is as we act that we are aware of ourselves" (p. 174). The "I" is present in our memories.

As the young male performs what he feels is an appropriate masculine role, he arouses in himself the attitude of others toward his performance. The young male responds to this attitude, and his response constitutes his "I." When the boy takes the attitudes of others he constructs the "me" aspect of self. When significant others call upon a boy to give an appropriate masculine response, the boy takes the attitudes of those others ("me" in process) and gives a response to the demand, constructing that response with knowledge of what is wanted and what the consequences will be—all aspects of the "me." It is within this context that the boy's "I" responds. Yet, the boy has not known what the response will be. It may be appropriate or it may not be appropriate. The boy's response as it is in his immediate experience constitutes his "I." When the boy reflects on his actions concluding that, indeed, he was "cool," "calm," and "collected," the way a "dude" would be, his "me" has arisen. The "I" then has entered into the boy's experience and become a part of the boy's "me." The "I" is what the boy was when he responded. This really means that the "I" is "free"; it initiates, and it is uncertain. The "me," in contrast, "represents a definite organization of the community there in our own attitudes and calling for a response, but the response ("I") that takes place is something that just happens (p. 178).

Stages of male self development. From Mead's perspective, the biological male goes through three stages of self development, each stage denoting an ability to engage in a progressively more complex form of role taking. A typical male goes through a *preparatory stage* which can be called a presymbolic period because the interactions which occur seem to lack meaning. The male infant or toddler during this stage does not really separate himself from others because he does not define objects with words and lacks any understanding of the meaning of his behavior and its relationship to others. Behaviors coming from the child during this stage are simply copies of others' behaviors. Yet, near the end of this stage, the child is on the verge of role taking and thus *prepared* to enter the *play stage.*

During the *play stage*, which Mead distinguishes as one of two in the full development of the self, the young male's self is made up of an organization of specific attitudes held by others toward himself and toward each other in specific social acts in which he participates. For example, a boy in the play stage of self development who interacts with other members during a family celebration is capable of assuming the attitude toward himself of each with whom he comes in contact. He can take the role of each specific other, and he can organize the specific attitudes toward himself and the ones of the others toward each other in the specific acts in which he and the others participate. Still, however, full development of the self has not occurred and awaits the *game stage*.

Self development for the social male reaches a peak when he enters the *game stage*. This third stage in the full development of the male self consists not only of the male's organization of specific attitudes of others toward self, but also the male's organization of the social attitudes of the generalized other or the group as a whole of which he is a member. "Only insofar as he takes the attitudes of the organized social group to which he belongs toward the organized cooperative social activity or set of such activities in which that group as such is engaged does he develop a complete self or possess the sort of complex self he has developed" (Mead 1934, p. 155).

If we want to understand how social groups, communities, and the like exert control over the individual male, it is important to recognize that it is in the social process, *generalized other*, that the group influences male behavior. Let us look at an example as it relates to the late adolescent and young adult male becoming, in popular parlance, a "dude."

The influence of the peer group on male socialization during adolescence is well documented. While this influence often runs counter to prevailing cultural norms and values (as was pervasive in America in the 1960s and 1970s), most peer-group influence is decidedly congruent with cultural values and norms (Reich 1970). Astin et al. (1984) have noted the distinctive cultural influence of peer groups in the 1980s toward conformity and tenets of the Protestant ethic with its emphasis on capitalism.

Developing alongside these peer influences embracing cultural attitudes and beliefs fostering conformity are those peer groups that embrace "cool" postures mentioned earlier. How is this possible? It is possible because of typical adolescent and early adult males' abilities to reflect on themselves from the roles of generalized others as well as take the roles of generalized others toward peer groups as a whole, their individual members, and the activities of the peer groups. Without such abilities to become objects unto themselves from the point of view of generalized others, the adolescent and early adult males could not become "dudes." Obviously, from a symbolic interaction perspective, when the biological male develops a fully functioning self, the process of becoming a "dude" is not a mystery. It involves no more and no less than the process of becoming a man or a guy.

Agents of Male Socialization

The human male undergoes a long socialization process whereby he becomes aware of himself as a male and develops sex role skills necessary for full functioning as a social male in society. Much of the emphasis in earlier sections of this chapter has been on self development. Just as important, however, is the sex role which the biological male must learn if he is to fulfill self and others' expectations of himself as a boy, a man, a guy, or dude. What is the nature of this sex role which must be performed if the biological male is to function fully as a social male? Two general male sex roles exist in American society: the *White male sex role* and the *Black male sex role*. These are general masculine roles assumed by American men which are ideal types subject to some deviation. On these two roles, I have stated:

> The two general roles assumed by American males are the *White masculine role* and the *Black masculine role*. I maintain that while subcultural, ethnic, racial and socioeconomic factors may modify the specific masculine role assumed by a specific male, the role that he makes and plays is derived either from the White masculine model or the Black masculine model. These models, I contend, have developed through a long historical process involving social, demographic, and socioeconomic factors. What this means is that masculine role assumptions *may* or *may not* be race-specific, although a race-specific pattern of masculine role assumptions is usually the case. Possible exceptions include those *few* Black males and white males who are exposed early to opposite-race socialization influences and live most, if not all, of their lives in opposite-race social and physical environments. . . .
>
> Undoubtedly, as many of you think about some of the above statements, questions about Native American men, Chicano men, Chinese-American men, Japanese-American men, Cuban-American men, and others arise. What about these men, and what

roles do they assume? My response to your probable question is that these men have not made the impact on American society that Black males have made, nor has society constructed specific strategies for meting out resources to these men. Men in the above ethnic groups usually find themselves assuming either the White masculine role or the Black masculine role. For these men, socioeconomic variables usually determine which masculine role model is assumed. (Franklin 1984, p. 45)

Based on societal expectations for Black males and white males in American society, the Black male sex role and the white male sex role are defined as follows: the Black male sex role refers to *a set of expectations and behaviors which emphasize physical strength, submission and dominance of women, angry and impulsive behavior, functional relationships between women and men, antifemininity, and strong male bonding*; the white male sex role is defined as *a set of expectations and behaviors which emphasize male dominance, male competition, male violence, the work ethic, and antifemininity*. Let us examine how one of these two sex roles becomes a constantly constructed feature of most American men's lives. A glance at some of the agents responsible for the development and maintenance of male socialization should contribute to an understanding of this process. The agents of socialization to be discussed are divided into those formally charged with the responsibility for male sex role socialization and those that have informal (and often latent) responsibility.

Purposeful Agents of Male Socialization

Each newborn male in society is expected to undergo a lengthy learning process to acquire appropriate male behaviors. Responsibility for this process historically lay with such societal agents as the family, religious institutions, educational institutions, the mass media, and adolescent and young adult male peer groups. A discussion of the roles of these agents in male socialization is presented in this section. Let us begin with the family.

The family. The family is a vital agent involved in teaching males appropriate attitudes and behaviors. From the moment the newborn is identified as male, a set of cultural expectations unfolds dictating what behaviors may and may not be displayed. The agent charged with initial responsibility for insuring sex role conformity with societal expectations is the family. Studies have suggested (e.g., Schau et al. 1980, and Fu and Leach 1980) that if the newborn is male, rather rigid cultural expectations exist for him to learn to give "male performances" in social inter-actions. This means that the socialization process for males is likely to be especially constraining, allowing little deviation.

Even more critical for many young males learning male sex role re-quirements is the presence of older males within the family who serve as role models. Often such males are the fathers of these young males, al-though all that seems necessary for partial male socialization is that older males are seen by the younger males performing certain roles within the family setting. Seeing older males' role performances within the family provides younger males with the opportunity to learn vicariously cultural expectations for their own behaviors.

Some studies have found that parents treat children differently de-pending on the sex of the child (Schau et al. 1980). Differential treatment of children according to gender has been observed in fathers who are much more likely to "rough it up" with boys than with girls (Parke and Suomi 1980; Power and Parke 1983). These differences in fathers' be-haviors toward their children depending on gender often follows stereo-typical directions. Interestingly, fathers' stereotypical behaviors in inter-action with their children follow parents' stereotypical descriptions of their newborns. Despite the lack of significant differences in birth length, weight, and APGAR scores, parents of daughters are more likely than parents of sons to give descriptions of their babies as "dainty," "pretty," "beautiful," and "cute" (Rubin et al. 1974). Certainly such differences in descriptions of children by gender may foretell parental behavioral differences by gender in parent-child interaction. We already know, for example, that parents of boys are much *less* directing of their offsprings' play than parents of girls. Such interferences by parents in the behaviors of girls may well affect girls' creativity and interests in ways inimical to their later independence and assertiveness. In the same vein, when parents of boys are less directing of their play, this begins to pre-pare boys for the independent and active male sex role many expect them to assume when they become adult males.

Other studies of parents' behaviors during the socialization of their children have produced mixed findings with respect to differential treatment of children by gender. Snow et al. (1983) found that parents responded differentially to some types of sex-typed behaviors in tod-dlers, but not others. In another study, fathers punished boys' cross-sex play behavior while mothers were found to punish and reward boys' cross-sex behaviors (Langlois and Downs 1980). These findings re-garding fathers' lack of tolerance for boys' cross-sex behaviors are consistent with our contention that male sex role socialization tends to be more restrictive than female sex role socialization, especially early in life. A final study which is instructive on this point is one by Eisenberg et al. (1985). In this study of mothers' and fathers' socialization of one- and two-year-olds' sex-typed play behaviors, several findings are notable. On the variables "parental choice of toys" and "parental reinforcement," parents of boys tended to choose neutral and masculine toys more than feminine toys, while parents of girls chose neutral toys more than the other two types. However, once parents had chosen toys for their children, they did not differentially reinforce them or neutrally respond to them for sex-typed or other-sex play. Eisenberg et al. concluded that "apparently, in the home, parents exert influence over their young children's play primarily via their selection of available toys" (p. 1512). Thus, parental opportunity to select and influence behavior may be a preferred method of socializing children's sex-typed behavior. Another finding from Eisenberg et al.'s study of interest is that parents reduced positive feedback for children's toy play with age. "Parents provided less positive feedback (and thus more neutral feedback) at age 26 to 33 months than at 19 to 26 months" (p. 1512). The reduction in parental reinforcement of play with age of the child occurred only for other-sex play activities, not neutral or sex-typed behaviors. This means that boys in all likelihood are aided in the development of gender constancy by continued parental reinforcement of sex-type play throughout childhood.

Findings regarding differential parental treatment by sex of child seem to be mixed at this point. Definite conclusions about differential parental behaviors by sex of child await further research. However, differentiated parental reinforcement may not be necessary for the development of sex differentiated behavior in children. Simply attending to behavior differentially may be enough. Consider a study by Fagot and Hagan et al. (1985). This study of thirty-four children in infant play groups revealed no sex differences in assertive acts and attempts to communicate verbally with adults at ages 13 to 14 months. However, the authors observed learning center teachers attending more to boys' assertive behaviors and more to girls *less intense* communication attempts. The result was that eleven months later twenty-nine of the same children exhibited sex differentiated behavior: boys were more assertive and girls talked more with adults. Thus, caregivers seemed to be responsible, in part, for the development of boys' and girls' sex differentiated behavior by guiding infant behaviors in stereotypical directions.

Educational institutions. It is well documented that there is a significant difference in what adults observe depending on whether the persons being observed are described as males or females (Condry and Ross 1985). Purported reasons for adult differential perceptions of children's behavior by sex vary. Some feel that adults may be differentially responsive to certain types of behaviors by girls and boys. For example, because girls are expected to be more verbal than boys, are teachers more attentive to girls' verbal behaviors than boys'? By the same token, because boys are expected to have more assertive interchanges in peer activities than girls, do adults attend more to boys' assertive behaviors than girls' assertive behaviors? If the answers to both questions are yes, then differential attention to certain behaviors of boys and girls result in adults' differential perception of boys' and girls' behaviors.

Another common assumption stemming from social learning theory is that adults directly socialize children to behave in sex-typed ways through differential reinforcement and punishment. This assumption is supported by Beverly Fagot's (1981) findings that teachers differentially reinforce boys and girls for high activity levels. Even the large school context seems to be more supportive of males than females. Males continue to hold the more prestigious positions in the school system, schoolyards remain sex segregated, and in general gender differences remain in confidence, self-concept, and problem solving behaviors. Certainly such differences are related to the educational system's reinforcement of gender differences and traditional sex role behaviors. For example, findings from Phillips' playground study (1982) were quite consistent with those of Janet Lever (1976), who had found in her analysis of boys' and girls' spontaneous games on playgrounds that the games were sex differentiated. Lever concluded that boys' games were less structured than girls' games, with less emphasis on ''turn-taking'' and invariable procedural rules. Moreover, girls played with fewer participants while boys' games emphasized more initiative, improvisation, and extemporaneity, encouraging within-group cooperation and between-group competition. Phillips also found in her study of school playground activities that school spaces provided for boys and girls encouraged sex-differentiated play activities. Boys had large play spaces supportive of large competitive groups for competitive games. Girls' play spaces were small and generally supportive of cooperative, dyadic, and/or triadic activities. The major play space for girls in Phillips' study was on the playground apparatus, which could be easily invaded by boys and on occasion *was* invaded by boys, with the girls submissively leaving the equipment until the boys no longer used it. Phillips concluded: "Boys' play was preparing them for future work roles that would consist of the networks of competitively based groups necessary for success and achievement in the work place" (Franklin 1984, p. 43).

Jeanne Block's (1981) summary of the effects of sex-differentiated socialization in educational institutions suggests that male socialization in the education institution (which encourages curiosity, independence, initiative, etc.) extends male experiences, while female socialization in the educational institution (which discourages exploration, emphasizes class supervision, stresses proprieties, etc.) restricts the experiences of females. While some changes in the educational institution have occurred in recent years, males and females still have sex-differentiated experiences throughout their tenures in educational institutions.

Religious institutions. Almost as influential in teaching males to assume the male sex role is another agent, the religious institution. The only reason the religious institution does not assume a more critical role in male socialization is that the typical child does not spend an inordinate amount of time in religious settings. The time that is spent, however, generally is time when gender distinctions are emphasized. Such distinctions, within Christianity for example, are seen as divinely inspired in that they support the ideal relationship between husband and wife. On this point, Patricia M. Lengermann and Ruth A. Wallace (1985, p. 239) state that calling for sex role equality, questioning patriarchy, and critiquing traditional male dominance and female submissiveness in marriage and family life are antithetical to the divine plan as visualized by many Christians. Such a posture on the part of religious agents supports traditional sex roles against gender equality. In the 1980s with the rise of evangelical Christian movements and retrenchment in Roman Catholicism, we can only conclude that the religious institutions in the United States remain staunchly supportive of traditional female and male sex roles.

Support for the above position is seen in "God Goes Back to College," an article appearing in *Newsweek*'s "On Campus" edition, November 1986. Noting the fervor with which college students on campuses across the nation (those mentioned included Brown University, Arizona State University, University of Illinois—Champaign-Urbana, University of Texas, Duke University, Washington University, and Northwestern University) are embracing fundamentalist religious beliefs. Two striking implications for sex role changes are discussed. These implications center around a great deal of sentiment among religious groups in these settings to deny gays equal rights and to thwart women's attempts to pursue careers. Increased religious proselytizing on college campuses in the 1980s frequently has resulted in support for homophobia and traditional sex roles for females and males.

Peer groups. A consistent finding in the literature on children is that American children show a preference for same sex peers by the beginning of their sixth year. This tendency toward peer-group sex segregation increases during middle childhood and reaches its peak right before adolescence (Hartup 1983). In addition, as Thompson (1985) found in his study, males in pre-adolescence are more peer oriented than females. Part of the reason for greater peer orientation among males undoubtedly is linked to greater encouragement of independence in males at an earlier age. What this means for male socialization is that boys at a relatively early age are more subject to peer-group influence than girls. Just as important is that such influence may be perceived positively and supported by parents as indicative of boys' independence.

If boys are susceptible to early peer-group influence, this also means that males' early-age peer groups may be responsible for a great deal of those sex role performances by boys. This is to be expected if Fagot's (1981) findings that boys who exhibit feminine behaviors receive negative feedback from peers are generalizable. Some support for peer-group influence on boys' sex role performances derive also from Eisenberg et al.'s (1985) study of a stronger match for males than females between same-sex peer interactions and neutral or sex-typed toy play for fifty-one four-year-olds. When boys play with boys they prefer sex-typed toy play. Eisenberg et al. (1985) felt that this is consistent with the notion that there is more pressure for males than females to avoid sex-inappropriate activities:

> Although initiation of and/or continuation of interaction per se may not be used consciously as a positive reinforcer by children, it could function as one. Thus, unintentionally as well as intentionally (Lamb et al., 1980), children, especially boys, may socialize peers into sex-stereotypic play behaviors. They may do so not only by initiating play with others in possession of sex appropriate toys, but also by inducing other children to engage in same sex play. (P. 1049)

There seems to be a logical relationship between children's play behavior and their everyday role performances. Indeed, when boys' play behaviors are channeled in a decidedly stereotypical masculine direction, certainly they learn that these same behaviors are expected of them by significant others in everyday situations. After all, parental brokering, approval, support, and reinforcement by early age peer groups function to inform the boy of the importance of this early socialization agent. An early study by Fling and Manosevitz (1972) on male socialization found that young males are encouraged to participate in activities that teach and reinforce male stereotyped roles. There is little reason to think that such participation has declined in the 1980s. Interestingly, peer-group influence over males tends to decline as the young male approaches late adolescence. While in late childhood and early adolescence, male peer groups are quite influential in boys learning competitiveness, aggression, violence, and antifemininity, young males also learn that they must become independent, self-reliant, and detached from the peer group. This latter socialization, in a sense, prepares young males for the role which must be assumed in adulthood, a role which minimizes male-male relationships. Yet, adolescent peer groups, for most males, are kinds of references groups providing information which the sixteen- or seventeen-year-old male actively filters, alters, and modifies to fit his own perspective. Typically, peer group information, standards, and values are some variant of those from other socialization agents, including nonpurposive ones discussed in the next section. Most young males experience a kind of socialization which teaches them societally approved sex roles, dysfunctional ones as well as functional ones.

The mass media. Mass media influences on sex role socialization are thought by many to be critical in the development and support of sex role stereotypes specifically and sex role inequality generally. The link between sex role stereotypes and sex role inequality is a direct one. Sex role stereotypes (expectations about and attitudes toward the sexes) lead to sex role inequality (inequitable actions toward a person based on the sex of that person). This linkage is consistent with findings in social psychological literature suggesting that stereotypes are better predictors of behavior than of attitudes.

Yet, how do sex role stereotypes relate to male socialization? Recalling that male socialization is a dual process, involving male self development and the learning of societal "shoulds" and "should nots" for males, one can see that much male socialization actually involves learning conceptions of males' "make-up" and "places" and females' "make-up" and "places." Undoubtedly, the mass media play critical roles in this process. When females in television commercials usually perform household duties and pamper men while males typically perform active roles outside the home and do not perform domestic duties, a message is given to viewers that housework is women's work and work outside the home is men's work (Mamay and Simpson 1981).

That television may play a powerful role in gender socialization is suggested by Drabman et al. (1979) since their findings indicate that young children (first graders), when shown videotaped presentations of males and females in counter-stereotyped occupations (such as male nurse and female doctor), tended to reverse sex role information in the stereotyped direction. For Drabman et al. this finding meant that television should be used in a specific way to modify sex role socialization in a more equitable manner for boys and girls. They state: "Television programming which directly informs the child nearly all life roles are available to both sexes might prove more fruitful in attempts to alter traditional gender stereotypes" (p. 388).

Not only is television a potentially powerful agent in the sex role socialization of males and females, but newspapers, comics, movies, and popular songs may also influence conceptions of gender roles. Lengermann and Wallace (1985) feel that such mass media are "a forum where critical views on gender equality are heard and aired, can affect the thinking and beliefs of men as well as women, and can be for both a resource for new meanings" (p. 222). To the extent that men and women are affected by such mass media changes and also participate in the teaching of males, the effects on male socialization are obvious.

To be sure, there have been some changes in the mass media toward presenting male and female images in a manner more consistent with sex role equality. Lengermann and Wallace point to the inclusion of women columnists like Ellen Goodman and Mary McGary in daily newspapers as evidence of changes in newspapers which can modify a man's thinking about a woman's place. They note also the emergence of Alan Alda, a popular television entertainer and self-described feminist, as a role model in the media for nontraditional men in contrast to more conventional male images like Bob Hope and John Wayne. Men's magazines, too, are thought to be sources of sex role changes in the mass media. Magazines such as *Esquire* and *Sports Illustrated* are thought by Lengermann and Wallace to reflect "new meanings." They cite the November 1982 issue of *Esquire* with a feature article entitled "Father Love" by Anthony Brandt and *Sports Illustrated*'s (Feb. 28, 1983) coverage of Louisiana Tech women's basketball team (a sign that women's sports are making strides toward parity) as evidence of further change in sex role meanings.

Yet, all is not progress in the 1980s on the issue of sex role equality in the mass media in America. For example, in an analysis of sex role stereotyping in the Sunday comics, Sarah Brabant (1976) found that males and females were overwhelmingly portrayed in stereotypical roles. Ten years later, Brabant, along with colleague Linda Mooney, finds minimal change in the portrayal of males and females in the Sunday comics. In fact, the authors are moved to state:

> Given that a cultural analysis of sex roles focuses on the shared meanings individuals use in their interactions, and that development of these symbolic meanings are, in part, dependent upon the mass media, it is especially disappointing to empirically document the continued depiction of a male-dominated society and the devaluation of women in everyday life. How far have women come? If Blondie, Gladys, and Alice are indicators, not very far at all. (P. 148)

Brabant and Mooney's findings are especially important in light of those from Sanik and Stafford's (1985) study of adolescents' contributions to household production. They found significant differences between females and males in the amount of time spent on household work in two-parent, two-child families; adolescent females clearly spent more time doing household work. Because first- and second-born boys and girls did not differ on any of the exploratory variables and their responses to independent variables were similar, Sanik and Stafford concluded that the higher participation in household work by females was due to the expectation placed on adolescents. A final statement by Sanik and Stafford on their findings underscores the necessity for media progress on the issue of sex role equality: "Until we witness equality in the sharing of work in the home during adolescence, we are not likely to witness it in the lives of husbands and wives of tomorrow" (p. 214).

Still, it is difficult to imagine significant changes in the mass media regarding the issue of sex role equality beyond employing token women in middle level positions, with minimal change in policy and philosophy on gender issues. Even when gender issues reach masses of people, often they take on an extremely negative tone. *New York* magazine senior editor Rhoda Koenig's September 1986 article in *Vogue* magazine entitled "How to Change a Man" is a case in point. Koenig begins her article with an acknowledgment of the existence of Men's Studies courses in what she says is "about a hundred colleges." Having some contact (it is not clear if all or some is face-to-face) with Robert Brannon (*The Forty-*

Nine Percent Majority), Michael Kimmel (who was then an assistant professor of sociology at Rutgers University), Steven Goldberg (*The Inevitability of Patriarchy*), Marvin Bressler (Chair[man] of Princeton University's Sociology Department), and Harry Brod (who was then assistant professor, University of Southern California), Koenig makes a great point of noting that most Men's Studies instructors (that she talked with?) belong to the National Organization for Changing Men and suggests that this group sounds as if "it, too, had something to do with diapers" (p. 370). From this point, Koenig's attack on Men's Studies moves on to the subject matter and topics taught in a Men's Studies class, class texts, class activities, the naiveté of the students taking a Men's Studies class at Rutgers, the professor's "patronizing, distorted view of the world," and finally Rutgers University itself for babying students.

Diane Petzke's "Men's Studies Catches On at Colleges, Setting Off Controversy and Infighting" in the February 1986 issue of the *Wall Street Journal* is hardly more positive than Koenig's. Petzke also zeroes in on Kimmel's class, emphasizing, with seeming amusement, a class activity which involved male students attempting to diaper a doll. Her major points, however, center on the controversial status of Men's Studies because of a *perceived conflict* with Women's Studies and a perception among some feminists that "men's courses aren't legitimate or are marginally useful at best" (p. 37).

In summary, some mass media changes in the last decade or so have been in the direction of sex role equality which would eventually lessen male dominance, male violence, male destruction, competition, and so on. Simultaneously, however, forces have arisen in the mass media which either support traditional sex role distinctions or at least suggest that change in men's behavior cannot occur or is trivial and of dubious value for society when it does occur. As we approach the end of the 1980s and move into the 1990s, it is hoped that the mass media will come to portray and reflect gender, especially the valued male sex role, in a realistic manner, that is, as sets of cultural expectations that are socially constructed.

Nonpurposive Agents of Male Socialization

Families, boys' groups, educational institutions, churches, newspapers, magazines, television, and radio are not the only socializing agents teaching males to be dominant, aggressive, violent, competitive, nonintimate, and non-nurturant. There are other agents in American society which are not charged with a learning function but which, nevertheless, teach males conceptions of themselves, other males, and what males should and should not do. Some of these agents are male-centered barbershops, sports events, taverns, and business meetings, where primarily males engage in social interaction. These are the same agents forming the core of men's culture which were discussed in chapter 2. In this chapter, two latent socialization consequences of the above agents are emphasized: (1) indirect socialization of young males and (2) reinforcement and support of traditional conceptions of the male sex role.

With some exceptions (e.g., unisex hair salons), male barbershops, topless taverns, male-dominated business meetings, sports events, and the like function as social settings/negotiation contexts where men negotiate masculinity. While the negotiation of masculinity is a complex process involving numerous contextual and social psychological variables, the emphasis here is on the process used by men in certain settings to arrive at conceptions of who men are and how men should and should not behave. At the same time, they also form conceptions about persons who are not men and masculine—women and others perceived as feminine.

The "particulars" of masculinity negotiations in various social settings will not be discussed here; however, a broad description of such processes includes verbal and nonverbal behavior by male participants in social settings which define appropriate male attitudes and behaviors. In such settings as barbershops and male-centered sports events, frequently young, impressionable males are present during the negotiation process. The young males learn not only what behaviors are expected from the primary male participants, but also the attitudes that they should hold about the negotiation process and what outcomes from the negotiation process are most desirable. For example, a young male attending a professional football game learns not only that the more "manly" team wins—the team that is more competitive, more aggressive subdues—but also how he is to respond to such characteristics. The young boy leaves the stadium *knowing* that dominance is a desirable trait for men to have. After all, an entire group of men have just been rewarded by a host of other men for displaying the dominance trait. Just as important, too, for the young boy is the low esteem many others hold for the losing team— the one that has been subdued.

Young boys generally do not go to topless taverns where women are seen in various stages of undress. Nevertheless, masculinity negotiations and male socialization are features of such settings. Men receive support and reinforcement from other men for certain behaviors they display. The swaggers, the yells, the obscenities, the sexual references all become permanently etched in their minds as appropriate behaviors for men. Those men who do not engage in the behavior nevertheless learn that if they want others to think of them as manly, all they have to do is display similar behavior. The "new" male in the topless tavern setting will know that he is engaging in appropriate male behavior when other males slap him on the back or shake his hand as he, too, screams and yells, "Take it off, baby."

5

Deviance

According to sociologist Howard Becker (1963), deviant statuses exhibit master status qualities—ones which overshadow all other positions held by persons in groups or societies. From this perspective, a deviant status is seen as taking precedence over all other identities an individual might have. Thus, when a man is defined as a deviant, this becomes his essential character, and others' responses to him are basically in terms of this deviant character. A man who is defined or typed as a member of a deviant category also has various auxiliary traits attributed to him, since they are believed to characterize all men so labeled. This same "master status" process goes on in other devalued categories based on race, sex, religion, and ethnicity. Schur (1984) alludes to the "hyphenization" phenomenon as a widespread cultural indicator of the master status tendency. He cites certain commonplace descriptions of women as "woman-doctor," "woman-athlete," "woman-executive" and "woman-driver" as examples of the phenomenon. He says further that while there may be a few such references to men (e.g., "male-nurse" and "male-secretary"), the hyphenization phenomenon is more than a convenient means of indicating numerically infrequent patterns. For Schur, there is at least implied occupational deviance in the hyphenization mentioned above. Moreover, because high status and prized occupations tend to be stereotypically male, hyphenization is a further "put-down" of women. Schur states:

> Because she is female, a woman is assumed not to have the same overall competence for the prized role that a man would have.

123

Hence, she should be described and assessed only relative to the occupation's other female occupants, rather than in terms of universalistic (i.e., sex-neutral) criteria. (Or, . . . she must be labeled an "exceptional" female.) (P. 25)

Typical consequences of categorical perceptions of women and their stigmatization in the United States include societal devaluation and subordination of women. Furthermore, dominant norms in American society automatically relegate women to deviant statuses. In fact, according to Schur (1984, p. 51), women frequently are subjected to contradictory social expectations regarding their behaviors. This means automatic deviance, because conformity to one standard "may be treated as deviance when viewed from the standpoint of the opposing one." Elements of this complex relationship between gender norms and female deviance, indicating a "Catch 22" situation for women as well as other aspects of the social construction of women's deviance, are presented in table 5.1, adapted from Schur's *Labeling Women Deviant* (1984, p. 53).

An interesting point about the deviance-defining nature of social expectations for women in America is that the relatively recent and minor changes in sex role expectations have, in many ways, exacerbated rather than attenuated the problem. This is seen in the tremendous amount of stress experienced by many women who are expected now to assume at least a partial breadwinner role while maintaining much of the traditional female sex role. Obviously, when women are placed in such positions they experience conflicting role expectations and feel much role strain.

In contrast to societal devaluation of women, men in America are valued, that is, as long as they conform to those norms existing for males. Masculinity is valued in the United States as long as it is exhibited by certain persons with the appropriate anatomical structure. Just as Schur finds it difficult to justify totally the devaluation of femininity but concludes that there is substantial devaluation of women, I believe pervasive valuation of masculinity exists with some major exceptions. These exceptions are noted in the discussions to follow.

Evidence for the devaluation of femininity rests on the existence of pronounced social and economic inequality of the sexes; widespread categorical perception and objectification of women; pervasive devaluation of women in cultural symbolism; and multitudes of specific deviance imputed to women (as evident in table 5.1) under a gender system signifying that femininity by its very nature is deviance.

On the other hand, societal valuation of masculinity is evidenced by

Table 5.1
Gender Norms and Female Deviance

Major Category of Norms	Typical "Offenses" and Deviance Labels
1. *Presentation of Self*	
a. emotions	too little emotion, (cold, calculating, masculine); *or* too much emotion (hysterical); *or* various wrong emotions (different types of mental illness)
b. nonverbal communication	masculine gestures, postures, use of space, touching
c. appearance	plain, unattractive, masculine, overweight, fat, old, drab, poorly made-up, *or* overly made-up, flashy, cheap
d. speech and interaction	unladylike, bossy, competitive, aggressive; *or* timid, mousy, nonentity
2. *Marriage/Maternity*	
a. marital	spinster, old maid, *or* unmarried, divorcée, widow; *or* unwed mother; *or* sleeps around
b. maternity	voluntarily childless (selfish); *or* had abortion (killer); *or* unwed mother; *or* unmaternal, unfit mother
3. *Sexuality*	
a. behavior	oversexed, nymphomaniac, promiscuous, loose, cheap, whore; *or* cock-teaser, cold, frigid
b. orientation	butch, dyke, queer
4. *Occupational Choice*	in a man's job, tough, aggressive, castrating, ball-buster
5. *"Deviance Norms"*	norm-violation "inappropriate" for females (e.g., armed robber, political revolutionary)

white male dominance and power in society's basic institutions; white male determination of the criteria for societal valuation; cultural symbolism as manifested in societal language, mass media imagery, and the like, depicting male privilege, power, and in general, male valuation; and, the culture's overall view that what is masculine is what is valued and most important for our society's survival. Even dysfunctional traits like destructive competition, unnecessary aggression, and violence—all linked with masculinity—frequently are assigned positive value in American society. If deviance is a constant companion of femininity, it is an infrequent companion of masculinity. In fact, when men are labeled "deviant," usually after much deliberation, generally they are stripped of the label "man." "Men" and "deviance" are carefully separated despite the sharing of similar characteristics (e.g., destructive competition, sexual aggressiveness, physical violence). Consider the fact that it is not unusual for the wife batterer to be referred to as "not a real man." Similarly, the man who chooses to deviate more passively from societal prescriptions that he assume breadwinner responsibilities for his family also earns the label "not a real man." Indeed, it is customary in American society to strip adult male persons of the label "man" when their behaviors fall outside of society's acceptable range of behaviors for men (a range of behaviors that, in actuality, includes a rather wide latitude of acceptable aggressive, violent, and other dysfunctional behaviors).

> From countless [people] we learned that our masculinity and therefore our self-esteem was always on the line. . . . The badge of manhood can be won only temporarily; it can be questioned or taken away at any time. One job poorly done, one failure, one sign of weakness—that's all it took to lose our membership in the charmed circle. . . . (Zilbergeld 1978, p. 16)

Through a relatively uncomplicated process, the typical American male learns that if his behavior falls outside vague boundaries of acceptable male behaviors, he will be delabeled. Little boys learn early in childhood that little boys don't behave in certain ways: "they don't whine"; "they don't cry"; "they don't sit on their mother's laps"; and so on. While little boys are not necessarily told what little boys do, the message, nevertheless, gets through, and many males' fears of being delabeled extend into adulthood where the message is, "*real* men don't. . ." More important, however, is the fact that in early boyhood a separation of male gender and deviance begins. Young males who behave according to society's sex role script are boys; those who do not are, well, they are *not* boys. Later on, some men who blatantly and undeniably heap violence upon women are *not men,* they are, well, *not real men.* After all, men cannot be deviant. As Schur points out, "imputed male superiority and male social dominance require female 'deviance' and subordination" (p. 47). Labeling men deviant, then, obscures the distinction between femininity and masculinity and diminishes male privilege; therefore, sustaining masculinity requires *separating* deviance and masculinity while *integrating* deviance and femininity.

Still, what is male deviance? Based on our discussion thus far, it would seem that the superior master status held by many males would make them immune to the deviant label. Yet, it is obvious that some males do become known as deviants. How does this happen? Generally speaking, if a male behaves in a way that violates social norms in American society, that behavior is deviance and technically he is a deviant. However, in order for the deviant label to stick, it seems that other social elements must also be present. These social elements must be attached either to the behaving male or to the behavior produced by the male. Moreover, such elements must be socially significant enough to separate the male and/or his behavior from masculinity before he is labeled a deviant.

The Social Nature of Male Deviance

The idea that certain social elements must accompany male social behavior before it is labeled deviant is not new. Sociologists Kai Erikson, Howard Becker, Edwin Lemert, Edwin Schur, and numerous others long have endorsed the idea that no behavior is inherently deviant. The social relativity of deviance, the differential power of the sexes to define acts as deviant, and the vagueness of boundaries separating permissible male behaviors from nonpermissible male behaviors all determine whether male behavior is deviant.

To begin with, definitions of behaviors as deviant change over time and also may differ from place to place, group to group, and situation to situation. For example, today throughout much but not all of the Untied States, a thirty-year-old male who makes sexual overtures toward a thirteen-year-old female is almost certain to be defined as deviant. Yet, prior to the companionate providing society in the United States (1920–1965), such overtures by adult males toward young females were commonplace and even expected, since numerous marriages took place between older males and very young females.

Similarly, two men locked in an embrace and kissing passionately in all likelihood are not thought to be engaged in deviant behavior by others in a gay establishment. However, if the same behavior occurs in a public park or in a city airport, the behavior is likely to be defined by others as deviance and the participants as deviants. What all of this means is that people at one time or another, in one group or another, in one place or another decide whether an act is deviant and react to it accordingly.

Given our earlier discussion, it would seem that the relative nature of male deviance along with a societal tendency to separate deviance from masculinity would mean that relatively few males in the United States are defined as deviants. Perhaps this would be so if males in America did not have differential power to make the deviant label stick and to resist the delabeling of masculinity. However, this is not the case. In point of fact, males do differ in terms of physical strength, wealth, political power, social privilege, and other valued resources. While we recognize that what is regarded as a valuable resource may vary by place, time, and circumstance, the fact that males differ in amounts of power possessed is important in our culture. Differences in male power mean that some males can impose their wills on others despite others' resistance. If some males decide that it is to their advantage to label some other males' behaviors deviant and the decision results in a deviant label, then behaviors defined as deviant in this instance involve power plays. Two examples illustrate this point, both related to what many feel is an ultimate form of male sexual deviance—homosexuality.

An adult male who voluntarily engages in sex with another adult male generally is thought to be gay and deviant, because he has violated a societal proscription forbidding intrasex sexual relations. However, homosexual liaisons are common occurrences in prisons as well as other total institutions. Ironically, within such settings it is not uncommon for both participants and participation in the sexual activity to undergo a redefinition process along the lines of deviance and nondeviance with gender implications. For example, a typical description of the participants in these sexual encounters is that they involve one inmate who deviates significantly from some masculine ideal (physically weaker, submissive, timid, passive, etc.) and one who displays some masculine image (physically strong, aggressive, violence prone, active). In prisons especially, those males displaying greater amounts of physical strength, aggressiveness, and violence as well as other forms of dominance frequently may participate in gay sexual activities (oftentimes assuming an "active role") and still not be labeled "sexually deviant" by other inmates or even prison caretakers. In fact, sociologists studying this phenomenon have constructed the descriptive concept "institutional sex," which often is used to define the behaviors of the "sexually nondeviant" prison inmate who participates in gay sexual activities. The behaviors distinguishing the "sexually nondeviant" participant from the "sexually deviant" participant are stereotypical masculine behaviors such as physical strength, aggression, violence, and dominance. The participant in gay sex in prison settings who displays these characteristics generally is viewed as "sexually nondeviant" and masculine. By the same token, a participant who is nonviolent, nonaggressive, physically weaker, and submissive generally is seen as feminine, as "a woman." Even in a setting where adult males typically experience being stripped of their masculinity, some vestiges of masculinity can be obtained if they engage in stereotypical destructive masculine behaviors. In a certain sense such males become "nondeviants" in settings composed of deviants (Nacci and Kane 1983; Nacci and Kane 1984).

A second example illustrating the idea of deviance from a power perspective as well as the separation of deviance from masculinity is found in a comment made by a respondent in an early study of bisexuality by Blumstein and Schwartz (1977): "There are four kinds of men: Men who screw women, men who screw men and women, men who screw men, and then there are the queers (i.e., the ones who get screwed)" (p. 43).

Vander Zanden (1986) has stated that "who is defined as deviant and what is defined as deviant depend on who is doing the defining and who has the power to make the definitions stick" (p. 123). Nowhere is it more evident that male power and male dominance frequently determine deviance and separate it from masculinity than in popular conceptions of the behaviors of nonwhite adult males. Native American males and other minority group males whose behaviors frequently depart significantly from white males' behaviors often are thought to be "unmanly," "not masculine," "irresponsible," and the like—all signifying male deviance.

On the other hand, some behaviors undergo a process of redefinition whereby they are delabeled as voluntarily deviant. This occurs when behavior previously defined as deviant and predominately engaged in by non-white men become pervasive behaviors among white men. Drug abuse, alcoholism, and wife battering are examples of such behaviors which have been found frequently among white men and which are increasingly being viewed as medical or mental anomalies. One cannot help but think that the redefining process is related to the "discovery" of large numbers of white male "offenders" who have the power to define what is deviant in American society. At the same time it must be remembered that large aggregates of American males by the very definition of masculinity and its link with deviance are always socially defined as deviant and of (at best) questionable masculinity (e.g., Black males, Chicano males, Puerto Rican males).

Another social element of deviance which interacts with male power and dominance in a way that causes much dysfunctional male behavior to go undefined as deviant behavior is the wide range of permissible masculine behaviors. Many males engage in specific behaviors that cross the boundaries of deviance, but because the boundaries are so nebulous, the behaviors are not defined as deviant. Actual instances of date rape, wife abuse, physical aggression toward other males, sexual harassment, various forms of white collar crime, and numerous other behaviors are examples of primarily male deviant behaviors that cross the boundaries of permissible male behaviors but often are not defined as deviant. This fact, along with the relative nature of deviance and male advantages in the power to determine deviant behavior all support the thesis that male deviance is socially determined. Succinctly, male deviance is determined in part by (1) a group of people deciding whether the behavior is deviant; (2) group norm boundaries distinguishing between deviant and non-deviant male behavior; and (3) differential power of the sexes and within the male aggregate to define behaviors as deviant. However, regardless of how male deviant behavior is determined, both individual and social consequences result. These effects are examined below.

When Men Don't Conform

One rationale for linking women and femininity with deviance while separating men and masculinity from deviance is that both societal features support men's power and men's dominance. Also important is the fact that when some males do not conform to societal expectations, they tend to be stripped of their masculinity and then defined as deviant. For example, the perpetual wife-beater long has been viewed by many as a sniveling coward with male identity problems and different from a "real" man. Only recently, as men are being studied as males, have scholars begun to point out that little difference exists between the discovered wife-beater and numerous other married men (some of whom beat their wives and others who express hostility toward their wives in myriad other ways). The murdering rapist is similarly demasculinized when discovered and described as a vile person who "isn't a real man" because no man would commit such heinous crimes.

The above examples of deviance are serious ones, but even less serious violations of social norms by males can result in attempts to demasculinize the violators. In some young men's peer groups, those young men not sharing ideas about women which frequently objectify them and lead to all kinds of sexist sexual innuendo, can expect to be thought of as "not quite manly enough." In a group when some members are suspected as having characteristics different from those of other members, group members gradually reach some consensus regarding what does and does not conform to group expectations. Thus, it can be expected that being perceived as "not quite manly enough" in a young men's peer group gradually will lead to being perceived as deviant by other group members.

Because men and masculinity are valued so highly in American society, most adult males who do not conform to societal expectations for men pay a high price. This is so regardless of whether the deviation is aberrant (Merton 1966), deliberately nonconforming, or due to an inability to conform.

Among other kinds of violators, men who break rules in order to gain personally fall into the aberrant deviant category. Most men who commit crimes become aberrant deviants just as those who are publicly admonished for sexually harassing women or engaging in other sexist behaviors in the work place. In contrast, some males deliberately do not conform to societal expectations for men as a "matter of principle." Those changing men in America who do not objectify and sexually exploit women; those men who are establishing warm, nurturing, nonsexual relationships with other men; and, those men who are leading the male profeminist movement to end violence against women all are deliberately *not* conforming to societal expectations for males in America. For these males, just as for the aberrant male deviant, the price that is paid includes demasculinization and the assignment of a male deviant label (e.g., wimp, sissy, weak male).

Also included among those adult males who do not conform to societal expectations for men are those unable to conform. This inability to conform generally is beyond the individual's control. Nonconformity by these males is due to the way that powerful males in the society define expectations for males which automatically excludes some males. Old males, handicapped males, ill males, economically disadvantaged males, and minority group males are examples of male persons who do not meet societal expectations for men in America and who pay high prices for their nonconformity. This point will not be explored further here because elsewhere in this volume there is discussion about those dysfunctional aspects of the male sex role in America which render men in these categories socially impotent.

Finally, unlike women, men as a group cannot be defined as deviant. Moreover, because groups of men that commit deviant behavior frequently are quite powerful and can vigorously resist being defined as deviant (e.g., the alleged secret sale of weapons to Iran by members of the National Security Council discovered in 1986), the phenomenon of male group deviance is difficult to grasp. Yet, there is a group of adult males in

America that has been subjected to the demasculinizing and labeling process so characteristic of males who violate normative expectations. That group's members, gay men, pay high prices individually and collectively. At an individual level the gay male may experience overt personal injustice, truncated relationships with others, and the like. The most pronounced collective cost experienced by gay men has been the social construction and enforcement of a pervasive homophobic norm. The homophobic norm, to be discussed in greater detail later, refers to an irrational fear and hatred of homosexuals designed to control men in their male roles. The existence of this norm affects greatly the destinies of gay men—and for that matter, non-gay men and women. The latest cost of this norm to gay men and society in general has been the proliferation of the deadly disease, Acquired Immunodeficiency Syndrome (AIDS). We will return to this point in chapter 6.

American society accepts a wide range of masculine behaviors as appropriate for adult males. Because of this broad latitude of acceptance, much male behavior is seen as functional for society, despite recent assertions that many effects of acceptable adult male behaviors actually are inimical to society's functioning. In this section our discussion will be devoted to those male behaviors that fall outside of society's acceptable range of male behaviors. As with any deviant behavior, some of the effects for society are disruptive and some are supportive for the continued functioning of society as a whole.

Confounding the determination of whether certain male behaviors facilitate society's continuation in the desired direction is the debate over what constitutes society's "desired direction." Are alterations in female and male sex roles desirable or undesirable for American society? Lack of societal consensus generally in answering this question renders the determination of male deviance a difficult task. For many years now social institutions, beliefs, values, and practices which support society's patriarchial ideology along with male privilege and prerogatives have been challenged. Yet, since the early 1980s such challenges to the traditional functioning of society have been met with counterchallenges from right-wing political groups, fundamentalist religious groups, and a general conservatism sweeping the nation. For purposes of our discussion let us assume moderate to little change in female and male sex roles in the United States since the early 1980s. Such a view is consistent with the opinions of such scholars as Frances Fox Piven (1985) and John Macionis (1987). This assumption enables us to discuss the positive and negative effects of behavioral nonconformity with the general male sex role.

Sociologist Albert Cohen (1966) provides a conceptual framework from which both social dysfunctions and social functions of male deviance can be explored.

Social Dysfunctions of Male Deviance

One outgrowth of the study of men as men has been the conclusion reached by some scholars that certain undesirable male behaviors such as rape, wife battering, overly zealous athletic behavior, general physical acts of violence and abuse toward others are not unusual male behaviors. Furthermore, the men who behave in these ways are not oddities or crazed persons. Rather, these men are seen basically as overconformists. In many ways they have learned the lessons of masculinity all too well— or, at the very least, they practice basic tenets of masculinity all too well.

In contrast to the kinds of deviance which occur because of overconformity to the male sex role is nonconformity to certain aspects of the male sex role. House-husbands, "changing men," male secretaries, male nurses, and openly gay men are examples of males who do not conform publicly to significant aspects of the male sex role. What does such public nonconformity mean? In terms of the male sex role as it stands for most men in America, public nonconformity may affect other men's desires to live up to some masculine ideal—to present a facade. Certainly, the gay liberation movement of the 1970s must have played a major role in ex–professional football player Dave Kopay's decision to go public with his gay sexual preference, just as it must have for ex–professional baseball player Glenn Burke. When relatively large numbers of men decide not to play the macho game, the game itself is called into question because decisions not to play the macho game frequently result in the social construction of ideologies and rationales which undermine morale and loyalty to a system embracing "the macho game."

When large numbers of men do not conform to traditional male sex role expectations, apart from destroying the willingness to conform among those who are inclined not to conform, such nonconformity may also impact on trust, on the feeling that others will, by and large, play by the rules. When these males violate aspects of the male sex role, others' motivations to conform are adversely affected. A case in point is the increasing numbers of males who are beginning to rethink their attitudes which lead to sexism and general oppression of women. While such attitudes by no means are on the verge of disappearing from American society, the emergence of men's groups to fight violence against women (e.g., rape, wife battering, etc.) attests to the emerging assault on trust and confidence in a system which supports violence toward women and the oppression of women. Increasing numbers of men's motivations to oppress women are being undermined by "deviant" males such as those who are in men-against-rape groups, men-against-violence-against-women groups, and numerous other groups which "violate" male sex role expectations.

In order for male privilege to remain an integral part of a society, individual actors within that society must cooperate at all levels to maintain it. If some men in strategic societal positions encourage women's efforts at upward mobility, or at least do not block such efforts, then the system of male privilege is in danger. Presently, a crack does exist in the iron wall of male privilege in American society, but it is a very small one. Yet there is a possibility that the crack will widen due, in part, to less oppressive men and the persistence of progressive women. These less oppressive men are our main concern, since they are conceptualized here as "male deviants." During the middle and late 1970s, the number and influence of such males increased dramatically. Since the beginning of the 1980s, increases in both numbers and influence of such males have been much less dramatic. In fact, men of an opposite persuasion seem to have become visible and certainly have become more influential in American society. These are men who have assumed powerful positions at the helms of society's religious, economic, educational, and political institutions. The result of such male conformity to societal male sex role expectations has been to slow down the gradual destruction of a system which perpetuates male privilege and power.

Social Functions of Male Deviance

In the above section, we deliberately presented a discussion of male deviance which focused on those aspects of male nonconformity which were inimical to society's functioning, as most of us are aware. In this section, how male deviance contributes to American societal functioning is considered, again drawing on the work of Albert Cohen.

Cohen felt that it would be a mistake to assume that deviance is necessarily destructive of organization. To the contrary, deviance may very well make positive contributions to a society. Deviance can perform a "safety valve" function, clarify social norms, increase group solidarity, enhance conformity, and illuminate defects in the system. What are the ways in which deviation from the male sex role performs these important functions for American society?

Male deviance is a safety value. The male sex role in American society specifies prescriptions and proscriptions for adult males. These are rules specifying the ways men "ought" to behave and the ways they "ought not" behave. One of the ways men ought *not* behave is sexually with other men. This is especially so if the man in question is married. Yet, there are numerous married men who apparently have desires that run counter to this societal proscription. Brian Miller (1978) defines such men as "trade husbands," who frequently engage in furtive and anonymous gay sexual activities. It can be argued that while such activities clearly violate normative expectations for married men, the deviant behavior for some males may be an alternative avenue to the satisfaction of their wants. Despite the "deviant" nature of the behavior, it may, as Cohen says, "perform a 'safety valve' function by preventing the excessive accumulation of discontent and by taking some of the strain off the legitimate order" (1966, p. 7). This would seem to be primarily what happens for trade husbands whose private and public identities remain heterosexual but who engage in impersonal gay sex in tearooms, public parks, adult bookstores, and the like. Even with the current AIDS scare, there seems to be no dearth of such men. These men are discussed in greater detail in the "Male Sexuality" chapter. Despite its offensive nature, some would argue that excluding the AIDS risk, trade husbands' sexual activities, like visits to prostitutes, satisfy illegitimate needs without seriously threatening the institution of the family.

Male deviance clarifies the male sex role. More than anything else in American society, male deviance enables us to understand clearly what men may do and what they may not do. It is through the clarification function of male deviance that we begin to understand the extensive nature of male power and privilege. Behavior often taken for granted as deviant because it seemingly violates societal norms suddenly takes on a different meaning when engaged in by certain "men" in American society.

An example of deviance clarifying the male sex role can be seen in the 1986 "Iran-contra" scandal involving the activities of Lieutenant Colonel Oliver L. North, former National Security Advisers John Poindexter and Robert McFarlane, and other U.S. officials. As the account unravels publicly it becomes increasingly clear that powerful men in high places in America have a great deal of latitude in obeying federal laws. It also becomes clear that the nature of deviance is indeed relative. Generally, prior to the scandal most Americans probably vaguely considered selling arms to Iran and transferring part of the money from sales to the contras in Nicaragua as constituting violated societal proscriptions. The decline in President Reagan's public approval rating immediately following disclosure of these activities and the public outcry against such activities left little doubt that the limits of deviance from overconformity to the male sex role had been reached. By overstepping the boundaries into the zone of deviance, once again powerful men in America have learned that there are limits to men's behaviors which are defined as acceptable. Hopefully, politically powerful men in America will come to understand more clearly than ever what can and cannot be legitimately done. As with the Watergate scandal, once again male deviance has clarified societal norms related to men's behavior.

Male deviance increases group solidarity. Unintended consequences of the involvement of a few men in the nonsexist men's organization N.O.C.M. have been labeling of the group as deviant by some persons and uniting of some masculinist men in support of traditional sex role expectations. The rationale for increased support of traditional sex roles is that organizations like N.O.C.M. contribute to the destruction of critical institutions which maintain society, such as the family. Supposedly, evidence for the breakdown of the family is seen in increased deviance rates, juvenile delinquency rates, teenage pregnancies, and other phenomena.

Actually, increased unity among some men opposed to alterations in the traditional male sex role can be expected in light of relatively recent findings from studies by Thompson et al. (1985) and O'Neil et al. (1986). Thompson et al. published findings indicating strong relationships between traditional male sex role endorsements by males and their support of homophobia, less self-disclosure to female friends, strong support of Type A behavior (generally defined as "aggressive" and "competitive"), and asymmetrical decision-making power with their intimate partner (power maintenance and control). Similarly, O'Neil et al. (1986) found that men who perceived themselves as masculine reported significantly higher scores on homophobia and restrictive affection between men than did expressive men.

Another way in which men's deviance increases group solidarity is through uniting group members in support of a deviant member via discounting the rule violated or saying that the violation was in the best interests of the group. This functional consequence of deviance seems to be a preferred method of handling the deviant behavior of powerful men. If the method is successful, there is no need to redefine the powerful violation; in fact, successful use of this method can lead to increased status for the violator, since his deviance will be viewed as being in the best interest of the group. An example of increased group solidarity through support of a deviant man is seen in a December 1986 statement by L. Brent Bazell, president of the National Conservative Political Action Committee. Bazell, speaking on behalf of the organization about North's involvement in the Iran-contra affair, said "our position is 100 percent behind North." Richard Viguerics, a leading conservative activist, also stated during this time that "he's one of us . . . we know him. We have felt he was part of our family. . . ." Simultaneously, President Reagan's communication director, Patrick Buchanan, endorsed by the White House, launched a campaign December 9, 1986, in the *Washington Post* to defend North by equating him with other American heroes "who have broken laws for good causes" (*Columbus Dispatch,* Dec. 9, 1986, p. 2a). In sum, men's deviance can promote group solidarity by uniting members in support of the deviant. Because of society's reluctance to define men as deviant, we can expect most men in America to continue their involvement with the deviant level.

Male deviance enhances conformity. Just as some males reject the stereotypical male traits of dominance, violence, aggressiveness, and sexist behaviors toward women, others cling tenaciously to such traits, believing fervently that they are appropriately "male" and that those who reject such traits are not masculine. Support for this position comes from throughout the society. For example, the "Rambo" phenomenon, the return of the "cult of bodybuilding," religious fundamentalist emphasis on male primacy, and pervasive homophobia among American males all are evidence of accentuated conformity in the face of male deviance. For those who are interested in the preservation of the traditional male sex role, some male deviance seems to be a rallying point for opposing male norm violation.

Male deviance serves as a warning signal. In this volume, the perspective has been taken that learning plays a critical role in male behavior. If this is so, then the fact that males are overwhelmingly responsible for much destructive, violent, and dysfunctional behavior in American society says a great deal about what males are learning. From stealing and rape to embezzlement and illegal shipments of arms to Iran, males seem to have a corner on deviant acts. In 1984 males were about four times more likely to be arrested for serious crimes than females. While the crime rate for males decreased 4 percent between 1975 and 1984, for females the crime rate increased 6 percent. Still, over three-fourths of the arrests for crimes against property were males (76.6 percent), while nearly 90 percent (89.3 percent) of the arrests for violent crimes were males.

Certainly factors other than sex of perpetrator influence deviance. Yet, one inescapable conclusion that has to be reached in analyses of deviance is that being male predisposes one to deviance. Moreover, if deviance is influenced greatly by learning, it would seem that one function of male deviance is to alert us to defects in the male socialization process. Many feminists have long alluded to this fact. Still, violence, aggressiveness, sexism, and destruction continue to be vital components of male socialization in a society with unlimited institutional supports for such learning. The warning light is on. If corrective mechanisms are instituted as a societal response, then at least men's widespread deviance will serve society positively beyond advancing male privilege and prerogatives.

Perspectives on Men and Deviance

General perspectives on deviance are defined broadly as biological, psychological, and social. Within the biological perspective on deviance are the contributions of Cesare Lombroso, William Sheldon, Eleanor Glueck, Sheldon Glueck, Patricia Jacobs, Muriel Brunton, and Marie Melville, among others. Lombroso was convinced in the latter part of the nineteenth century (1876) that male prisoners had distinctive physical characteristics, like peculiarly shaped foreheads, protruding jaws and cheekbones, long arms, and as Macionis (1986) puts it, apelike characteristics. As criminologists have pointed out, Lombroso's conclusion that such physical features (characteristic of infra-humans) were linked with criminal behaviors was neither logically nor empirically well-founded. Because Lombroso's research involved only males in prison, the finding that these males were not significantly different from male noncriminals had to await the research of others (Goring 1972).

Psychologist and physician William H. Sheldon, believing that weeding out the socially harmful constitutional types was the only effective means of social control, in 1949 proposed another biological explanation of men's deviance. After analyzing detailed physical and biographical data on 200 male youths at a rehabilitation home for boys in

Boston, Sheldon characterized the boys in terms of his constructed typology of body types. The typology included: the endomorph, who is described as soft and round; the mesomorph, who is hard and rectangular; and the ectomorph, described as lean and fragile. Sheldon associated personality characteristics with the body types as follows: endomorphs tended to be easy going, sociable, and self-indulgent; mesomorphs were restless, energetic, and insensitive; and ectomorphs were introspective, sensitive, and nervous (Cohen 1966, p. 51). While a link between body type and male youth deviance was suggested, Sheldon did not say that there was a causal link between body type and male youth deviance. Nevertheless, Sheldon did suggest some ways in which body type could relate to male youth deviance. For example, the mesomorph seems especially suited for delinquency because he is highly driven, active, impulsive, adventurous, and insensitive—a predator who takes what he wants. Now, mesomorphs do not have to become deviants. If intelligent and in the proper environment, mesomorphs could be redirected and their traits could be expressed in societally acceptable ways, in politics, industry, and the armed services.

Later, Eleanor Glueck and Sheldon Glueck (1950), in a much more sophisticated and methodologically adequate study, also would conclude that an association exists between mesomorphic body type and male youth deviance. Five hundred delinquent boys were compared with five hundred nondelinquent boys on frequency of body type within each category. In addition, Eleanor Glueck and Sheldon Glueck compared the frequency with which each of sixty-seven personality traits and forty-two sociocultural factors was associated with each of the body types within the two groups. They concluded that significantly more of the delinquents than nondelinquents were predominantly mesomorphic (Cohen 1966, p. 52). This led the Gluecks to suggest the following: (1) mesomorph body type provides only a potential for deviance; (2) deviance in mesomorphs as well as others may be related to one's feeling about one's body, which is social; and (3) mesomorphs may simply be overrepresented among the deviant because their bodies are well suited to street life and delinquency, which rewards strength, agility, and physical toughness.

Most criminologists have been reluctant to infer a causal relationship between body type and criminality despite reported association between the two variables; instead, a social explanation has been suggested for the preponderance of mesomorphs among male deviants. For example, Gibbon (1986) implies that young males with muscular and athletic builds may have the "right stuff" for engaging in deviant behavior. After all, certain forms of deviance call for physical traits like agility and physical aggressiveness, which are characteristic of mesomorphs. Moreover, as Macionis states (1986), we may expect muscular and athletic boys to be more physically aggressive than others, thus we treat them accordingly and provoke the very behaviors we expect.

Another line of research within biological explanations of deviance has been chromosome pattern research. It was pointed out in chapter 1 that females have an XX chromosome pattern, while males have an XY chromosome pattern. Occasionally, however (about 1 case in 1,000), because of a genetic mutation, a male is born with a XYY chromosome pattern. In early studies, many such males were found in prisons and mental institutions, leading some to believe that a causal link existed between the XYY chromosome pattern in males and male deviance. Further research has shown, however, that XYY males are not significantly more prone to violence than XY males.

Recent research on the role of the genetic component in deviance using pairs of twins and allowing variability in criminality to be environmentally inferred or genetically inferred has led to some interesting conclusions (Rowe 1983; Rowe and Osgood 1984). According to Rowe and Osgood's findings, juvenile deviance is best explained by a combination of genetic factors and environmental experiences. Sociobiologists James Q. Wilson and colleague Richard Hunstein recently reviewed research in juvenile deviance and concluded that the probability of persons engaging in deviant behavior is due in a small part to biological factors. Still, the critical factors determining deviance seem to be lodged in the social environment.

Not all students of deviance who search for the causes of deviant behavior within the individual believe that the causes are innate. Some believe (e.g., Becker 1963; Reckless and Dinitz 1967; Eysencek 1977) that deviance is a function of defects in the personality that make some persons more prone to deviant behavior than others. It is important to note that most personality defects and much "proneness to deviance" are functions of socialization, with the exception of a relatively small number of personality disorders linked to heredity or to congenital defects.

Psychological perspectives frequently are used to explain men's deviance. For example, learning the male sex role means learning to behave in certain ways, which in some situations can be labeled deviant. Date rape on college campuses is an example of such behavior which often is analyzed from a psychological perspective. Following a psychological line of thought, a critical part of male sex role socialization is learning to be aggressive in female-male dating situations. Males learn that they are expected to take the lead in romantic and/or sexual encounters. They also "learn" that females must not appear to be eager for such encounters, although this does not necessarily mean that they do not want to have sex at a particular time. Succinctly, males "learn" as a part of the male sex role to objectify, fixate on, and conquer females, while ignoring what females want. Date rape is a part of males' faulty socialization, according to the psychological perspective.

As Albert Cohen suggests, psychological perspectives on deviance tend to consist of "kinds of people" theories responding to the question, "What kind of man would do that sort of thing?" The superior status assigned to men in our society distorts the frequent response, "He is not a man, he belongs to some other species." The tautology is complete. The male who committed the heinous act is not a man, because men do not commit such acts. Thus, deviance remains detached from manliness.

Recently, sociologist Allen Liska (1987) noted that attempts to explain norm violations as functions of personality traits are not very successful. A cursory examination of published research in the area (Schuessler and Cressey 1950; Waldo and Dinitz 1967; Tennenbaum 1977) reveals mixed findings on the causal relationship between personality characteristics and deviance. According to Liska, one of the major criticisms directed toward psychological theories of deviance is that they emphasize rare and abnormal personalities as explanations of deviance while ignoring those aspects of present situations which may contribute to deviance. Biological and psychological explanations of deviance also fail to consider deviance as a social construction. Yet many disruptive behaviors seem to occur within particular facets of our social system. For example, different kinds of deviant acts seem to be variously distributed within American social structure. What is it about this structure that creates regular patterns of wife battering, rape, sexual harassment, destructive competition between men, and other forms of deviant behavior? The patterns persist in America in all socioeconomic classes, racial groups, ethnic groups, and religious groups. Wife battering, rape, sexual harassment, and destructive competition between men are properties of American society. From the social perspective, these deviant acts often committed by males are social facts rather than individual facts. In the next section these deviant acts are viewed as social facts, taking into account the importance of social meaning in male deviance.

Structural-Functionalism and Male Deviance

Of all the social perspectives on deviance, structural-functionalism more than any other provides a reasonable explanation of minority group male deviance in American society by focusing on inconsistencies in the social order. At the same time structural-functionalism supports our argument that deviance among minority group males generally is socially constructed, and that the social construction of male deviance involves a demasculinizing process.

Particularly important for our purposes are the contributions of Robert Merton (1957) and Richard Cloward and Lloyd Ohlin (1960). Presented first in 1938, Merton's views on deviance, which focus on incongruences between societal goals and means for attaining these goals as causes of deviance, seem particularly relevant in understanding the pervasiveness of deviance among minority group males today. Cloward and Ohlin's extension of Merton's ideas enriches this applicability. Merton's ideas were extensions of early sociologist Emile Durkheim's concept of *anomie,* a lack of regulation by the collective conscience (Turner 1982).

Merton goes beyond this definition, emphasizing anomie as a state of normlessness which occurs when dominant cultural goals and legitimate normative means do not regulate the behaviors of persons (Turner 1982, p. 84). He listed four "deviant" modes of adaptation to anomic situations: (1) *innovative,* acceptance of society's goals but rejection of the means for attaining these goals; (2) *ritualism,* acceptance of society's means for attaining its goals, but rejection of society's goals; (3) *retreatism,* rejection of both society's goals and means; and (4) *rebellion,* rejection of society's goals and means while substituting new ones. That these modes of deviance seem to characterize much deviance among minority group males is seen especially in deviance among Blacks, Chicanos, Puerto Ricans, Cubans, and Native Americans.

It is precisely because males in the above minority groups typically have racist and discriminatory experiences that they learn to reject societal means for achieving societal goals. After all, what good is it to accept and learn societal means for achieving desired societal goals when discriminatory practices will block utilization of the means? According to Cloward and Ohlin, it is precisely along this line of thought that the potential "deviant" proceeds as he takes advantage of an opportunity to learn and use innovative (illegitimate) means. Undoubtedly numerous minority group males' social experiences in American society prod them to seek and take advantage of opportunities to learn deviance.

This should not be a surprising observation to anyone familiar with the plight of minority group males. A more surprising observation is that many more minority group males do not fail to accept societal means for attaining societal goals. The argument that, in American society, a relatively high proportion of minority group males reject societal means for attaining societal goals and take advantage of illegitimate opportunities cannot be denied. It is important to keep in mind from this perspective that while individual males violate societal norms, the violations are functions of societal characteristics—discrepancies between societal ends and means.

Minority group males are not the only ones who may become innovative deviants. The male sex role in general, with its restrictive, conflicting, and stress-filled expectations, creates situations for many men which result in a need to innovate. The emphasis on male acquisition of wealth, power, and prestige makes even the most conforming males susceptible to learning and using deviant means for goal attainment. Acts of embezzlement and/or corporate theft are examples of male deviance in high circles along the lines of male innovation.

Merton and Cloward and Ohlin's contributions are remarkable all the more for they allow a special comment about ritualism as a form of deviance characterizing the behavior of many males, especially minority group ones. If ritualism can be viewed as a form of goal de-escalating, whereby frustration and stress are reduced by aligning goals with what is possible (Liska 1986), then it may define much male behavior ordinarily thought to be conforming. Most minority group males, especially Black males, are acutely aware that certain societal goals are beyond their reach. Few Black males believe that they can become presidents of large, male majority group-run corporations or become heads of economic, political, or religious institutions in society. Yet, the conforming Black male, or other minority group male, often gives the appearance of accepting societal goals by continuing to use means which would get him to the top if he were not a minority group male. Actually, the Black male who truly believed in societal goals and refused to accept the inevitable probably would not be mentally capable of using societal means. Undoubtedly ritualism is a deviant mode of adaptation numerous minority group males are forced into because of societal constraints and thus, societal means-ends inconsistences.

If ritualism characterizes the behavior of many minority group males even when the behavior is thought to be conforming behavior, what is the nature of their obviously deviant behaviors with high male proportions, such as mental illness and alcoholism?[1] Merton argued that such pathologies were forms of social retreatism. The question that arises for us is, What causes large numbers of males to drop out of society and into different worlds as manifested by their numerous social pathologies?

I believe the answer to this question lies in the high incidence of ends-means discrepancies existing as a result of unrealistic societal sex role expectations for males. Males in American society not only are expected to strive for success, but are expected to be successful. Being a "successful" man means achieving a certain measure of wealth, power, and status. Just how much of each must be achieved remains vague, since striving behavior is continual and never ending. It is safe to say that in America no man ever achieves so much that he can rest on his laurels. There is always another height to climb. For most men these lofty goals are impossible to attain, due to their lack of cultural means. Even some highly successful men whose experiences for long periods of their lives are ones of learning to use various societal means for attaining societally approved goals eventually face means-ends discrepancies. This occurs because male sex role expectations are conflicting and often contradictory, as pointed out in chapter 2. The successful male corporate executive who gradually rises to his "level of incompetence" is a highly visible example of a candidate for social retreatism. For years, he sacrificed close relationships with family and friends to reach certain goals only to find that there were even higher goals to be attained and inadequate means to attain them. It is not unusual for such a man to retreat to alcohol, mental illness, or drug addiction.

Other less "successful" men may realize even earlier that goals established for them by the social order are not really theirs and that they are unwilling to use societal means to obtain societal goals. Often what is referred to as a "midlife" crisis characterizes such a "realization" by many men, and the result is a rejection of the male sex role. Because of the dominant position of males in American society, rejecting most as-

---

1. The National Institute on Alcohol Abuse and Alcoholism reported 18 million persons eighteen years old and over were alcoholics in 1986. Of this number, 67 percent were male and 33 percent were female (*6th Special Report to the U.S. Congress on Alcohol and Health*, 1986).

On reported cases of mental illness in America resulting in inpatient care in 1986, the National Institute of Mental Health released figures for 1983–84. According to the report there were 117,084 inpatients in public facilities, of whom 58.2 percent were male and 41.8 were female; 16,079 persons were reported as private facilities inpatients, with 53.2 percent and 46.8 percent being male and female, respectively (*Special Report on Mental Health Organizations in the U.S., 1983–84*, 1986).

pects of the male sex role frequently means perceiving clearly the discrepancies existing between societal goals and legitimate means for attaining them. For many males (it seems to be an increasing number), perceptions of societal ends-means discrepancies lead to social retreatism—dropping out of society.

Periodically in American society, men arrive on the scene who do not conform nor do they engage in innovative, ritualistic, or retreatist behaviors. Like retreatists these men reject cultural goals and means, but unlike retreatists they advocate new goals and means. In the late 1960s and early 1970s such men were quite visible in America. Some males in the youth movement, Black males in the modern day civil rights movement, and males in the gay liberation movement all rejected for a while cultural goals and means while advocating new ones. These men did not drop out of society; they tried to change society. In other words, they used the rebellious mode of adaptation. To a certain extent society did change as a direct response to their efforts, although some may claim that the change has not been substantial. Today, a new breed of rebellious men has arisen as a response to ends-means discrepancies in American society. Men who are active in movements such as the one against nuclear war, for gay liberation, against violence toward women, for men nurturing, and the like are, in fact, rebellious male deviants.

The Chicago Perspective on Male Deviance

The Chicago perspective on deviance has been one of the most influential in sociology. The foundation for most of this work on deviance lies in the early ecological interests of University of Chicago sociologists such as Ernest Burgess, Louis Wirth, Clifford Shaw, Henry McKay, and E. Franklin Frazier. These scholars and others studied the relationship between patterns of city development and ecological processes (e.g., competition, invasion, succession), the etiology of city development and influence of ethnic-racial cultures within cities and upon zonal patterns, the patterning of deviance in physical space, and the relationship between industrialization, urbanization, social disorganization, and social deviance, among other things. Quite generally, scholars at the University of Chicago in the early twentieth century (e.g., Frazier 1932; Shaw et al. 1929; Shaw and McKay 1931), who were interested in social ecology and social deviance, first sought to understand the link between ecological processes and culture. A critical question asked by many of the scholars of this period was, Which cultural and ecological processes operate to produce social order? (Liska 1987, p. 63). Because behavior

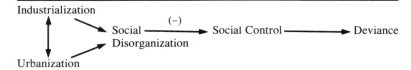

Fig. 5.1. Causal structure underlying the theory of social disorganization. Arrows describe the direction of causal effects; a double-headed arrow means that the effect flows in both directions; and a minus sign means that the effect is negative (an increase in one variable results in a decrease in another variable). Generally, the figure shows that industrialization and urbanization increase social disorganization, which decreases conventional social controls, which in turn increases deviant behavior. (Liska 1987, p. 62)

standards were synonymous with conventional societal customs and norms of the time, spatially distributed ecological processes like competition, population mobility, migration, invasion, etc. were seen as "disruptive processes" leading to deviant behavior.

Liska alludes to an important theoretical issue related to the Chicago perspective. The issue has to do with a basic assumption made by many adherents of the perspective and involves the notion that *social control processes in urban areas are disruptive.* This assumption leads to a second one, which is *urban areas are disorganized.* The causal structure underlying the above argument has been outlined in figure 5.1.

Figure 5.1 has some interesting implications for the link between men and deviance. Couched within the broad confines of Charles Darwin's *Origin of Species* (1859) and the works of aforementioned University of Chicago sociologists, the Chicago perspective emphasizes the survival of humans and their adaptation to their environment. The fact that some aspects of the environment are conducive to the survival of only some humans is recognized as others are thought to survive only through adaptation to the environment and to each other (Liska 1987, p. 60). Because humans develop cultures, the ecological processes of competition, cooperation, symbiosis, and cyclical change are restricted. Within this general framework, however, it is possible to understand the unique link between men and deviance which has existed and continues to exist in the United States.

In the first place, I have argued that there is a societal rationale for separating men and deviance. Much male deviance in the United States has been explained using the model presented earlier. Specific miniature theoretical explanations include differential association theory (Sutherland and Cressey 1970), social learning theory (Burgess and Akers, 1966), and social control theory (Hirschi 1969). The specifics of these explanatory systems are discussed elsewhere. What seems essential here is the fact that such explanations of male behavior support separating men and deviance. For example, those undesirable male behaviors which can be found among some Native American males, Hispanic males, Asian American males, other racial-ethnic males, and poor white males are not seen as behaviors engaged in by *men*. Rather, these are thought to be the behaviors of "poor misfits" who are products of an inadequate physical environment or inappropriate socialization or some combination of the two. These "poor misfits" are seen as males who cannot compete successfully, but they are not seen as men—men and deviance remain separated and attention is diverted from the dysfunctional deviance-producing aspects of male competition. Ironically, "humanitarian" societal efforts even "excuse" some male deviance by making attributions to the environment and/or the nature-nurture dichotomy. Support for this position can be seen in the seemingly constant decline in penalities for many deviant acts committed primarily by males, such as rape, assault, robbery, and even murder. Alterations in the biotic process of male competition seems to await further progressive changes in American society.

Let us turn our attention briefly to two popular theoretical models from the Chicago perspective on deviance: differential association and social control.

Differential association and deviant males. Numerous miniature theories and/or conceptual schemes have emerged from the Chicago perspective on deviance. One such theory is differential association; its basic tenets have been outlined by Edwin Sutherland and Donald Cressey (1970). The tenets suggest that deviant behavior is learned primarily in social interaction within intimate personal groups. The nature of this learning process is rather complicated and includes techniques of committing deviant acts as well as learning the specific direction of motives and drives from definitions of the legal codes as favorable or unfavorable. What determines whether a person becomes deviant is an excess of definitions favorable to deviance over those unfavorable to deviance. Critical variables in the learning of deviance via differential association are frequency, duration, priority, and intensity of deviant associations relative to conventional ones. In other words, the number of deviant definitions to which a person is exposed as well as the length of time of exposure, age during exposure, and the level of affection between the person and the source of deviant exposure all play critical roles in determining deviance. Deviance, like nondeviant behavior, is learned through patterns of social association and like nondeviant behavior is an expression of general needs and values, although it is not explained by them.

The implications of this perspective for our approach to male deviance are significant. Deviance among men is not thought to be inborn, yet it is thought to be pathological, something relatively rare and unusual. We do not hesitate to think of the male who violently aggresses against others as "crazy," as "some kind of nut," or worse. Still, there is the tendency in our society to avoid linking much male deviance with male socialization. Several researchers (Cullen et al. 1979; Felson and Liska 1984) report that there is little empirical support for gender explanations of deviance, suggesting that gender role expectations and socialization do not explain differences in male-female deviance. Still, many studies using self-concept, gender role expectations, sex role attitudes, and the like fail to capture the essence of "being a social male in American society." "Being a social male" in American society often means learning to behave in ways that are on the edge of deviance and, given specific situations, actors, and definitions, also learning behaviors and engaging in behavior quite likely to be defined as deviant at some time, in some place, and by some people. From our approach and this perspective, some male deviance probably occurs because of differential association. However, some males act deviant not because they experience differential exposure to conventional and nonconventional means, but because they learn the male sex role. This means that the seeds for deviance are sown during the male socialization process for most males in American society. Why some males are singled out for deviance when engaging in some behavior while others are accorded the status manliness when engaging in the same behavior cannot be explained via any cultural transmission theory of deviance. Perhaps the explanation, indeed, lies in the inferred ecological assumption that conventional customs and societal norms produce and are manifestations of social order. Let us turn our attention to a second model emerging from the Chicago perspective—social control.

Social control and male deviance. The assumption that there is a conventional social order in America which can be identified and that deviance is a violation of social norms supporting this social order are basic ideas underlying social control theory. Liska (1984) suggests, however, that social control theory is different from many of the Chicago perspective-based socialization theories of deviant behavior. The difference lies in the main question posed by proponents of social control theory: *What are the social structural factors weakening social constraints for certain aggregates of persons within certain urban areas?* The question is raised with the underlying Hobbesian-based assumption that all persons would commit deviant acts if there were no social constraints. The implications for males in American society are obvious. Due to a variety of reasons, males generally have much more freedom to commit deviant acts and fewer social constraints inhibiting deviance than females. Moreover, within the male aggregate there exists differential social constraints which inhibit deviance. On the one hand, extremely powerful males have fewer social constraints than less powerful males. On the other hand, once male power goes beyond some minimum level, fewer social constraints inhibiting male deviance exist. According to this perspective, then, male deviance can be expected to be pervasive among extremely powerful males and among those males with no power or only a modicum of power at best.

Two types of social control which inhibit deviance are said to exist: internal and external. Scholars like Walter Reckless and Simon Dinitz (1967) have focused on the former type of control with what they call containment theory, while a chief proponent of control theory, Travis Hirschi, has devoted attention to a combination of inner and external controls emphasizing such elements as belief, attachment, commitment, and involvement. From Reckless and Dinitz's social containment theory we would surmise that deviance is more pervasive among males because they have weaker bonds with conventional others than females have. Coupled with this is also the idea that males are more sensitive to peer pressure and school bonds than females while being less sensitive to parental bonds than females. Datesman et al. (1975) found some support for the above, but Shover et al. (1979) and Canter (1982) reported findings that were mixed, suggesting that females have stronger family ties but males seem to be more sensitive to family ties.

Taking Hirschi's social control theory into account when considering the pervasiveness of male deviance leads to some interesting speculation. Relative to females in the United States, males in general may be characterized by low internalization of conventional norms, minimum social rewards for conforming behavior, low social attachment to others, and low involvement in conventional activities. These variables which characterize the bond between persons and society (Hirschi refers to them as belief, attachment, commitment, and involvement) in numerous everyday examples are manifested by males enacting the male sex role in our society. First of all, while social control theorists may assume that some conventional social order exists, many males have no idea of its nature. In fact, the sex role strain paradigm which characterizes the modern male sex role suggests that most males experience extreme difficulty internalizing conventional social norms, since for them they are innately conflicted. This is thought to be basically true for males in general and even more so for certain aggregates of males not in mainstream society.

Not only is internalization of conventional social norms problematic for many males but commitment to conventional norms also may be quite difficult. On the surface, it would seem that there are numerous social rewards for males who conform and therefore the commitment element is a powerful social control factor. Yet, close scrutiny of the male sex role reveals, as we have seen, numerous lethal aspects. Because of its conflicted nature, the male sex role can be devastating to males physically, psychologically, and socially. Also critical for the person-society bond, as pointed out above, is the attachment element. Are men less sensitive to the opinions of others? Are they relatively unconcerned about the status and respect associated with conformity? These are perplexing questions, because the answers are both no and yes. Some discussions and studies (e.g., Hall and Halberstadt 1981; Franklin 1984) have suggested that some men may be less empathic and display less ability in decoding because of internalized gender expectations. On the other hand, I contend that when some men desire, they become quite empathic—that is, when it is beneficial to them. This would lead us to conclude that generally men are sensitive to the opinions of others. However, because of the nature of gender relations in American society and the complexity of the male sex role, men also may be primarily interested only in the opinions of other males. The literature on homophobia certainly suggests that this is the case. Because other males too have conflicting ideas about what conforming behavior means, it is entirely possible that the social attachment variable means little to many males. In fact, "being a man" may, for many males, mean ignoring social attachments (e.g., professional decisions, bureaucratic activity, etc.). Finally, "being a man" means for many people low involvement in social activities which inhibit social deviance although there may be high involvement in conventional activities associated with men's professions and occupations. Most men, however, may not be expected to be highly involved in religious activities, family activities, and other social activities. In fact, men's deep involvements primarily in occupational or professional activities may even *afford* opportunities for deviance. Thus, it may not be low social involvement per se which contributes to male deviance but low involvement in certain kinds of social activities.

The Labeling Theory Perspective on Male Deviance

A final perspective on men and deviance to be considered is labeling theory. Labeling theory emerges from a perspective in social psychology associated closely with the University of Chicago—symbolic interactionism. Essential tenets of symbolic interactionism are: (1) persons react to objects on the basis of the meanings that objects have for them; (2) meanings of objects grow out of social interaction; and (3) meanings of objects are modified by an individual interpretive process (Blumer 1969). These three tenets can be seen throughout the works of chief proponents of the labeling perspective, such as Edwin Lemert (1967), Howard Becker (1963), Edwin Schur (1971, 1984), and Thomas Scheff (1966), as well as numerous others.

Generally, from a labeling perspective deviance is seen as a social definition some persons and groups assign to the behaviors of others. There is an obvious relationship between social process and the ability to make a deviant label stick, since labeling theory actually is societal reaction theory. Three major questions are raised by labeling theory: What kind of behavior is defined as deviant behavior? Who are the people defined as deviant? and What are the consequences? Much of labeling theory is devoted to answering the second and third questions. Additionally, embedded in most of the work of scholars interested in the labeling perspective are conflict theory assumptions about competition between societal interest groups and social power and dominance. Quite simply, some groups' norms within society are closely aligned with societal norms, while other groups' norms are not so closely aligned and may even be in direct opposition. Still, the major thrust of labeling theory is in the direction of determining who is labeled deviant beyond social structural considerations.

Edwin Lemert (1967) postulated two types of deviance: primary and secondary. Primary deviance arises in numerous social, cultural, and psychological contexts and affects only minimally persons' psychic structures. It is omnipresent among persons. In contrast, secondary deviance refers to norm violations which are socially defined responses to problems created by societal reaction to their deviance. It involves persons' adjustment to overt and covert problems created by subsequent societal reactions to them (Lemert 1951, 1967). Primary deviance may or may not lead to secondary deviance. If, however, persons are publicly stigmatized, their relationships with others as well as their self concepts will be affected, leading to greater entrenchment and/or involvement in deviance (secondary deviance). For Lemert it is secondary deviance which should be the main focus of labeling theorists.

On the other hand, and critical in the thinking of Schur, some primary deviants may successfully negotiate a nonstigmatized social label or defend themselves successfully against others, accusing them of deviance but still consider themselves deviants. For Schur, deviant self concepts are manifestations of secondary deviance. Support for this comes from Warren and Johnston's (1972) report that while some closet gays may never be publicly labeled gay, they nevertheless may consider themselves gay.

Certainly the deviant label is not applied as easily to men who violate social norms as it is to women who violate social norms. This should not be surprising, since women in ordinary social interaction are treated as deviants (Schur 1984). Moreover, many of the patterns and restrictions that oppress women (which could be labeled deviant) actually are considered by many in society to be normal patterns of interaction (p. 20). Going a step further, for some men violating social norms, the influence of societal reaction on secondary deviance is not mediated by structural opportunities, interpersonal networks, and self concept which ordinarily are mediators. For example, because powerful men in our society often are able to successfully resist a stigmatized label despite norm violations, there is little or no reduction in their legitimate opportunities. And since powerful men often are able to alter what is acceptable behavior and what is unacceptable behavior in a society, primary deviance on their part does not lead to a deviant label, patterning opportunities of interaction and resulting in secondary deviance. To the contrary, it is not unusual for some such men to actually expand their legitimate economic opportunities after their previous deviant ones are recognized. Several Watergate defendants in the mid-1970s are excellent examples of powerful males who did not become locked into secondary deviance because of expanded legitimate opportunities.

The issue of societal reaction resulting in an increase in illegitimate opportunities which result in secondary deviance also is quite complex when applied to men in American society. Much primary male deviance does not lead to secondary deviance per se because the acts are considered "masculine" rather than deviant. What is considered an illegitimate interpersonal network becomes a legitimate interpersonal network. Males engaging in certain forms of violence, for example, increase their interaction in illegitimate interpersonal networks but only in the sense that the forms of male violence become a part of the networks of large numbers of males with whom they will interact. In sum, the violence becomes a part of the acceptable male sex role. The past popularity of chewing tobacco among high school male athletes, though not an external violent act, is a case in point. Until a very effective national campaign was waged emphasizing the health hazards of such deviance, being a high school male athlete increasingly was beginning to mean nationally "chewing tobacco."

A final point on the relationship between labeling and men's deviance is that (1) society encourages a separation of the two, and (2) alterations in self concepts for many norm violating males do not occur. Much of this chapter has been devoted to the first point and no further comments are made. On the second point, because men control society and a great deal of their behavior is highly revered in our society, much norm violating behavior by men simply results in a redefinition of behavior from deviant to acceptable. What is considered a hard-core pornographic magazine enjoyed primarily by men, for example, has changed tremendously in much of American society in the past decade. *Playboy, Hustler, Penthouse, Gallery,* and other magazines, once considered hardcore pornography, presently are referred to as "soft porn" if they are seen as pornography at all. One can only speculate that the redefinition is due to the multitude of "conforming men" securing and partaking of the magazines.

On Theories of Deviance

General explanations of men's deviance have been explained in this chapter. A prominent feature of the explanations is that all are rooted in social facts. From Merton's conceptualization of deviant modes of individual adaptation (also referred to as "strain theory") to labeling theory, deviance is considered as a form of social behavior even though each theory discussed offers different ideas to explain norm violations, including men's groups' differential power to control and enact norms and laws.

Despite the fact that some have criticized strain theories of deviance (Hirschi 1966) for assuming that a set of societal goals can be identified,

Merton's contributions are significant ones. They are important because they describe quite adequately the plights of many minority group men. These men, frequently facing limited means and avenues for goal accomplishment, are almost automatically relegated to lives of deviance by a society valuing only some majority group members of its male population.

From the Chicago perspective sketched in this volume comes differential association theory, which has been criticized for its generality and the fact that it fails to explain why deviant behaviors occur, focusing instead on the social construction of deviance. A position taken in this chapter and throughout this book is that the "why" of male deviance becomes clear when one examines closely the nature of the male sex role and the socialization process experienced by most American males. Inherent in both are the seeds of male deviance which are nurtured to full bloom by a patriarchial, male-valued society.

Because acceptance of certain aspects of one explanatory system does not necessarily negate the utility of other explanatory systems for understanding certain kinds of male deviance, social control theory seems quite valuable. It cannot be denied that some male deviance probably occurs because of males' greater freedom to violate social norms. Traditional features of the male sex role discussed in earlier chapters are quite compatible with a lack of intimate attachments to parents, teachers, and peers. According to social control theory, as we have seen, such a lack of social attachment and freedom from conventional norms allow many men the freedom of norm violation without social disapproval. Control theory, however, does not provide information about the frequency with which different men have impulses to break rules (Conklin 1987). However, if we recognize that many men's "impulses" to break rules may be related to their perceptions of power, our understanding of the relationship between key variables in control theory and men's deviance will be enhanced.

Studying the process by which behavior becomes labeled deviant and how this affects the status of a man and/or his self concept, giving rise to entrenched deviance, was a final perspective discussed. Labeling theory is seen as particularly unique in explanations of men's deviance, because men and deviance are carefully separated in our society. Some men do not get labeled deviant because they have the power to resist the deviant label. Still, this does not tell us why initial acts of male deviance occur, nor do we learn from labeling theory why some men who break rules change their self concepts even when they are not labeled (Gove

1980). By the same token, it may be noted that some men do not change their self concepts even when they are labeled deviant. Perhaps in the future further synthesis of the labeling perspective with conflict theory focusing closely on differences in men's power, prestige, and privilege within the male aggregate, as well as between the male aggregate and the female aggregate, will contribute greatly to our understanding of men's deviance.

6

Men's Sexuality

A persistent belief in our culture and in many cultures throughout the world is that men's sexuality is natural and/or instinctive. This belief undoubtedly has supported the construction of numerous myths surrounding men's sexuality. The myths are quite varied, and a full listing is impossible. Nevertheless, psychologist Bernie Zilbergeld (1981) provides in his book on male sexuality a summarized version of ten myths which most influence male sexual conduct. They are as follows:

Myth   1: Men shouldn't express certain feelings.
Myth   2: Sex is a performance.
Myth   3: A man must orchestrate sex.
Myth   4: A man always wants and is always ready to have sex.
Myth   5: All physical contact must lead to sex.
Myth   6: Sex equals intercourse.
Myth   7: Sex requires an erection.
Myth   8: Good sex is increasing excitement terminated only by orgasm.
Myth   9: Sex should be natural and spontaneous.
Myth 10: In this enlightened age, the preceding myths no longer have any influence on us.

A cursory examination of the above myths actually should suggest to us that much of what is regarded as the natural sexual inclination of human males is a function more of social variables than of biological ones. This means, quite simply, that men's sexual behavior, rather than being innate, largely is learned through a sexual socialization process and through vicarious and direct experiences. Instead of consisting only of physical or biological responses, the human male's sexuality also is affective, cognitive, and behavioral. Feelings about sex, thoughts and ideas about sex, and ways of behaving sexually accompany those biological components of men and together make up men's sexuality. Men's accounts of their earliest recognition of their own sexuality give credence to the importance of the social. Excerpts from the writings of three men are presented below, each illuminating the social aspects of men's sexuality.

The one thing that remains hidden about male sexuality is its complexity. Male sexuality generally is thought of as simple and straightforward. Few people, for example, can envision a ''real man'' not being turned on sexually when a ''desirable woman'' seems willing to engage in sexual activities with him. Despite the current AIDS scare, the man who does not at least give serious consideration to the possibility of a sexual encounter with this woman will be thought of as ''unmanly,'' ''strange,'' or as a victim of some sexual dysfunction. Certainly such a perspective presupposes that men's sexual behaviors are primarily biological and/or instinctual. It is commonly believed that men are ''always ready for sex'' and can always ''get it up,'' that is, if they are *real* men.

The main line of thought in this chapter is that such views of men's sexual behavior are fraught with misconceptions, myths, and downright untruths. The argument put forth is that much of men's sexual behavior comes about through vicarious and deliberate socialization. Male sexuality is similar to other kinds of human behavior in that affective, cognitive, behavioral, and physiological components are involved. Most males become sexual humans because they acquire certain knowledge, feelings, and behavioral repertoires and are physically capable of participating in a sexual act. Thus, while physiology/biology plays a role in men's sexuality, other components are just as important, if not more so. Let us consider the thoughts on early sexual experiences of two men: Julius Lester and Bill Cosby. Excerpts from their accounts illuminate the critical roles played by social variables in male sexual functioning.

> As boys go, I wasn't much. I mean, I tried to be a boy and spent many childhood hours pummeling my hardly formed ego with failure at cowboys and Indians, baseball, football, lying, and sneaking out of the house. When our neighborhood gang raided a neighbor's pear tree, I was the only one who got sick from the purloined fruit. I also failed at setting fire to our garage, an art at which any five-year-old boy should be adept. I was, however, the neigh-

borhood champion of getting beat up. "That Julius can take it, man," the boys used to say, almost in admiration, after I emerged from another battle, tears brimming in my eyes but refusing to fall.

My efforts at being a boy earned me a pair of scarred knees that are a record of a childhood spent falling from bicycles, trees, the tops of fences, and porch steps; of tripping as I ran (generally from a fight), walked, or simply tried to remain upright on windy days.

I tried to believe my parents when they told me I was a boy, but I could find no objective proof for such an assertion. . . .

Through no fault of my own I reached adolescence. While the pressure to prove myself on the athletic field lessened, the overall situation got worse—because now I had to prove myself with girls. Just how I was supposed to go about doing this was beyond me, especially because, at the age of fourteen, I was four foot nine and weighed seventy-eight pounds. (I think there may have been one ten-year-old girl in the neighborhood smaller than I.) Nonetheless, duty called, and with my ninth-grade gym-class jockstrap flapping between my legs, off I went. . . .

God, how I envied girls at that moment. Wherever it was on them, it didn't dangle between their legs like an elephant's trunk. No wonder boys talked about nothing but sex. That thing was always there. Every time we went to the john, there it was, twitching around like a fat little worm on a fishing hook. When we took baths, it floated in the water like a lazy fish, and God forbid we should touch it! It sprang to life like lightning leaping from a cloud. I wished I could cut it off, or at least keep it tucked between my legs, as if it were a tail that had been mistakenly attached to the wrong end. But I was helpless. It was there, with a life and mind of its own, having no other function than to embarrass me.

Fortunately, the girls I danced with were discreet and pretended that they felt nothing unusual rubbing against them as we danced. But I was always convinced that the next day they were all calling up all their friends to exclaim: "Guess what, girl, Julius Lester got one! I ain't lying!"

Now, of course, I know that it was as difficult being a girl as it was a boy, if not more so. While I stood paralyzed at one end of a dance floor trying to find the courage to ask a girl for a dance, most of the girls waited in terror at the other, afraid that no one, not even I, would ask them. And while I resented having to ask a girl for a date, wasn't it also horrible to be the one who waited for the phone to ring? And how many of those girls who laughed at me making a

fool of myself on the baseball diamond would have gladly given up
their places on the sidelines for mine on the field?

No, it wasn't easy for any of us, girls and boys, as we forced
our beautiful free-flowing child-selves into those narrow, con-
stricting cubicles labeled female and male. I tried, but I wasn't
good at being a boy. Now, I'm glad, knowing that a man is nothing
but a figment of a penis's imagination, and any man should want to
be something more than that. (Lester 1973)

While Lester's account is one of some confusion about the male sexual role even to the point of being confused about male erections and their
causes, Cosby's account is much more social in nature.

First reported in *Playboy* magazine in 1966, Cosby's childhood sexual socialization involved an incident between Cosby and a friend he refers to as ''Rufus.'' While the two were engaged in throwing a football,
Rufus inquires about Cosby's relationship with a girl called ''Rosemary.'' Upon receiving an affirmative answer to the question of whether
they were boyfriend and girlfriend, Rufus then asks Cosby, ''Did you get
any yet?'' Of course Cosby replies, ''Get any what?'' Rufus responds by
asking Cosby, ''Did you get any p-u-s-s-y?''

Cosby says to Rufus that he really doesn't do that kind of thing, or in
today's vernacular that he isn't ''into that.'' Rufus immediately challenges Cosby by asking him if he would engage in sex if a girl would offer
him sex and hesitantly Cosby implies that he would have sex with the
girl.

As the story unfolds, one learns that Cosby knows nothing about female genitals and sexual intercourse. He sees graffitti on the walls and
sidewalks in his neighborhood saying that ''pussy is good,'' but he really
has not grasped what this means. Cosby points out that he had even over-
heard older guys in his neighborhood making statements that some girls
have ''goooood p-u-s-s-y'' but he didn't really know what they meant.
While older boys fixated on girls' legs, even suggesting that they liked to
see girls' legs way up in the air, Cosby, at eleven years old, was confused, he reports. His response to older boys' comments about girls' legs
in the air was, ''You like to see people fall down, or what?''

Bill Cosby's story becomes, quite frankly, hilarious as he recounts
how Rufus' challenge leads him to approach Rosemary about the possibility of having sex with her. The only problem for Cosby is that he does
not know how to have sexual intercourse. He says, ''You know, and I'm
trying to ask people questions about how they get some p-u-s-s-y and I
don't want guys to know that I don't know nothing about getting no p-u-s-

s-y.'' Using 'round-a-bout ways to elicit sexual technique information
from older boys, Cosby asks one boy, ''Well, man, what is your favorite
way of getting it?'' The older boy says, ''The regular way,'' to which
Cosby replies, ''Yeah, good ol' regular way . . . good ol' regular way of
getting that p-u-s-s-y.''

Cosby reports that he experienced a good deal of anxiety trying to
figure out how he was supposed to have sex without allowing anyone to
know that he was a virgin. Cosby also reports that he was anxious about
engaging in the act itself without knowledge of what he was to do. He
states that because he was a male he didn't feel that he should admit to
Rosemary that he didn't know what to do.

Cosby's anxiety grows as the time nears and he has gained no information about how to engage in sexual intercourse. As Cosby approaches
Rosemary's house, the following account describes his dilemma and his
feeling about his would-be first sexual experience:

> So I keep walkin' and the closer I get to the house, the more
> scared I get. And I get to the house and now I *don't want to do it*. I
> mean, I *don't want none*, 'cause it's nasty . . . and it's *dirty* . . .
> and you will *go to hell* and she could get pregnant and my mother's
> gonna cry, and my father's gonna cry, and I'll probably get a
> beatin' . . . so I really don't want to do it now, I'm not gonna do it
> to her. But I go and knock on her door. And I'm not shaking or
> nothin', it's just that I'm knocking on the door and I don't want
> any. And I'm gonna tell her as soon as she opens the door that I
> don't want any. Because it is nasty and you could get pregnant from
> it and all those things. (Cosby 1966)

Zilbergeld's (1981) personal account of his early masturbatory activities also underscores the role of learning sexuality even in such a solitary sexual activity. After having gone to summer camp at age thirteen
where he saw and heard his older roommates masturbating in his cabin at
night, Zilbergeld practiced the activity. Attempting the activity first at
camp without success and without an erection, Zilbergeld termed his first
sexual investigations a ''flop'' (p. 14). Sometime afterward, when he
was alone at home, Zilbergeld says, ''absentmindedly stroking my penis
and thinking that I would have to retire from such pursuits unless more
rewarding results were forthcoming, I became aware of some pleasurable sensation'' (p. 14). He went on to say:

> I kept stroking, my penis got hard, and the sensation felt better
> and better. Then I was overcome with feelings I never had never

before felt and, God help me, white stuff came spurting out the end of my cock. I wasn't sure if I had sprung a leak or what. . . .
    As I look back at those days, I can see how much I had to learn. The first ejaculation fired my curiosity—they were certainly interesting—but they didn't feel all that great. I wasn't sure what to make of them. Only gradually did I begin to experience them as extremely pleasurable, perhaps more pleasurable than anything else. (P. 14)

It is probably correct to say that, in the past decade or so, sexual knowledge has been more available, and there has been greater societal permission to be interested in such knowledge. Still, the sexual script most men develop comes about prior to their access to accurate sexual information. Few parents, even today, participate actively in the social construction of their son's sexuality. More than likely, the maturing boy develops sexual thoughts, feelings, and behaviors in much the same way as Lester, Cosby, and Zilbergeld did. If there is some parental participation in a son's sexual socialization, it is likely to be along the lines of disseminating information that is misleading, inaccurate, and even dangerous.

With minimum parental participation, maximum peer group participation, and sundry other vicarious sexual socialization experiences, boys learn to be sexual—they learn a general sexual script from which they individually improvise. The script involves sexual ''knowledge,'' sexual ''feelings,'' and sexual behavior. The nature of this script and men's responses to it are discussed below.

Men and Sex: The Male Heterosexual Sexual Script

One feeling more than any other is learned by American males early in their lives and permeates all of their sexual and intimate relationships with others. Gregory Lehne (1976) and Perry Garfinkel (1985) contend that this feeling, ''homophobia,'' is one of the major barriers to intimate relationships *between* men. As a point of departure for our discussion, homophobia is seen as perhaps the most critical factor shaping American men's sexualities—heterosexuality, bisexuality, and homosexuality. An irrational fear and hatred of homosexuals and homosexuality permeates the sexual scripts for men who participate in sex with women; for those men who engage in sexual activities with men; and for those men who have sex with women *and* with men. Homophobia, along with misogyny (hatred of women), facilitate men's constructions of heterosexual sexual scripts which all too often lack intimacy. Homophobia alone could not affect men's sexual scripts so profoundly. It is necessary for homophobia to be accompanied by another social pathology, misogyny, in order for sexual scripts to exist as barriers to men's intimacy in relationships. Let us consider the roles of both homophobia and misogyny in men's constructions of sexuality.

The Role of Homophobia in Male Sexuality

Homophobia is best conceptualized from (1) a cultural perspective and (2) a personal perspective. From a cultural perspective, homophobia is a belief system which supports negative myths and stereotypes about homosexual people; and from a personal perspective, homophobia refers to an irrational and persistent fear, dread, intolerance and/or hatred of homosexuals (G. Weinberg 1972; Morin and Garfinkel 1978; Lehne 1976; MacDonald 1976).

Morin and Garfinkel identify aspects of American culture which support negative myths and stereotypes of homosexuals. Such cultural aspects include (1) belief systems which justify discrimination on the basis of sexual orientation; (2) verbal symbols (language) which are offensive to persons whose sexual orientations are homosexual; and (3) belief systems which devalue homosexual life styles. Certainly, the fact that most religious institutions hold firmly to a literal interpretation of the tenets of Leviticus 20:13 supports the denigration if not annihilation of homosexuals. The verse states:

> If a man also lie with a man kind, as he lieth with a woman, both of them have committed an abomination; they surely shall be put to death, their blood is upon them.

Of all Biblical verses, this one more than many others, seems to be one that a growing number of "straight" men are willing to subscribe to, given the tremendous increase in "gay bashing" activities. The case of Timothy Lee, a twenty-three-year-old Black gay man, who is believed to have been raped and/or murdered in Concord, California by Ku Klux Klan members on November 2, 1985, is but one example of the growing number of gay bashings and killings in the late 1980s. Gay newspapers, magazines, and other gay media also report increased use of language (e.g., queers, faggots, fruits, etc.) offensive to gay men. Finally, prejudices and discrimination against homosexual men also come from other, often unanticipated, segments of the culture. For example, the 1986 Supreme Court *Hardwick* decision in Georgia upholding Georgia's state sodomy law; the refusal of hospitals, undertaking services, and law enforcement officials to recognize homosexual attachments as ones where the participants enjoy any legal rights; and even political attempts to denigrate persons seeking public office who support gay rights all point to belief systems supporting the oppression of gay people in general and gay men in particular.

While homophobia, the irrational fear and hatred of homosexuals, often is referred to as the unspoken barrier inhibiting close and intimate relationships between men (Garfinkel 1985), just as critical is the fact that homophobia does more to men than inhibiting intrasex intimacy—it also contributes to the way men construct their heterosexual sexual scripts. First of all, men's sexual roles in heterosexual sexual encounters are becoming more and more explicitly defined, because sexual orientation increasingly is becoming *the* component defining masculinity. Due to recent shifts in the definition of masculinity (Pleck 1981; Franklin 1984), heterosexuality increasingly is emphasized when the concept of masculinity is defined. Herek (1986) states: ''. . . although past American notions of masculinity have implicitly included the component of heterosexuality, that component is now more salient and often must be explicitly avowed as part of one's (masculine) identity'' (p. 571). Herek feels, further, that the tendency to include explicit heterosexuality in definitions of masculinity is likely to increase because of (1) the AIDS epidemic and (2) the superficial flexible behaviors of many routine masculinist men (see Franklin 1984). The latter reason for increasing the importance of the heterosexual component of masculinity is not too different from football players who can express tenderness toward each other on the football field after an extremely strenuous ''masculine'' performance (first, ''proof'' of heterosexual masculinity is established, and then tenderness is expressed).

Herek feels that heterosexual masculinity embodies personal characteristics of success, status, toughness, aggressiveness, dominance, and independence, which usually are manifested by social relationships exclusively with men and sexual relationships exclusively with women. Moreover, as alluded to earlier, heterosexual masculinity means *not being feminine* in behavior, feelings, and physical appearance *and not being homosexual* or overly intimate with men—and in some instances, being homophobic. Men's sexualities are affected profoundly by the latter. Men's fear of homosexuals means that they must engage in behaviors which they perceive set them apart from gay men. Sexually speaking, this means that instead of being "submissive," "compliant," and "passive," men must be "aggressive," "forceful," and "eager" for sex. All of this translates into internalizing and playing out a men's sexual script characterized by what Jack Litewka (1979) calls the "socialized penis" and Leonore Tiefer (1986) refers to as "the perfect penis."

Jack Litewka (1979) has distinguished three components of the "socialized penis" that are aspects of a male's environment which must be present if he is to become sexually stimulated while interacting with a female. The elements *objectification, fixation,* and *conquest* together constitute features of a kind of sexual script denoting *sexual dominance* which most males in America learn during their early years. Given what some have termed men's achievement orientation to sex (Slater 1976), significant components of the script can be outlined.

Teaching young males to be homophobic frequently means teaching them to sexualize their relationships with others—men as well as women. As pointed out earlier, men learn to be extremely cautious in their relationships with other men; they learn to sexualize such relationships, subjecting them to numerous homophobic standards and barriers which limit intimacy. Learning to loathe homosexuality and homosexuals, men also learn to constantly question their own feelings and behaviors as well as the behavior and feelings of other men. It becomes essential for men's heterosexuality to take on a distinctive flavor—after all, gay men, too, are sexual. But heterosexuality is different from homosexuality, and a different sexual script must be followed. The nature of this sexual script, though, is a direct outgrowth of men's sexual socialization, stressing homophobia, male dominance in sex, and an achievement orientation to sex.

The idea that frequently men internalize an achievement orientation to sex is related to Alan Gross' (1978) idea that sexuality becomes a critical component of masculinity for males at an early age. Because of social forces (peer pressure, parental expectations, etc.) and biology (anatomical structure, involuntary erections, etc.), boys probably masturbate earlier than girls. Early masturbating activities may lead to an early genital focus because of the link established early in boyhood between sexual desire/feeling and the penis. What all of this means, according to Gross, is that men, more than women, learn early to isolate sex from other aspects of their lives, leading them to separate sex from intimacy. This view is consistent with Mercer and Kohn's (1979) finding that sexuality was more integrated into the overall personality of females than of males in their study. Mercer and Kohn found that for males, sexual urges predicted both frequency of sexual contacts and number of sexual partners. For females, sexual urges predicted only frequency of sexual contacts, while attitudes and values better predicted the number of sexual partners. For males, attitudes and values did not predict male sexual contacts or number of sexual partners.

The heterosexual male's sexual script which emerges in part from the homophobic norm can now be outlined. Males learn early to achieve and this achievement orientation extends to sexual matters. During the period in which young males learn to achieve, they also learn to focus on their genitals and probably begin to engage in masturbatory activities. Both the achievement orientation and genital focus lead young males to become preoccupied with sexual climax as an indicator of sexual accomplishment, meaning that sex can be isolated from other aspects of social life. For example, several men in Shere Hite's 1981 study reported how they felt following their first ejaculatory experience:

> I felt that I had arrived and now I was one of the "big guys" too.

> When I finally ejaculated at thirteen, I felt great! "Hooray, I'm a man!" The world was complete.

> With my first ejaculation at fifteen, I thought of it as a big thing, quite macho. Something to brag about to the guys.

> After I came while masturbating, I thought I was a great guy who was gonna lay every chick in sight. (Hite 1981, p. 606)

Such a view of the sex act is quite consistent with the young male's views of females, which often accompany the development of components of male sexuality. From other young males, older males, the mass media, and other sources, boys learn that to be masculine is to *objectify* females (any female will do) and to concentrate on (*fixate* on) parts of females' bodies—their legs, hips, breasts, and so on. They also learn that erections often can accompany such fixations and this becomes associated with possibly deriving pleasure from erections if sexual climax can occur. (Frequently, young males initially accomplish this via masturbation.) Males also learn that females do not actually have to be present for this scenario to develop; they can simply imagine females and portions of females' bodies and erection will occur, leading to pleasurable sensations. The final act in the script occurs when males learn to use women for sexual gratification. The accepted notion is that, after all, if women are not used for this purpose, one just might be—God forbid—gay! Thus, *conquering women* becomes an outgrowth of the homophobic norm, because it affirms a man's masculinity and reassures him that he is *not* homosexual. Moreover, when a man shares this experience with other men, they reward him with admiration, and he learns quickly that the more often he repeats the scenario, the more rewards (trophies) he will receive. Conquest of women, then, becomes a central part of male sexuality, inextricably linked with homophobia.

As stated earlier, homophobia alone cannot account for the predominant sexual script followed by many American men in their heterosexual sexual encounters. Probably due to a tendency for persons in our society to make gender assumptions about men whose sexual preference is other men, the construction of masculine sexual scripts involves also establishing sufficient distance from women and femininity.

The male sexual script outlined above, which includes *objectification, fixation,* and *conquest,* certainly is not the only one followed by American males. Yet, it cannot be denied that men's use of this script is pervasive in American society. Evidence for this contention comes from increasing rates of heterosexual rape, child sexual assault, and women's laments about lack of empathy in their romantic relationships with men. All of this seems to indicate that men in America often construct sexual scripts which reflect relatively low levels of involvement with their female sex partners. Constructing such a sexual script means that men in general have a wider latitude of partner acceptance than women do. As Litewka (1979) states, ''Any number of lips or breasts or vaginas would do—as long as we can objectify, fixate, and conquer, an erection and (provided there is some form of penile friction) ejaculation will occur'' (p. 105).

To explain why many heterosexual men construct such sterile and hostile sexual scripts means recognizing misconceptions and false stereotypes about gay men and the dislike of women and femininity inherent in the predominant male sexual script. Lehne (1976) points out that a popular stereotype of gay men is that they are similar to women despite empirical evidence that the vast majority of gay men are not suspected of being gay (approximately 80 to 85 percent). Moreover, psychological testing of gay men reveals that they cannot be differentiated from straight men, which means that women and gay men tend to be quite dissimilar. Still, the stereotype exists, and the implications of the stereotype are important for our consideration.

Homophobia, Misogyny, and the "Perfect Penis"

Lehne (1976) implies in his analysis of homophobia that the norm functions to constrain men in the male sex role. He feels that homosexuality is not the main issue; rather, the real thrust is change in the male sex role. The male sex role is constructed and maintained by men as well as the norm of homophobia. Men use homophobia to control other men in their sex roles. The male role is quite powerful in American society, and maintaining power is very important for many men. Gay men are perceived as not supporting the dominant male role, not having a vested interest in oppressing women, and not using power to further male interests—all of which pose a threat to the continuation of male power (pp. 78–80). The influence of the homophobic norm in heterosexual men's constructions of their sexual script is mediated by a subtle dislike and hostility toward women and femininity (misogyny). In sum, many men in America often construct heterosexual sexual scripts reflecting socialized penises that can perform only when there are low levels of sex partner involvement and wide latitudes of sex partner acceptance. Understanding of this phenomenon is enhanced when it is recognized that our society constrains men by a homophobic norm and by misogynistic attitudes.

Leonore Tiefer (1986) contends that sexual virility is a major social expectation associated with masculinity. Of concern to many scholars, especially since around 1970, has been "the ability of men to fulfill the conjugal duty, the ability to procreate, sexual power, potency" (p. 579). This was also the time that the modern-day women's movement began to move ahead full steam. We can only surmise that increased attention devoted to impotence in the psychological literature is in some way related to increased concern with the topic in everyday life. Tiefer notes that use of the comparable pejorative term for women, frigidity, has declined dramatically since that time. Both Jack Litewka (1979) and Bonnie Allen (1983) recount incidents indicating that men in sexual encounters who cannot follow the traditional male sexual script emphasizing male dominance and prerogatives in the sexual arena seem not to be able to "get it up," or in more proper terms, they experience impotence.

Tiefer feels that male sexual competence is by far the major force consolidating and confirming masculinity regardless of whether a given male is inclined toward "traditional" masculinity or "progressive" masculinity. She recognizes and accepts Gagnon and Simon's (1973) explanation of the genesis of men's genital foci. During adolescence masturbation is perhaps the chief sexual activity engaged in by most boys. Erection and orgasms are viewed by them as signs of power and achievement. Frequently such views are manifested by adolescent male peer groups which place great value on members' erection and orgasm abilities. Such peer group emphasis undoubtedly results in erections and orgasms becoming viewed by many males as the major components of their sexuality. Unfortunately, when male sexuality assumes the ability for potent function, demands on men become extremely stressful. Tiefer outlines her own version of sexual beliefs drawn from the writings of Zilbergeld (1981), Doyle (1983), and LoPiccolo (1985). They are:

1. Men's sexual apparatus and needs are simple and straightforward, unlike women's.
2. Most men are ready, willing, and eager for as much sex as they can get.
3. There is suspicion that other men's sexual experiences approximate ecstatic explosiveness more closely and more often than one's own.
4. It is the responsibility of the man to teach and lead his partner to experience pleasure and orgasm.
5. Sexual prowess is a serious, task-oriented business, no place for experimentation, unpredictability, or play.
6. Women prefer intercourse to other sexual activities, particularly "hard-driving" intercourse.
7. All really good and normal sex must end in intercourse.
8. Any physical contact other than a light touch is an invitation to foreplay and intercourse.
9. It is the responsibility of the man to satisfy both his partner and himself.
10. Sexual prowess is never permanently earned; each time it must be proven. (Tiefer 1986, p. 581).

Easily recognizable in Tiefer's "sexual beliefs" that many men in America subscribe to are basic elements of the male sexual script which include genital foci, isolation of sex from other aspects of social life, and emphasis on competent sexual performance. The latter is defined as a strong erection, technical mastery, and ejaculation. Ejaculation is thought by a majority of men to be absolutely essential to a full sexual performance, despite the report by many men in Shere Hite's (1981) male sexuality study of over 7,000 men (1981) that ejaculation is not synonymous with the experience of full orgasm. Comments from three of Hite's respondents on the subject of ejaculation and orgasm are as follows:

Anybody can ejaculate. You just do the physical thing and you ejaculate. But to orgasm, you must follow an emotional scenario.

Orgasm is satisfying; ejaculation is not. In orgasm, there is a gap, a moment where you lose consciousness, a break.

An ejaculation without orgasm is a nothing—no feeling of any sort except the wetness and the muscle contractions.

When she wants to fuck and I'm just too high, or too uninterested to respond, I ejaculate but I don't come. (Pp. 472–73)

The kind of orgasm described above by the first respondent seems to be similar to what Donald Mosher refers to as (1) ecstatic role enactment; (2) total absorption in a special sexual orientation; and (3) the deepest, and core-centered, involvement with a sex partner where consciousness of self and partner is lost in the experience of mystical union (Mosher 1980).

It should not be surprising that most men seldom experience the kind of orgasm described above. The chief impediment to such an experience seems to be the sexual requirements and demands men place on themselves. In their search for what Tiefer calls "the perfect penis," men often find that erections and ejaculations enhance their immediate self-esteem, massage their egos, and maintain their masculine reputations, but leave them still unfulfilled as sexual and human beings. But, increasing numbers of men are finding themselves unable to find "the perfect penis" and are turning to medicine for answers to their sexual dysfunction. Tiefer claims that such medicalization of male sexuality has led to an escalating use of medicinal remedies for male impotence, the long-term effects of which are unknown and seem in some cases to be harmful. In addition, when male sexuality is medicalized, human experience is mystified and dependence on professional help and experts is increased. Such medicalization also leads people to believe that the absence of erections is unhealthy, and thus medical authorities are left to decide the norms and standards of sexual conduct. Perhaps the major disadvantage of the medicalization of men's sexuality, though, is that it obscures the social causes of male sexual dysfunction, and impotence, for example, becomes the problem of an individual man. Tiefer says:

A rigid, reliable erection is necessary for full compliance with the script. The medicalization of male sexuality helps a man conform to the script rather than analyzing where the script comes from or challenging it. . . . The demands are so formidable, and the pressures from the sociocultural changes . . . so likely to increase that no technical solution will ever work. (P. 595)

The Sexual Intercourse Orientation of Men

From our discussion thus far, it is possible to conclude that male sexuality is distinctively sexual-intercourse oriented. Such a view of male sexuality is supported by Shere Hite's 1981 report that the overwhelming majority of men she studied reported that sexual intercourse which culminated in orgasm was perceived to be the essence of male sexuality. In fact, most men in the study "did not want to have sex that did not culminate in intercourse and male orgasm" (p. 335). This would seem to imply that, for men, sexual intercourse is the greatest sexual pleasure that a man can have. Yet, the Hite report also reveals that most of the men studied experienced a stronger orgasm when they masturbated than when they had sexual intercourse.

Why, then, is sexual intercourse so central to men's sexuality? Certainly, the physical pleasure men experience when they engage in sexual intercourse is important as are the emotional and psychological rewards, including feelings of being loved and accepted as well as giving love and celebrating emotional and physical closeness with a loved one. Shere Hite alludes to still another reason why men often define sex and intercourse synonymously: "the pressure of tradition—and the traditional symbolism of intercourse" (p. 346). As stressed throughout this section, male sexuality in America involves a male sexual script which emphasizes masculinity and male dominance. Both men and women in America (a patriarchial society) are taught that intercourse symbolizes masculinity and male identity—an erect penis ready to engage in sex and an accepting vagina both constituting the validation of masculinity. Hite reports that many men in her study implied in one way or another that much of their desire for sexual intercourse was related to the cultural expectation that *this is what they should want.* In addition, Hite found that, for many men, as we stated earlier in this chapter, sexual intercourse also symbolized the male's power and dominance—the man had, indeed, conquered the woman (p. 350).

Undoubtedly, the male "sex drive" or male sexuality has been one aspect of a broader ideology stressing male dominance in American culture. Such an ideology often has meant that men have felt that they needed to have sex frequently in order to live up to some masculine ideal. In many cases this has extended to include numerous different sex partners—both frequency of sex and number of different sex partners being equated with masculinity. But in the late 1980s, male sexuality is on the verge of undergoing some alteration. What evangelical religious leaders, irate wives, girlfriends, lovers, and literature stressing the development of in-depth male sexual involvement all have been unable to do, a deadly virus seems quite capable of doing—that is, forcing some sexually active men to limit the number of sexual partners and in many instances even to maintain monogamous relationships. But, heterosexuality is only one of several sexualities of men. Let us consider others.

Men's Ambisexuality

Male ambisexuality, involving the ability of a man to eroticize either males or females under certain circumstances, is a male sexual alternative which has gained increased recognition in the waning 1980s. Frequently referred to as male bisexuality, the term denotes the tendencies of those males who are attracted to both males and females. Because many people perceive ''bisexuals'' to be equally attracted to both sexes and because the concept gives a misleading sense of fixedness to sex-object choice suggesting equidistance from heterosexuality and homosexuality, Phillip Blumstein and Pepper Schwartz (1976) suggest substituting the concept ''ambisexual.'' They feel that the term ''ambisexual'' focuses on the individual's sexual behavior, while the term ''bisexual'' focuses on the person's ''sexual place.'' Utilization of the term ''ambisexual'' means that adequate descriptions of persons' sexual behaviors with both men and women can be given regardless of whether these behaviors occur simultaneously within a given period or within separate periods of time.

Men's ambisexuality is a sexual alternative practiced by many men today that is increasingly being understood. Long seen by some as a phenomenon of the world of arts and entertainment, male ambisexuality until the middle 1980s was thought to be rarely associated with the sexuality of most heterosexual men. This was so despite Shere Hite's report that 6 percent of the men in her sample enjoyed sex with both men and women, while another 9 percent enjoyed and preferred sex with men.

One reason ambisexuality presently is being recognized as a sexual alternative of some men is due to the rapidly increasing number of heterosexual AIDS transmissions. Heterosexual AIDS cases previously were recognized as products of intravenous drug abuse and sexual activity with infected persons. Increasingly, however, bisexual activities practiced by many men are the foci of attention as possible sources of AIDS transmissions. *Time* magazine (Feb. 16, 1987) reported a forthcoming study by Dorothea Hays of Adelphi University which indicates that 80 percent of the wives of bisexual men in her sample were ignorant of their husband's gay activity (p. 52). While this finding may seem shocking to some, it is quite plausible when the nature of male bisexuality is understood.

The Nature of Male Ambisexuality

The definition of male ambisexuality stated earlier, emphasizing the ability of men to be erotically attracted to both men and women, does not enhance our understanding of the phenomenon. Weinberg and Williams (1974), for example, note that gayness is viewed both as a "condition" and as a "status." When viewed as a condition, it becomes necessary to decide how much of the condition must be present before the individual is labeled "gay." On the other hand, if being gay is a status, then the behaviors are not important; rather, importance is attached to the expectations and typifications surrounding those defined as gay and whose self-conceptions are affected (Weinberg and Williams 1972, p. 276). "Heterosexual," "homosexual," and "ambisexual" can refer to numerous things, like inclinations, activities, statuses, roles, self-concepts, and so on. Yet, it is precisely the tendency to define these concepts in ways other than "activities engaged in" which politicizes the concepts, often rendering them meaningless. For this reason, the position assumed in this volume is that "activities engaged in" is the critical variable defining the sexual orientation of a man. Regardless of how a given male defines himself, if he engages in sex with men and women during a period of time, or with one sex exclusively during a period of time followed by sex with the other exclusively for a period, or in some combination, the ambisexual activities define him as "ambisexual."

A definition of ambisexuality such as the above allows us to define those men who only occasionally engage in ambisexual activities regardless of self-definition as ambisexual. It also means that regardless of a heterosexual man's fantasies about engaging in sexual activities with men (and many do have these fantasies, according to Hite), if he does not act upon such fantasies, he is defined as heterosexual, not ambisexual. By the same token, a man who considers himself heterosexual, has an active sexual life with women (or *a* woman), and also regularly or irregularly visits adult bookstores where he engages in "glory hole" sexual activities anonymously with other men is defined as ambisexual. There is no dearth of such self-labeled heterosexual men. They go to public parks, roadside stops, adult theaters, and other places for the express purpose of engaging in tearoom sexual activities, and thus are defined in this volume as ambisexual men.

I contend that no criterion other than *voluntary* participation in ambisexual sexual activities is necessary to define the male as ambisexual. Excluded from the definition of male ambisexuality are those men who are sexually violated by other men. Such sexual violations are common occurrences in prisons and other total institutions, and are increasing occurrences in everyday life. While the victims of such crimes are not labeled ambisexual here, the perpetrators *are* labeled as such, albeit criminal ambisexuals.

High incidences of ambisexuality have been reported consistently by social researchers such as Humphreys (1970), Kirkham (1971), Ross (1971), Ponte (1974), Blumstein and Schwartz (1976), Bell and Weinberg (1978), and Bozett (1987). Still, the fact that particular men are ambisexual often is masked, denied, ignored, or labeled something else. The only conclusion that can be drawn from this is that our homophobic teachings aid us in constructing a rationale that says that a voluntary homosexual or gay image *is worse* than a perverted macho image—one that allows a male to participate in "gang banging" a gay man, or an abusive animal-like prisoner to violently rape a fellow male prisoner, or a "happily married" middle-class man to engage in anonymous gay sex in tearooms with willing participants and later publicly denounce gays, gay rights, and gay activity.

Matteson (1988) has suggested that "the discovery that a married man is gay threatens the safe division of the world into the neat categories of gay and straight." As a result, ambisexuality, especially when a heterosexual marriage is involved, often is hidden from and/or rejected by the mainstream community. Still, there is no dearth of such male sexuality.

Types of Ambisexual Men

Brian Miller's (1978) typology of gay husbands, in his brilliant article on adult sexual resocialization, describes three kinds of ambisexual husbands and one gay husband who moves completely into the gay world. According to Miller, there are three types of married men who at least partially construct or participate in an ambisexual world. A fourth type of married man (the faggot husband) gradually gives up an ambisexual existence for total submergence in the gay world. The faggot husband's private and public identities become totally gay. This male sexual alternative is discussed in greater detail in the next section.

Of more relevance for our discussion of ambisexuality are Miller's trade husband, homosexual husband, and gay husband. These types represent varying degrees of involvement in the gay culture and in the heterosexual world. The *trade husband* is seen by Miller as the married man who engages in ambisexual sexual activities; he has the least involvement with the gay culture. He is the ambisexual who would seem to experience the most self-identity problems and psychological difficulties, although Weinberg and Williams' (1974) study did not provide support for this contention. Failure to find support for this contention may be due to the fact that trade husbands are difficult to locate, since they tend not to be involved in the gay subculture nor do they define themselves as gay.

Miller suggests, however, that occasionally trade husbands progress to another status, *homosexual husband.* The homosexual husband is a type of male ambisexual who broadens his involvement in the gay subculture and "extends his knowledge of a gay 'trick' beyond sexual contact." How can this happen when the homosexual husband wants to maintain, at least initially, minimum involvement in the gay world? Miller suggests that the homosexual husband's broadening involvement may come about unexpectedly through repeated encounters with a former trick at a tearoom or when he goes to a former trick's home. Such contact allows the homosexual husband to develop positive images and conceptions of the gay world as knowledge of the gay world extends beyond "glory holes," penises, and so on to include feelings, emotions, and knowledge of other aspects of the gay world.

The homosexual husband remains cautious about revealing his ambisexuality to others even though he admits it to himself, which often means increased anxiety and feelings of guilt. Thus, many heterosexual marriages involving homosexual husbands are conflict-ridden. While some of these marriages end in divorce, many others remain intact because of the ambisexual man's commitment to his children and/or because he does not perceive viable alternatives to his situation. This leads us to the third type of ambisexual husband discussed by Miller, the *gay husband.* The gay husband is close to giving up his heterosexuality. He has entered the gay world totally. His private identity is totally ambisexual although he remains heterosexual to the public at large. Such men often tell their wives and children and actively seek resolution of their problems through divorce. Still others seek resolution through the establishment of what has become known as the "new couple." This couple is discussed later in this chapter.

Characteristics of Ambisexual Men

Blumstein and Schwartz (1976) recognize several patterns of commonality among men who engage in ambisexual sex: (1) early sex experience; (2) an ambisexual period during adolescence, followed by a heterosexual period and then an ambisexual period; (3) absence of homophobic socialization experiences; and (4) broad involvement with sexual partner(s). Certainly there are men who have these experiences and who are not labeled ambisexual by others or by themselves.

This point raises an interesting issue about ambisexuality: Is ambisexuality a condition, a status, or a sexual activity? Weinberg and Williams (1974, p. 296) imply that ''gay'' can be more profitably viewed as a status than a condition. ''The status of gay refers not to behaviors themselves but to the expectation and typification surrounding those defined as gay.'' Defining gay in this way means that the typification rather than the sexual behaviors affect the self-conceptions of those perceiving self as gay. Weinberg and Williams also suggest that ''gay'' can refer to inclination, activity, role, status, or self-concept and that a person does not have to be equally gay in all respects (p. 296). They point to the male hustler as an example of one who engages in gay sex but denies the self-concept; and the heterosexual married man who has a gay inclination but does not act on the gayness. Finally, male ambisexuality based on Weinberg and Williams' definition can be defined as male sexual attraction to both males and females (p. 450).

While the foregoing discussions of and definitions of ambisexuality seem harmless enough, they do not distinguish adequately between those men who, with societal constraints, resist what some researchers suggest is a ''natural inclination'' toward ambisexual sexual activities those who actively construct their sexualities along ambisexual lines. Allowing some men to decide whether they are ambisexual via self-definition means allowing the societal homophobic norm to operate fully, and in many instances to increase in intensity. The so-called straight, macho-type male who occasionally makes forays into the tearoom culture after which he viciously beats his sex partner is a case in point. By allowing such a man to construct and maintain a heterosexual sexual image rather than forcing him to accept an ambisexual image, *society supports the heaping of violence on the man's male sex partner.* This is like the scenario followed in male-male rapes. In essence, homophobia supports the separation of *voluntary* male ambisexual sex from male definitions of self as ambisexual, and, as a result, support is also given to the further denigration of gay and self-labeled ambisexual men.

One cannot help but wonder about the proportion of men in America who are gay and/or ambisexual if male ambisexuality is defined in terms of periods of active same-sex sexual activity, either exclusively or in conjunction with opposite-sex sexual activity. I believe that placing great emphasis on men's *voluntary* sexual behaviors after adolescence gives us a more accurate picture of the true nature of men's ambisexuality, heterosexuality, and gay sexuality without the intervening influence of the homophobic norm. The time variable also may be quite useful in assessing the sexual alternatives followed by men in a given society. Numerous factors other than inclination, self-concept, and the like may influence whether a man voluntarily engages in ambisexual sex. Presently, a factor in America influencing all of men's sexual alternatives is the spectre of AIDS. We seem to gain very little by defining some people as heterosexual, gay, or ambisexual in terms of their sexualities if, in fact, they are self-sexual or celibate. The sexual activities engaged in constitute more than biology. Sexual beings *construct* their sexualities before, during, and following a sexual act. A mental set which says ''I am bisexual,'' ''I am gay,'' or ''I am heterosexual'' no more defines the true processes of these sexualities than the stereotype frequently associated with them. For these reasons, it is instructive to identify several patterns of men's ambisexual activities.

Patterns of Men's Ambisexuality

The suggestion is made that most men probably would engage in ambisexual sexual activities under the right circumstances. Societal constraints and ensuing personal inhibitions are very powerful and probably render many men in American society quite incapable of ambisexual sexual activity. Nevertheless, it is recognized that there are some men in America ordinarily not defined as ambisexual who should be so defined if there is interest in obtaining accurate descriptions of their sexualities. Let us look more closely at the patterns of men's ambisexual activities listed above.

The work of Weinberg and Williams (1974) shows that patterns of men's ambisexual activities are: (1) predominantly gay ambisexual behavior; (2) predominantly heterosexual ambisexual behavior, and (3) ambisexual behavior with approximately balanced gay and heterosexual sexual activity.

Predominately gay ambisexual men. A common belief among people in American society is that gay men dislike women and/or fear them. Many people cannot imagine gay men ever having been sexually involved with a woman. We know, however, from research studies on gay men that most gay men have biographies which include heterosexual coitus at some point in their lives. Bell and Weinberg's (1978) survey of 1,500 gay men revealed that about two-thirds had engaged in heterosexual coitus at least once in their lives. Others (Schofield—34%, 1965; Saghir and Robbins—48%, 1973; and Weinberg and Williams—51%, 1974) have reported lower incidences of gay men having experienced heterosexual coitus. Though estimates of such incidences vary from source to source, what is significant is that a relatively high proportion of gay men have experienced heterosexual sex.

The above discussion may be useful in debunking the myth that gay men have *never* experienced heterosexual coitus, but it says nothing about the extent to which predominantly gay men engage in heterosexual coitus within a period of time which would enable us to define such men as ambisexual. It is possible to identify predominantly gay men who engage in heterosexual activities cyclically or alternatively within a relatively short period of time. From the studies of Saghir and Robbins (1973), Weinberg and Williams (1974), and Bell and Weinberg (1978), we find that between 10 and 18 percent of predominantly gay men reported engaging in heterosexual coitus during the year in which they were respondents in the studies. These findings would seem to indicate that a significant minority of predominantly gay men do experience opposite-sex sexual involvements. As Nahas and Turley (1979) point out in their study of relationships between gay men and women, while all gay men may not express interest in having opposite-sex sexual involvements, some gay men do view such relationships as viable alternatives. They desire to integrate sexual relationships with women into their lives without denying their primarily homosexual orientations (pp. 208, 282). Nahas and Turley distinguish two kinds of relationships predominantly gay men have with women which also involve sexual activities—the "traditional couple" relationship and the "new couple" relationship.

Typically, a traditional couple consists of a predominantly gay man and a heterosexual woman who are married or sexually involved and who attempt (usually unsuccessfully according to the authors) to fit their relationship into a conventional heterosexual mold. Most often the man's gayness is hidden, but once revealed it typically results in efforts being made to change him into a heterosexual, conceal his gay life, or pretend that it does not exist. Rarely do such relationships last for an extended period because "the partners believe they cannot resolve their difficulties" (p. 10). Undoubtedly, at any given time in American society, there exists a significant indeterminate number of such relationships.

The "new couple" consists of a predominantly gay man and "a woman who understands and accepts the man's homosexuality" (p. 11). While these couples often integrate sex into their relationships, "it is usually not the most compelling reason that the man and woman are together." Nahas and Turley state:

> Most often other influences predominate, such as compatibility, mutual acceptance and support of each other's desire for autonomy, and a shared need for companionship of a sort which the gay life of the male and the heterosexual experiences of the female have not provided. (P. 12)

Critical in the new-couple relationship is the ability of the partners to alter the rules of courting, lovemaking, and commitment to meet specific and unique aspects of the relationship. A woman in such a relationship realizes that the man has wanted other men sexually and in all likelihood will continue to want other men. The woman also realizes that the relationship with her predominantly gay partner may or may not be a permanent one. The relationship seems to be one characterized by a mutual granting of freedom which began with a close friendship and gradually extended to sex without commitment. Sexual activities may be cyclic with periods of exclusive heterosexual activity and periods of exclusive homosexual activity. Often such male partners engage in both types of sexual activity during the period of the relationship. Nahas and Turley's analysis of new couple relationships is quite similar to Blumstein and Schwartz's (1976) discussion of gay men's ambisexuality. Blumstein and Schwartz point out that when gay men become sexually involved with women, typically (1) the women are personal friends who are aware of the men's gayness; (2) the men themselves are secure in their gayness; (3) the men do not experience fear or anxiety about heterosexual coitus; (4) the men do not feel that they must commit to a permanent relationship; and (5) the sexual relationship is enjoyable but not as erotic as their relationship with men.

Quite a few predominantly gay men become sexually involved with women. While this may have been difficult for many people to believe a few years ago, the fact that AIDS has been transmitted to heterosexual women by gay men is well known and in all likelihood has made many aware of the ambisexuality of many gay men. Whether such awareness means that fewer women will become involved with gay men is an empirical question. Certainly, sexual experimentation with multiple sexual partners is on the decline in the face of the AIDS threat. Whether this means ambisexuality will diminish, only a speculative answer can be given. It seems unlikely that ambisexuality will decrease. What does seem likely to occur are "new arrangements" which minimize contracting the AIDS virus but allow those so inclined to engage in "new couple" type relationships. As Nahas and Turley contend, "the new couple is one of several alternative relationships developed to accommodate the changing needs of contemporary men and women" (p. 283). Some men and women so inclined may opt for exclusive and "safe" sexual arrangements with several persons which allow individuals to be gay, hetereosexual, and ambisexual.

Another researcher, David Matteson (1988), conducted extensive research on what he calls mixed-orientation marriages (marriages where one of the spouses is gay). His research reveals a greater prevalence of mixed-orientation marriages where the husband is the gay spouse, and thus, becomes quite relevant for our purposes.

Matteson, in contrast to Miller, has found that mixed-orientation marriages where the husband is gay can stabilize if the couple survives an initial crisis period that occurs upon discovery or disclosure of the man's ambisexuality. If high levels of trust and intimacy have been established prior to disclosure or discovery, and if these are not eroded, chances for marital stability are great. Matteson does recognize an alternative arrangement which can develop, however. He points out that some ambisexual men decide not to tell their wives, which results in a "conspiracy of silence," and frequently creates "a spiral of mistrust and distance." If disclosure or discovery occurs, a crisis period follows that either quickly ends the marriage or leads to renegotiation of the marriage contract as an acknowledged mixed-orientation marriage. Matteson contends that once the initial crisis is over, it is possible for these marriages to stabilize and for the ambisexual man to develop congruent sexual identities that affirm his gay component. Matteson states: "A positive gay identity is far more difficult to achieve in traditional marriages in which the husband's bisexuality is not acknowledged by the wives" (p. 16). Moreover, Matteson has found that the most serious crisis in mixed-orientation marriages is not disclosure but "establishment of the primacy of the marital relationship" (p. 16).

Predominantly heterosexual ambisexual men. A striking finding from Shere Hite's 1981 survey of 7,000 men was that 31 percent of the men in her study with a heterosexual orientation had tried being anally penetrated, an activity that is usually thought of as a homosexual activity. More important than this, however, is the Hite finding that most of the men (both heterosexual and homosexual) who had been penetrated by a finger, whether by themselves or another person, *liked it,* and many of those experiencing penis or penis-sized object penetration had also liked it. Hite also found that 10 percent of the men who had not tried anal penetration said they would be interested in trying it in some form (p. 517). Quotes from some of these men expressing a heterosexual sexual preference include the following (pp. 527–28):

> I would try a penis for the experience. It's all the other freight that would necessarily accompany it that turns me off.

> The only desire I have in the way of homosexuality is to feel a penis in my anus.

> I fantasize a lot about being taken in this way by another man. Given the proper man and occasion, I would try it.

> I have often wondered about it, but I don't think I could ever bring myself to submit to it (finger or penis). Some of my fantasies concern other men penetrating me, but I really couldn't let it happen.

While the foregoing quotes from heterosexual men are related only to anal intercourse, another form of sex, used overwhelmingly by gay men—fellatio—also had been tried by 19 percent of heterosexual men in the Hite sample. Most of them were enthusiastic about the activity (p. 548). Given our discussion thus far, it should not be surprising to find that there are many predominantly straight men who have sex with men. What kind of man who prefers women sexually gets involved sexually with men? The answer is, a man who engages in sex with women most of the time but who also seeks out men for anonymous sexual activities some of the time. There is no scarcity of such men in our society. Laud Humphreys' (1970) classic tearoom study consisted of a large proportion of married participants (54%). Other studies, too, report large proportions of married men participating in gay sexual activities.

Some men's ambisexuality appears to be a function of socialization experiences which teach them to separate sexual activities from love and affection. When men learn that they are supposed to have strong sex drives and be interested in sex most of the time, they also learn that it is shameful to be erotically attracted to other men. Nevertheless, this does not prevent some men from constructing their sexualities along ambisexual lines even though their primary sexual orientation is heterosexual. Certainly, not all men who are sometimes erotically attracted to other men engage in sexual relations with men. But there are many who do so, even those whose primary sexual attraction is to women. A trade husband is one such type of man. Also included in this group would be men who assume active roles in prison sex. While some social scientists may be reluctant to include such men in this group, since it is commonly thought that they return to exclusively heterosexual sexual activities once their incarcerations have ended, I submit that this is an empirical question. In actuality, follow-up studies of these men's sexual activities after leaving prison are nonexistent. Aside from this, however, a critical question remains: Why do some heterosexual men in total institutions construct their sexualities along active homosexual lines, while others do not? The answers to this question would no doubt bear some similarity to answers to why some predominantly heterosexual men outside of total institutions occasionally engage in gay sexual activities. Some portion of the answer may be related to Bell and Weinberg's (1978) statements: "Homosexuality-heterosexuality is not necessarily an either-or proposition. Rather, people can be distinguished on the basis of the degree to which their sexual responsiveness and behaviors are limited to persons of a particular sex (male or female)" (p. 53); and "Homosexuality is not an all-or-nothing phenomenon, and many people have learned to respond in varying degrees to both males and females" (pp. 295–96).

Gay Men's Sexuality

No aggregate of people in the United States is more hated, reviled, persecuted, and misunderstood than homosexual men. This is so despite the fact that a large proportion of the adult male population has engaged in homosexual sexual activities to the point of orgasm at some point in their lives following adolescence. Estimates of the percentage of such males vary, but prior to the relatively recent AIDS crisis, hovered around the Kinsey figure of 39 percent. Even if this percentage has decreased because of the overall curtailment of sexual activities due to the fear of AIDS, there is little reason to feel that the homosexual urges, fantasies, or desires of postadolescent males have diminished. Given that there is no shortage of males who have such feelings, why do attitudes of hostility and revulsion toward male homosexuals exist? The answer lies within the genesis of American homophobia. In the discussion to follow, not only will it be possible to see how homophobia exhibited by heterosexuals toward homosexuals affects greatly the lives of gay men, but also we will begin to grasp how homophobia affects gay men themselves. Let us consider first, however, the nature of the conceptualization "gay men."

The Concept "Gay"

Writing in 1972, psychotherapist George Weinberg stated, "I would never consider a patient healthy unless he had overcome his prejudice against homosexuality" (p. 1). Weinberg recognized that male homosexuals themselves often have this prejudice and feels that it bars easy expression of their own desires. With these thoughts in mind, Weinberg noted that the word "gay" in its homosexual connotation and association had existed since the very early 1960s and was "a testimony to the selection process going on in the minds of many homosexuals who are deciding on self-referent words" (p. 121). Weinberg felt such decisions about self-referents were positive because they would serve to shape the view homosexuals would hold of themselves in the future, since "all heritage of attitudes is cultural and not hereditary" (p. 121).

As Weinberg discusses the "healthy homosexual," a rationale for the concept "gay" unfolds beautifully. "Gay man" refers to a man who has an erotic preference for men *now* and who acts sexually on this preference in a "healthy" manner. Weinberg suggests that a man may be homosexual for a minute, an hour, a day, or during his entire sexual lifetime. Recognizing this, and that there are degrees of homosexuality, the perspective taken here is similar to Weinberg's in that men's recent past and present behaviors are the foci of attention: A man is gay "when he regards himself as happily gifted with whatever capacity he had to . . . be free of shame, guilt, regret over the fact that one is homosexual, that the searchlight of one's childhood vision of human beings shined more brilliantly on members of one's own sex than on those of the other. . . . To be gay is to view one's sexuality as the healthy heterosexual views his" (p. 70). A gay man does not question himself about the reasons for his homosexuality. He does *not* feel that it is a disease nor does he feel in need of therapy, because he does not have misgivings about his homosexuality. Finally, when a man is gay, he feels free to explore his preferences and desires in sexual roles of his own choosing without feeling the need to justify his behavior. He knows that his homosexuality *does not render him any less masculine than other men* and, thus, there is no capitulation to a homosexual stereotype. Succinctly, being gay means making a "political statement." This political statement has enabled many homosexual men to become gay men with as much diversity as their heterosexual counterparts.

Gay Men's Lifestyles

A not surprising impression of gay men that some people have is that they frequent public restrooms (tearooms), public parks, and so on, looking for sex. Others who are slightly more sophisticated about gay men's lifestyles realize that not all gay men frequent tearooms, but that many, if not most, have been, and some still are sexually active with multiple partners. Of course, the AIDS crisis has altered much of this behavior and probably some perception of gay men's sexual activities. What is critical here, however, is the fact that diversity in lifestyle always has existed among gay men. Bell and Weinberg (1978) present composite pictures of five types of gay men, which translate (for our purposes) into five lifestyles that characterize gay men in the United States: *dysfunctional gay lifestyle, functional gay lifestyle, open-coupled lifestyle, close-coupled lifestyle,* and *asexual lifestyle.*

Before describing the above lifestyles, it is important to emphasize that drastic changes have occurred in gay men's lifestyles since the middle 1980s. As a result of the AIDS crisis, proportions of gay men in America falling into each category have been altered—perhaps, forever. For example, while a large percentage (approximately one-third) of Bell and Weinberg's sample of gay men fell into the functional category (characterized by a high number of sexual partners), this category today undoubtedly has shrunk considerably.

Bell and Weinberg constructed the above typology by using five highly discriminating variables related to their respondents' lifestyles. The five variables were as follows: (1) whether the respondents were coupled; (2) how much they regretted being gay; (3) how many sexual partners they had in the past year; (4) the amount of cruising (looking for potential sexual liaisons); and (5) the level of sexual activity. In Bell and Weinberg's study, 14 percent of the respondents were close-coupled; 25 percent were open-coupled; 21 percent were functional types; 18 percent were dysfunctional types; and 23 percent were asexual. Let us explore the typology in more detail and the implications of the AIDS virus for each group.

A *close-coupled lifestyle* is characterized by two gay men bound together closely in a relationship in which they turn to each other rather than outsiders for sexual and interpersonal fulfillment. These men experience few sexual problems and regrets about their gayness. They are likely to lead a "happy couple" life, spending evenings at home during the working week and planing and spending leisure time together. Close-coupled men lead gratifying sexual lives characterized by use of a wide variety of sexual techniques. They demonstrate superior adjustment with good communication between partners.

The *open-coupled lifestyle,* the modal type in Bell and Weinberg's study, undoubtedly has undergone a decline among gay men in the late 1980s. This lifestyle is characterized by a man living with a special sexual partner but likely to seek sexual satisfaction outside of the relationship. Partners in this relationship are less well adjusted than those in a close-coupled one, since they worry continuously about public exposure due to cruising activities and that their partner will become aware of their activities. An added fear is contracting one of the great variety of venereal diseases, especially AIDS.

A third type of gay men's lifestyle, one which certainly has declined in frequency, is the *functional lifestyle.* Once considered strikingly similar to the idea of "swinging singles," this lifestyle rapidly is becoming a part of the past. While in previous years, gay men leading a functional lifestyle were single, cruised frequently, and had high numbers of sexual partners, few sexual problems, high involvement in the gay world, and few regrets about their gayness, much of this is undergoing change. This lifestyle is centered around sex—sex with many different partners. "Functionals" in the past were second in adjustment only to close-coupleds. Necessary changes in the functional lifestyle in all likelihood have resulted in decreased numbers of gay men falling into this category. Some gay men have tried to hold onto aspects of this lifestyle by practicing "safe sex" techniques designed to prevent the transmission of bodily fluids between sex partners. They range from "circle jerk" (masturbation) activities engaged in by numerous men or a couple individually, where there is no risk of contracting the AIDS virus, to anal intercourse or fellatio, with the penetrator wearing a condom so that there is less risk of AIDS transmission. Still, it is a safe bet that many gay men have ceased to live a functional lifestyle, opting for a category less threatening to their lives.

Given society's historical and present constraints on and past hostility toward gay men, it is not surprising that almost a fifth of Bell and Weinberg's respondents were classified as leading a *dysfunctional lifestyle.* Poor adjustment is the chief characteristic of gay men leading this lifestyle. It is a lifestyle filled with regrets about being homosexual, sexual problems, worry about maintaining a partner's affection, high amounts of cruising (looking for sex partners), high numbers of sex partners, feelings of sexual inadequacy—the list goes on and on. In all likelihood, gay men leading this lifestyle are the most conflict-ridden of all gay men. They are described quite adequately by the term "tormented homosexual." Again, the AIDS scare has diminished the numbers of such men leading this type of lifestyle. This does not mean, however, that gay men inclined to fall into this category have solved their problems. In all likelihood, some such men are beginning to lead another lifestyle—the *asexual lifestyle*.

In Bell and Weinberg's (1978) study, 23 percent of the gay men respondents were considered asexual. Asexual men are not coupled, have little sexual activity, and complain chiefly about inability to find a suitable sex partner. Interest in sexual activity is also low, and there is much regret over their homosexuality. These men are covert, less exclusively homosexual, and tend not to consider themselves sexually appealing to other men. Finally, asexuals seem to be characterized by poor overall adjustment.

Given the current climate in the gay community, which is one of fear because of AIDS and social fallout from the linkage of AIDS and gay men, it is likely that the percentage of asexual or at least self-sexual gay men will increase. Many of these men often voice intentions to engage primarily in self-sexual behavior. Only time will tell if this lifestyle becomes the predominant one among gay men—at least until a cure for AIDS is found.

Early indications are that some form of altered gay male sexuality is occurring. In February 1988, Anthony Fauci, director of the National Institute of Allergy and Infectious Diseases and coordinator of the U.S. government's AIDS research agencies, pointed out that testing a vaccine among gay men in San Francisco would be difficult due to the relatively small number of new infections. Other indications that gay men's sexual lifestyle has changed are the proliferation of articles in gay magazines and other gay literature promoting safe sex techniques as well as advertisements of safe sex paraphernalia, including the promotion of solitary sex aids ranging from masturbatory erotica, such as videos, to gay fantasy telephone talk.

Sexism, Racism, and Ageism as Political Factors in the Gay World

Sexism and gay men. It has been stated in this section that there are many similarities between gay men and straight men, which may be one of the reasons why intimacy between straight men is often discouraged or at least not supported by many requirements of the male sex role. These similarities include negative traits as well as positive ones associated with men and masculinity. Just as heterosexual men learn to devalue women and femininity, gay men have similar socialization experiences. The result is that some gay men are not distinguishable from some straight men on the gender issue of sexism. In fact, the denigration of femininity can be seen as a persistent, albeit negative feature of many gay men's values. While gay men generally do not tend to exhibit hostility toward women nor do they generally dislike or exhibit overt prejudice toward women, manifestations of the devaluation of femininity are reflected in their attitudes toward certain gay men and gay sexual techniques.

Generally, gay men who do not present a stereotypically masculine image are less preferred as a sex partner than those men who do (Bell and Weinberg 1978, p. 92). In a gay establishment, at any given time, where there is substantial patronage, one can expect to hear statements denigrating gay men who appear ''too feminine.'' Such statements as ''look at that girl,'' ''she is a real bitch,'' ''she's too nelly,'' and ''he's a hunk . . . a real man'' all reflect a devaluation of femininity and a valuation of masculinity consistent with prevailing societal norms and values.

Ordinarily one may think that sex between men is sex between equals with no need to divide the sexual roles according to gender. Gender divisions, however, not only are made with respect to gay men's personal appearance (e.g., facial hair, eye features, muscular build, body hair, etc.), but also emerge in the techniques gay men use in sexual activities. One or more sexual techniques predominant, as discussed by Bell and Weinberg (1978) and others (Saghir and Robbins 1973; Franklin 1984). These techniques or some variation on them include the following: (1) body rubbing; (2) fellating a partner; (3) being fellated by a partner; (4) masturbating a partner; (5) being masturbated by a partner; (6) being the insertee in anal intercourse; and (7) being the inserter in anal intercourse. In terms of frequency of occurrence among gay men, Bell and Weinberg reported the following: (1) fellatio; (2) masturbation; (3) anal intercourse; and (4) body rubbing.

With respect to gender politics, many gay men define being fellated by a partner, being masturbated by a partner, and performing anal intercourse as *masculine* sexual roles. Given these definitions of gay male sexual roles, it should be apparent that the complementary ones consisting of fellating a partner, masturbating a partner, and accepting anal intercourse are seen as feminine sexual roles in the gay world, with body rubbing being the most egalitarian. Of interest here is the fact that the latter role is *least preferred;* the *most preferred* sexual roles among gay men are reported as receiving fellatio and performing anal intercourse—both gay-male defined as *masculine* sexual roles.

The implications of the above discussion should be obvious. Those men who prefer assuming ''feminine'' sexual roles are valued less in the gay world than those who prefer assuming the ''masculine'' sexual roles in sexual encounters. Close-coupled gay men tend to be diverse in the roles assumed in their sexual activities. Regarding gender distinctions in the gay world, a correlation between personal appearance and the sexual role to be assumed often is expected. Thus, just as the stereotypic masculine image and sexual role are more desirable traits and acts in the heterosexual world, they are also more desirable in the gay world. Thus, masculinity and femininity make political statements even in a ''world'' where gender distinctions could be minimal.

Racism and gay men. Just as gender distinctions are made between men within the gay world, race and age distinction are also made. It can be said that race and age problems in the gay community mirror those in the larger society. Many minority gay men in America feel a double sting of prejudice and discrimination because of their minority group status and their sexual preference. Black gay men represent the largest visible gay male minority in America and probably are the main targets of discrimination and prejudice within the gay culture. Most often prejudice and discrimination directed toward Black gay men assume subtle forms. Occasionally, acts of discrimination are more blatant. For example, gay establishments may require Black men to present several items of photo-identification before being admitted, while requiring only one or none for white men. Employment discrimination also occurs in the gay community with an infinitesimal number of Black gay men hired as employees in gay owned hotels, lodges, bars, restaurants, and the like. In sum, unlike white gay men, Black gay men remain largely unrecognized and/ or invisible. As gay writer Joseph Beam (1986) puts it:

> Visibility is survival. It is possible to read thoroughly two or three consecutive issues of the *Advocate,* the national biweekly gay news magazine, and never encounter, in words or images, Black gay men. It is possible to peruse the pages of 212 magazines special issue on Washington, D.C. and see no Black faces. It is possible to leaf through any of the major gay men's magazines, *In Touch, Drummer, Mandate, Blue Boy,* or *Honcho,* and never lay eyes on a Black adonis. Finally, it is certainly possible to read an entire year of *Christopher Street* and think that there are no Black gay writers worthy of the incestuous bed of New York's gay literati. We ain't family. Very clearly, gay male means: white, middle class, youth-

ful, nautilized, and probably butch; there is no room for Black gay men within the confines of the gay pentagon. (Pp. 14–15)

Of course prejudice and discrimination against Black gay men are not only institutionally based. On an interpersonal level, daily, Black and other minority gay men are victims of prejudice and discrimination within the gay community. Consider the following excerpt from Thom Beame's "Racism from a Black Perspective":

> It's easy to see why San Francisco's called a gay mecca . . . but it's not a mecca for gay Blacks . . . the base of gay power in San Francisco is the white gay propertied and merchant class. It's white gays who hold elected offices, own small businesses, and own the Castro. . . . Yet as a rule they don't share useful information or interface socially or professionally with other ethnic factions in the gay community. . . .

The Black gay man's social position within the gay community is no different from his counterpart's social position in the larger culture. Either Black gay men experience personal rejection in the gay community similar to that in the straight world or they are sought out for sexual reasons similar to those for which Black men have been sought out for historically (sometimes with deadly consequences). Beame's account of a conversation between men occurring on a hill in Pacific Heights overlooking Lafayette Park in San Francisco continues:

> It's easier for whites to hire, sleep with and socialize with other whites. It's easier for them to exclude us. . . . Gay power means white gay male power . . . gay hiring policies, renting policies, banking policies, social customs haven't changed from the status quo . . . we're fine for show during Gay Pride Week when a little color is needed, or for a quick fuck in the dark, when none of their friends are looking, but middle-class whites don't want to pass along any useful job or investment information or include us in their social circles. They don't hire us to work in their bars and businesses, and after a roll in the hay, they just may not speak the next time they see you. . . . (1983, pp. 57–58).

Efforts to combat racism in the gay community have been made by two organizations which were established for this precise reason. The express purpose of the National Coalition of Black Lesbians and Gays includes the following: "to actively work against racism, sexism, ageism, classism, homophobia and any other form of discrimination within the black community and the gay community" (Beam 1986).

NCBLG, the autonomous national Black lesbian and gay organization, is a network of 3,000 people with local chapters in San Francisco, New Orleans, Washington, D.C., and Minneapolis dedicated to ending lesbian and gay oppression in general and Black lesbian and Black gay oppression specifically. Separate from but coterminous with NCBLG in aims and goals is another international organization, Black and White Men Together, which was begun in 1980. This organization, consisting chiefly of Black and white men, exists to promote harmonious and cooperative relations between Black and white gays.

Ageism and gay men. Like racism, sexism, and gender discrimination, ageism is a recognized problem within the gay community. There, as in the straight world, people are accorded different rights and opportunities on the basis of their ages without due regard to their individual abilities. In the past, the gay world has placed much emphasis on youth, but perhaps this emphasis has been no greater than the youth emphasis in the culture as a whole. Gay men experience problems as they age; however, some researchers feel that the problem of older gays are no greater and maybe even less than the problems experienced by their heterosexual counterparts (Kimmel 1978; Frencher and Henkin 1973).

Still, if older gay men experience the same kinds of problems that the nongay elderly experience, an ageism problem exists within the gay community. American society values youth, and this valuation *is* reflected in the gay community just as it is in the larger society. Ageism, like sexism and racism, in the gay community is symptomatic of a greater problem that is endemic to the culture as a whole.

Acquired Immunodeficiency Syndrome (AIDS)

The cover of the February 16, 1987, issue of *Time* magazine reads "The Big Chill: How Heterosexuals Are Coping with AIDS." In the same issue, William A. Henry writes a eulogy for Wladziu Valentino Liberace, who died in February of complications from the AIDS virus. Liberace, in death, joined a growing list of public figures, such as Rock Hudson, Perry Ellis, Willi Smith, Michael Bennett, and others who died from or were rumored to have died from the disease. Undoubtedly the list of names will grow longer as the disease continues "to cast a shadow over the American sexual landscape." As of February 1988, over 60,000 cases of AIDS had been reported in the United States. More alarming, however, is the report that 1.5 million people in our society may be carriers of the virus. The current prediction from the Center for Disease Control in Atlanta is that over the next five years 270,000 people will contract AIDS with the number of deaths rising to 179,000. At first it was believed that only 10 percent of those infected with the AIDS virus would develop full-blown AIDS. Now the prognosis is that 50 percent or more of those testing positive for the virus will develop full-blown AIDS.

At present, AIDS is concentrated among high-risk groups: gay men, ambisexual men, and intravenous drug users. The latter group consists overwhelmingly of the inner-city poor, who tend to be Black or Hispanic. Heterosexuals most at risk are those likely to engage in sexual relations with this element of the population. The result is that two-thirds of the heterosexual AIDS cases in early 1988 were Black and Hispanic. However, this does not mean that AIDS is going to remain an inner-city disease for heterosexuals any more than AIDS remained a "gay males sexual preference" disease or an affliction of drug addicts. Many people are beginning to recognize AIDS as a growing threat to the heterosexual population. An increasing percentage of persons not in the high risk groups have contracted the disease. Heterosexual sex partners of intravenous drug abusers, ambisexuals' sex partners, and children infected with the AIDS virus at birth signal additional ways the virus enters America's population—its heterosexual population included. By 1991, the percentage of persons who contract the disease in these ways is expected to increase considerably. Another critical point, too, is that AIDS is bidirectional—it is passed from men to women and from women to men.

AIDS specialists have become particularly concerned about the latter fact and that many young heterosexual men seem not to be particularly concerned about the disease. Many people do recognize that ambisexuality is a route of AIDS viral transmission to the female population, but fewer seem to understand that men can get AIDS from women. Education certainly is the key in the immediate future to halting the spread of AIDS. The discovery of a cure lies in the future; presently only therapeutic drugs like azidothymidine (AZT) and dideoxyeytidine (DDC) exist which interfere with viral reproduction but do not eliminate the virus. It is hoped that DDC will be less toxic and free of the serious drawbacks of AZT, which include severe bone marrow damage and anemia.

Educational campaigns directed at gay men urging decreases in numbers of sex partners and use of safe sex techniques show dramatic decreases in the number of new AIDS infections in San Francisco. *Time* reported that the rate of new AIDS infection in San Francisco fell from an

18 percent increase each year between 1982 and 1984 to only about 4 percent in 1985. If it can be understood by our society that many gay men's pattern of numerous sexual encounters with numerous sexual partners is related directly to their "masculinity" rather than to their sexual preference, stemming the deadly tide of AIDS in the heterosexual community may be possible. Heterosexual men will, like many gay and ambisexual men are doing presently, re-examine and reconstruct their sexuality along less dangerous and irresponsible lines. In the long run this may mean that men, for the first time, will begin to experience the integration of sex and other aspects of their social lives and simultaneously bring to a halt the dramatic spread of a deadly disease.

7

Social Institutions
and Social Change

As we have seen, there are critical social issues in American society related to sexual regulation, reproduction, and child-rearing; goods production and distribution; power and political change; the transmission of knowledge from generation to generation; and the changing forms of agencies responsible for giving persons their senses of purpose and meaning. American society, like other societies, has constructed social institutions, which are values, norms, and strategies centered around the above concerns in a society. We will view men's and women's roles in five social institutions: the family, the economy, the polity, the educational institution, and the religious institution. Because they are so intertwined, the economy and the polity are discussed under one heading. Let us begin with the norms, values, and standards related to men's roles concerning sexual regulation, reproduction, and child-rearing in American society. We will explore first men's roles in the family, then men's roles in other institutions. We should keep in mind during our discussion that we are exploring a portion of the means through which our lives become patterned and organized.

Men's Roles in the Family

Men's social roles have been variously defined in this volume. For our purposes in this chapter men's social roles will be defined quite generally and discussed according to Bruce Nordstrom's (1986) rather loose categorization: the "traditional" male role and the "less traditional" male role. Defining men who fulfill the traditional male sex role in the family as "traditional men," Nordstrom delineates numerous characteristics of traditional men in the family. These characteristics include men who basically are "responsible providers," seeking from their wives companionship, marital support services, and self-validation. A conspicuous characteristic of many such men, Nordstrom found, is that they often are uncertain about why they chose their particular wives other than that their wives met certain criteria: the chosen woman has a similar social, educational, and maybe religious background, coupled with a willingness to validate the man's self, accept his ideas, and the like. Traditional men approach and live their marriages on "wishes to be married" rather than feelings about a particular woman leading inevitably to marriage and family life.

"Traditional men" also demand that their wives fulfill the traditional "housewife role," again de-emphasizing a particular woman in marriage. Finally, traditional men simply "add" their wives to their lives, requiring them to adapt to their lifestyle and to "support" them. Frequently such men bring latent generalized romantic feelings to marriage, which actually means that there is nothing about their particular wives that creates the feeling of romantic love. Moreover, such men often do not describe their wives as "people." When asked how they know their wives are right for them or what they like about their wives, traditional men typically do not describe personal characteristics of their wives; rather, they describe and discuss roles assumed by their wives (what their wives do, for example, cook well, keep the house clean, are good mothers, supportive, etc.). In summary, the traditional male role in marriage and the family, according to Nordstrom, is one primarily of provider-protector. In turn, the man expects a traditional female role performance from his wife as reflected in his inability to define his wife apart from the myriad roles she assumes.

Nordstrom's less traditional men assume somewhat different roles in their marriages and families. These men, too, value their marriages because they share feelings, values, and companionship with their wives. However, less traditional men speak less of their wives merging their lives with the men's lives and more of two people coordinating and accommodating their lives to each other. Less traditional men marry their wives partly because of the women's personal qualities as well as because the women are able to merge with their lives ("she wants what I want out of life, she makes a good wife and mother, she loves me and accepts me").

The less traditional man, according to Nordstrom, sees his wife as an interesting woman with whom to share his life. This may mean that he too must sacrifice and accommodate in order for his wife to realize goals which she brings to the marriage. The less traditional man does not expect his wife to conform to a predictable role and knows that he has to always take her into account. These men "enjoy just being with and talking with their wives, and the freedom from rigid expectations a marriage without set roles provides" (p. 49). Later we will see how both types of men respond to functions associated with the family.

Thought of as the most basic of all institutions, the family is the fundamental unit in American society despite numerous contemporary pressures. These pressures have been so great in recent years that some feel the American family is on the verge of collapse. That most American men and women engage in premarital sex; teenage sex and teenage births are common occurrences; 20 percent of births in America occur outside of marriage; half of all marriages begun in the 1980s are expected to end in divorce; and, single-parent households are an increasing phenomena are seen as indications of the declining significance of the American family. So, what is this unit called "the family"?

Defining the Family

By no means is "family" an easy concept to express, devoid of ethnocentrism. To many Americans the family is a social unit made up of a married man and woman and their offspring living together. Yet, such a definition would exclude basic family units in some societies where the kinship group is the basic family unit rather than a married couple and their offspring (Vander Zanden 1986). An alternative definition of the family that many find acceptable suggests that psychological bonds are the critical variables denoting the social unit, family. This means for our purposes that a family is "a group of people defined by the members of a community as a household unit" (p.255). Persons in such units may be related by blood, marriage, adoption, or agreement, and they cooperate economically. Of critical importance, according to Vander Zanden, is "(1) the social unit offers more or less standardized solutions that serve to direct people in meeting the problems of social living and (2) the relatively stable relationships that characterize people in actually implementing these solutions" (p. 255). Given this rather liberal definition of the family, let us explore the relationship between the two general men's roles discussed earlier and the family as a social unit.

Men and Family Functions

Sexual regulation. Sexual behavior is regulated in all societies, and American society is no different. Since 1630, our society has placed restrictions on sexual behavior. Such restrictions forbid sexual intercourse between certain kin within families, between members of certain racial/ethnic groups, between persons of the same sex, and between persons of certain ages, among others.

For the most part, men primarily have been both the ones to enforce societal restrictions on sexual activity and the ones most likely to deviate from societal norms, values, and standards related to sexual activity. This says, in effect, that in American society the male role in sexual regulation is a very powerful one. As stated in another context in the previous chapter, men are in charge of the sexual arena. Unlike sexual views in some periods of American history, today women in families are recognized as sexual beings. Still, men are expected to take the lead in sexual matters. A major point related to sexual regulation, however, is that the family today is much less influential in people's sexual lives. A poll conducted by *People* magazine in February 1987 through the New York polling firm Audits and Surveys posed forty-one questions to thirteen hundred students in sixteen high schools, sixteen hundred students in ten colleges across the country, and five hundred parents of teens in twelve cities. Excluding impoverished inner city and rural students from the survey, the pollsters found that 57 percent and 79 percent of high school and college students, respectively, had lost their virginity. The average age at which teenagers first had sex was 16.9; and, 33 percent of the teens polled engaged in sex from once a month to once a week; the percentage for college students was 52 percent. Regarding the family's role in sexual regulation, two other findings shed additional light: 81 percent of the parents polled believed their children responded honestly to questions about sex and 9 percent believed they responded somewhat honestly; 22 percent of teens in high school said they were totally honest when talking with parents about sex; and 27 percent of college students responded similarly. Clearly, according to these findings, the role of the family as a sexual regulator may be in doubt. Still, men decide how ''free'' sex is to be in American society, what persons can be sexual with each other, what sexual acts are appropriate, and which times are appropriate for sexual activity.

Despite the fact that change seems to be occurring in the family's role of sexual regulation of its members, males seem not to have experienced a radical decline in power in the sexual environment. If anything, males may have increased their sexual regulatory power. After all, because males always have enjoyed greater sexual freedom than females, and due to aspects of the traditional male role complemented with sexual freedom (e.g., aggressiveness, violence), greater sexual permissiveness among women may mean simply greater opportunities for males to "fulfill" their traditional sexual roles (one of sex without responsibility).

Because women can now approach sex in the same nonintimate manner as many men traditionally have done does not mean that men experience a reduction in power in the sexual arena. A reduction in gender power in the sexual arena refers on one level to a loss of one gender's ability to control sexual encounters, and on another level, a loss of that gender's ability to regulate sexual activities for both males and females. In the first place, most men remain in control of their sexual encounters. Greater sexual permissiveness among females generally has not been accompanied by the expectation that women basically should take charge in sexual matters. In fact, when women do "take charge" in sexual encounters, denigrating ideas about them are likely to surface.

Given all of the above, there still is much evidence that the family no longer regulates the sexual lives of its members to the extent that it did in the past. Evidence of the declining significance of the family in the regulation of family members' sexual activities includes the phenomenal increase in premarital sexual activities and extramarital sexual activities for both sexes. Certainly, men traditionally have enjoyed greater sexual freedom than women, who prior to the middle 1960s were constrained greatly by sexual proscriptions. Yet, we must consider recent trends indicating greater liberalness regarding male and female sexualities at earlier ages. This is so despite the increasing threat of AIDS. These changes in male and female sexualities are related both to the family's role in the regulation of sexual activities and the family's role in reproduction of societal members. Let us turn to two other family functions related to men's roles: child-rearing and emotional security.

Child-rearing. The male role related to child-rearing in the family has changed significantly throughout American history. Elizabeth Pleck and Joseph Pleck (1980) recognized several phases in America during which changes in the male's child-rearing role took place. During what was defined early in this volume as the agrarian patriarchal period (a period extending from Puritan times through the Colonial period into early Republicanism), men assumed responsibility for overseeing and teaching children appropriate morals and values. Ensuring that children received an education and "proper" upbringing were major responsibilities of "good" fathers. This was to be accomplished by providing children with a model of good Christian living and socializing children in the scriptures of the Bible. During the commercial and strenuous life periods of masculinity (Pleck and Pleck 1980) described in detail earlier, shifts in the father's role within the family occurred. Centralized industrialization characterized these times, and the father's role was reconceptualized largely in terms of breadwinning. This conceptualization lasted from approximately 1850 to the 1930s (Pleck 1976).

Throughout the companionate providing period in the 1960s up to the middle 1970s, another aspect was added to the male role within the family. The new conceptualization of the male role emphasized moral teaching and breadwinning, but the major focus was being a sex role model. Lamb (1986) points out that numerous books and articles in the professional literature lamented the high incidence of fathers not fulfilling this new responsibility well. Frequently such literature focused on the need for strong sex role models. Levy's *Maternal Overprotection* and Strecker's *Their Mothers' Sons* are cited by Lamb as examples of professional literature admonishing fathers to more properly assume the sex role model aspect of the reconceptualized father role. Lamb contends that inadequacies in men's role assumptions were "underscored in dramatic works such as *Rebel without a Cause* and were ridiculed in comedies and cartoons, for example, *Blondie* and *All in the Family* (Ehrenreich and English 1979)" (Lamb 1986, p. 6).

From the middle 1970s to the present, still another aspect of men's roles in families has emerged. Fathers are increasingly expected to assume a father's role that is both active and nurturant. While the father role in the family still involves overseeing moral teaching, breadwinning, and being a sex role model, especially for sons, a "good" father today also increasingly is being measured by the *nurturance yardstick*. As Lamb (1986) states:

> Fathers fill many roles . . . the relative importance of each varies from one context to another . . . active fathering . . . must be viewed in the context of the various other things that fathers do for their children (for example, breadwinning, sex role modeling, moral guidance, emotional support of mothers). (P. 6)

In sum, the male role in the family has been expanded over time despite the fact that during each phase of American history a particular component of the role has been emphasized or has been dominant. The last reconceptualization of the male role to occur has been the redefinition of fatherhood in the family. Generally, this redefinition has involved an alteration of ways fathers influence their children as they participate in the child-rearing process. Most fathers have influenced their children indirectly because their participation in the family was indirect. Fathers were the primary breadwinners (in the vast majority of two-parent families, they still are) and thus contributed indirectly to their children. They also functioned as sources of social support for mothers, thereby enhancing socioemotional relationships within the family.

In less traditional families, fatherhood is taking on a new look. Because such families are likely to have two wage earners, fathers today are assuming much more dynamic and direct roles in child-rearing. Fathers influence their children directly by participating in child-related housework, which helps prevent mothers from experiencing role overload and simultaneously provides children with positive role models. Additionally, fathers in less traditional families also influence their children directly through greater face-to-face social interaction, for example, playing, teaching, and care giving (Lamb 1981). On this latter point, more and more we are learning that men, too, can and often do assume nurturant roles with their children characterized by high sensitivity and responsiveness. In a series of studies by Parke and his colleagues, evidence emerged which showed that first-time fathers were just as sensitive and responsive to their infants (rocking them, kissing them, talking to them) as mothers, if not more so. But, following this early stage characterized by high parental involvement, the majority of fathers cease care-giving activities. What has emerged from these findings, however, is that fathers are just as competent as mothers in assuming care-giving responsibilities, but gender role norms may dictate more maternal involvement in child care than paternal involvement (Berman 1980). As Lamb (1986) suggests:

> Both men and women can be effective caregivers of infants and young children; what distinguishes them in the traditional family are the roles they assume in relation to young children, not characteristics associated with gender per se. (P. 71)

Increasing evidence shows that, contrary to popular opinion, fathers can and oftentimes do become very much involved with their infants and toddlers (e.g., Clarke-Stewart 1980; Yogman 1977; Power and Parke

1982). Much of fathers' involvements with their young children involve play activity. In fact, not only does research show that play is a significant interaction activity for fathers and their young children but also there is ample evidence that fathers play with their young children more than do mothers. In addition, fathers play with their children in qualitatively different ways than mothers do (Belsky 1979; Lamb 1977; Power and Parke 1982; Yogman 1977). Fathers tend to play physically active and rough games with their children, while mothers play more passive games (e.g., pat-a-cake, peek-a-boo) as well as those that are centered around toys.

Another feature of father involvement in child-rearing is that the paternal role expands as children get older. As children develop, special needs accompany their development. Needs related to the child's gender socialization, intellectual development, social competence, and social responsibility must be met if he/she is to develop into an adequately functioning human being. Evidence exists suggesting that fathers become more intimately involved with their children as their children get older.

Fathers apparently play vital roles in gender socialization; they interact with sons differently from daughters. This difference continues throughout childhood with fathers encouraging sons to be active in play and setting different standards for them than for daughters. Fathers emphasize task performance for boys while concentrating more on the interpersonal aspects of learning for girls. Fathers provide consistent reinforcement to their children for engaging in normative sex-typed behaviors (Langlois and Downs 1980). Reviewing a large number of studies related to paternal influences at later ages, Thompson (1986) concludes that in traditional families, "paternal influence is an important contribution to the gender socialization of boys and girls" (p. 74).

Fathers in traditional families also affect children in other ways. Paternal influences seem to be important in academic achievement, intellectual development, social competence, and social responsibility, especially for sons. Radin (1981) has reviewed research which points clearly to fathers' influence on sons' achievement and intellectual development when they nurture and encourage their sons. While such research indicates sex differences with respect to paternal influences, when fathers are involved with their daughters and encourage them to achieve, girls, too, are affected positively, as evidenced by improved cognitive competency and intellectual growth. Father involvement also impacts positively on the development of social competence and responsibility in boys. Hoffman (1981) suggests that fathers facilitate their sons' acquisition of moral values by serving as identification figures.

Fathers who participate in child-care activities are found in both traditional families and nontraditional families such as dual-career families and shared care-giving families. While further research is needed on these kinds of families, evidence exists at this time that child-care responsibilities remain largely with mothers (McHenry, Price, Gordon, and Rudd 1986). Fathers in dual-career families do not seem to increase significantly their own child-care responsibilities. Pederson, Cain, Zaslow, and Anderson (1982) provide us with striking findings from their comparative study of traditional and dual-wage-earner families with firstborn five-month-old children. Pederson et al. observed that working mothers were more highly interactive with their children than the other parents in the study, while their husbands were the least interactive with their children. In interpreting these findings, Pederson et al. used an explanation similar to one used in a 1980 study of parent-child and husband-wife interactions observed when the child was five months old. The explanation is that the father relinquishes the time period to the mother that would ordinarily be used by the father for parent-child interaction. Still, these findings relate to father interaction with relatively young children. There is no reason to believe that father involvement with their children in dual-career families as the children grow older is qualitatively different from father involvement in traditional families.

It is clear that fathers do not always assume child-care responsibilities when mothers work. However, increasingly fathers are electing to adopt child-care responsibilities and thereby reduce role overload for mothers. When a father makes such a decision, the family is recognized as a shared-care-giving family. When fathers share care-giving, they seem to experience closer relationships with their offspring (Russell 1982, 1983). Radin found only minor effects of increased father involvement in child care, such as children being more likely to perceive that they were in control. Studies by Field (1978) and Pruett (1983) indicate that child development continues in an uninterrupted manner when fathers are primary care-givers. The reason for this is that when fathers increase their care-giving in shared-care-giving families, they also seem to behave in ways strikingly similar to traditional mothers, while retaining ways characteristic of traditional fathers. Fathers behave quite nurturantly toward their infants, and the infants in such families tend to develop strong attachments to their fathers. In sum, present research shows that fathers in shared-care-giving families merge ''maternal'' and ''paternal'' behaviors, and the result is that children thrive.

While some changes in father participation in child-care activities have occurred in the last two decades, the changes have been small (Lamb, Pleck, Charnov, and Levine 1985). A question which can be asked at this point is, Are relatively small changes in paternal involvement with children necessarily negative or positive for child development? What happens to children when men don't participate directly in the child-rearing process? Does father noninvolvement have negative effects on children's relationships with fathers, their sex-role development, their achievements and achievement motivation, their school performance, their moral development, and their psychological adjustment?

The above questions are difficult to answer because simple yes-no responses cannot be given based on available evidence. Lamb, Pleck, and Levin (1986) feel that it is misguided to believe that paternal involvement is a universally desirable goal. An alternative and more viable strategy, these scholars believe, is one designed to increase options available to fathers and mothers "so that those who want to be more involved in their children's lives can become so" (p. 142). Lamb et al. (1986) allude to the fact that evidence exists pointing to both positive and negative effects for increased paternal involvement in children's development. In fact, increased paternal involvement is likely to produce desirable effects on children's development only when this kind of involvement is perceived positively by both mother and father (Lamb et al. 1986).

At this point let us zero in on some specific effects on child development of father noninvolvement reported in the literature. Two kinds of literature may help us in discussing this kind of father-child relationship. Child development research on children with fathers displaying "traditional" male sex role attitudes and behaviors toward family participation as well as children with fathers absent will be considered data sources of childhood development effects when fathers are uninvolved directly in child rearing. Langlois and Downs (1980) point out that fathers more than mothers consistently reinforce and punish sex-typed behaviors. Biller's (1981) review of literature on boys' sex role development in father-absent and father-involved families reveals that these boys tend to develop either more or less sex-typed attitudes and interests than those with fathers involved who are physically present. Still, most boys regardless of father presence or involvement develop "appropriate" sex roles. After all, sex role development is not determined only by father facilitation; rather, it is a function of multiple determinants (e.g., school, peers, mothers, etc.; see Fagot, 1977; Lamb, Easterbrook, and Halden, 1980; Nash and Feldman, 1981, among others).

On the issue of increased father-involvement effects on children's achievement and achievement motivation, research findings do not justify a definite conclusion. Radin (1976, 1981) has found that high achievement motivation seems highly correlated with parents who are warm and encourage independence rather than those who are authoritarian. By the same token, Barnett and Baruch (1978) found that high achieving women tend to have warm fathers who encourage them, even though the fathers may have been low in parental involvement in child rearing. Radin (1981) found that father-absent children seemed to be characterized by poorer school performance than children from two-parent families, but the results were most pronounced for lower-class children. Because the ''class'' variable seems to intervene in the latter relationship, socio-economic stressors affecting the mother may be more directly related to children's poor school performance than simply father absence. However, Radin (1982) did find, as stated earlier, that children with highly involved nurturant fathers manifested more cognitive competence and internal loci of control. Yet, are fathers-present-and-involved effects on academic performance some function of fathers' associations with high achievement and superior occupation or, instead, reflections of dual parent high stimulation of and involvement with children?

Moral development and psychological adjustment are additional areas where father participation in child rearing is thought to affect children positively and father uninvolvement is thought to negatively impact children. In 1970, Hoffman suggested that parents play critical roles in the development of their children's internalized controls. All in all, however, a dearth of literature exists on the relationship between father involvement and societally sanctioned moral development. In addition, as Lamb et al. (1986) point out, ''Although some studies show that boys whose fathers are absent display less moral internalization and are more likely to become delinquents than boys whose fathers are present, the preponderance of the evidence indicates that mothers have a much greater influence on moral development than fathers do'' (p. 151).

Finally, research on the relationship between father involvement/ presence and psychological adjustment suggests that children who experience parental separation resulting in father absence show more signs of psychological maladjustment (Biller, 1981). The nature of this relationship is unclear, primarily because it is difficult to extricate marital disharmony from father absence. At present, there is no satisfactory evidence suggesting that paternal involvement is related in any way to children's psychological adjustment. On the issue of paternal involvement, Russell (1982, 1983) quite appropriately points out that it is difficult to discern the effects of paternal involvement when there is no longitudinal evidence. This is so because fathers have attitudes, values, and standards *before* they become involved with their children. Such attitudes and values, as well as other father variables, may directly account for "effects" on children more commonly attributed to father presence/involvement. As desirable as increased paternal participation may seem in families experiencing change and becoming what some would call "more progressive"—recognizing mothers' as well as fathers' individual preferences and values—an important fact remains:

> There is no evidence that in any of the aspects of (child) development, the father's role is necessary. In his absence, development usually proceeds quite normally, because development is multiply determined. The implication is that while increased paternal involvement may increase the magnitude of paternal influence, it does not have effects on children sufficient to justify a conclusion that increased paternal involvement would be beneficial to all children. (Lamb et al. 1986, p. 152)

What happens when only fathers participate in child rearing? Father-headed families are increasing in number dramatically in the United States. Masnick and Bane (1980) have projected that the increase will continue up to 1990. The U.S. Census Bureau reported that in 1985, 896,000 children under eighteen years of age were living in families headed by single men with no spouse present. (Of course, 6,006,000 children lived in single-mother homes.) Research on such families is limited three major ways: (1) most studies of single fathers have relied on interviews without direct observation of father-child interaction; (2) findings obtained from previous studies of single fathers may be of limited generalizability due to the fact that widowed, abandoned, and divorced fathers were not distinguished in the studies and the circumstances under which fathers become single parents may impact the father-child relationship; and (3) most of the existing studies on single fathers relied on interviews conducted sometime after the adjustment to the single parent role.

The first limitation is a possible source of biases in existing studies because of the potential for father reports to be optimistic about children's adjustments to single male parent households. The second limitation underscores the possibility that fathers' satisfactions with parenting and, therefore, the parent-child relationship itself may be affected by whether the father has fought for custody of his child or has assented to custody. Needless to say, the circumstances under which fathers become single parents may affect children's adjustments to male-headed households. The third major limitation of single father studies implies that when reports of the father-child adjustment period (which occurs at the inception of the alternative family) are retrospective, the relatively stable current period may influence such reports, giving them a somewhat optimistic flavor. Given these limitations, let us review briefly what existing research seems to indicate about fathers who rear children alone and children who are reared by fathers only.

In contrast to what some believe, single fathers are not at a loss where child rearing is concerned. Given the necessary cautious interpretation of data from studies on single fathers in light of the above mentioned limitations, single fathers, according to Wallerstein and Kelly (1980), go through a stressful period following divorce. This is a period during which they have feelings of low self-esteem, inadequacy, and role overload. Following the beginning period of their single-father head-of-household status, however, these men begin to feel comfortable, competent, and successful in their newly acquired care-giving role. Single fathers report that they are organized in their domestic duties and feel that they provide for their children's nurturance needs, although they express some concerns about this. Generally, single fathers express satisfaction with their children's social development and adjustment to the father-child single-parent relationship (Lowenstein and Koopman 1978; Luepnitz 1982).

In the one study comparing direct observations of parent-child interaction and interviews with children in single-father homes with those in single-mother and intact two-parent homes, positive child adjustment was found to be very much related to the child living with the same sex parent. Using measures of maturity, sociability, and independence as indicators of social competence, Santrock et al. (1982) and Warshak et al. (1983) found that boys in homes with single fathers fared much better on social competence than girls in homes with single fathers. Moreover, these boys scored higher on social competence than boys from intact families. In single-mother homes, girls were found to be more socially competent than boys in single-mother homes. When ratings of social competence were derived from interviews with children, similar findings were obtained, as reported by Warshak and Santrock (1980) and Santrock et al. (1982).

Overall, then, it seems that single fathers frequently are quite competent when they must give care to children once they have gone through a period of adjustment.

Religious Institutions

As a kind of cultural universal, the meaning of human existence intrigues people all over the world, and people in American society are no different. Curiosity about the meaning of life results in systems of beliefs and practices based upon faith which give people a sense of purpose. In this section, men's relationships to cultural patterns and social structures related to beliefs about the purpose of life and the meaning of human existence are explored. Following the lead of sociologist John Macionis, no judgment will be passed on religions in our society as an element of human experience nor will we attempt to assess whether religion is good or bad. We will explore, however, portions of the operation of religion as well as the consequences (both positive and negative) of the religious institution as related to men in society.

Religion Defined

Similar to other cultural patterns devised to solve social problems of everyday living and promote the relatively stable relationship between persons solving the problems, the religious institution is a critical instrument characterized by social sharedness in thinking, feeling, and acting. What distinguishes religion is the nature of its focus on solving problems related to social living. According to the early work of Emile Durkheim (1965), religion encompasses salient issues related to "all sorts of things which surpass the limits of our knowledge" (p. 62). Distinguishing between socially shared meanings attributed to objects, events, and the like, Durkheim pointed out that human beings recognize both the *profane* and the *sacred*. *Profane meanings* refer to socially shared understandings of the social that are ordinary or commonplace. *Sacred meanings* are those socially shared understandings of that portion of reality related to the forbidden, the extraordinary, the mysterious, the awe-inspiring, and so on. Within Durkheim's view of the profane and the sacred lies the nature of religion. *Religion is a social institution—a system of beliefs, meanings, values, and practices which are centered on the sacred.*

Religion and Gender

Of the six world religions (Buddhism, Christianity, Confucianism, Hinduism, Islam, and Judiasm), Christianity is the largest (approximately 1 billion persons) and is the most dominant in the United States. About 87 percent of Americans identify with the Christian religion, although only 60 percent are formally affiliated with a religious organization according to N.O.R.C. (1983), Gallup (1984), and U.S. Census Bureau (1985) data.

As one of the world religions, Christianity embraces an ideology based on love between all mankind and womankind, because all are siblings in Christ. From the idea of brotherhood and sisterhood in Christianity comes the derived ideology that all are equal in the eyes of God. Christianity, as the dominant religion in the United States, is monotheistic (recognizes a single divine power).

Men's relationship to Christianity in the United States is similar to men's relationship to all of the major world religions in that patriarchal control clearly exists. While men assume the leadership positions in religious institutions in the United States, women have higher participation rates. According to the 1984 Gallup Poll, 43 percent of American women and 37 percent of American men attend religious services on a regular basis. Students of religion (e.g. Chalfont et al.) have alluded to the relatively low status of women in Christian churches, where men hold positions of higher status while women are encouraged to devote their time to menial chores and providing-for-others tasks. The duties are demanding (church secretary, Sunday School teacher, food preparer, child care giver, etc.), the pay is low or nil, and recognition is practically nonexistent. Chalfant, Beckley, and Palmer (1987) point out that while women in the United States have had primary positions in the church, seldom have they had a significant voice in making policy decisions. Even when women have been *allowed* membership on ruling boards and councils of their local churches, they have been made "to feel inferior and are treated as tokens." According to Chalfant et al. (p. 117), what male dominated power structures of congregations seem to be saying is, "We have to give women the impression they have a part in governing the church, but they must also understand that they are not really supposed to do anything to upset the status quo."

Obviously, a major component of leadership in religious groups is the role of ministers and priests. Just as obvious is the fact that women remain in an inferior position on this dimension. Although women seem to be making some strides in the ministry, the Roman Catholic church still does not ordain women to the priesthood and women still are less successful than men in obtaining ministerial assignments once they have been ordained (Lehman 1985).

Like many organized religions in the world, Christianity provides role definitions for men and women. Jack Nichols (1978), who wrote one of the pioneering works related to the male sex role, suggests that the

Christian system quite early gave men the reins of power and dictated that women should assume submissive roles in the church. Furthermore, says Nichols, dominant sex role practices in our society are derived from the Judeo-Christian tradition which retains woman as property and shows the most concern for men. Nichols states:

The Genesis story of the Creation and the commandment on adultery retained women as property along with servants and mules. She was, after all, a sort of after-thought, a reshapement of Adam's rib. The Judaic tradition has always shown the most concern for males, segregating the sexes at worship through the centuries so that women were able to look out of shuttered chambers while their husbands, sons, brothers, and nephews took care of application to the Divinity. (Nichols 1978)

Judaism is an important influence in America. There are approximately 1 million Orthodox Jews in the United States practicing traditional beliefs and values. Conspicuous features of the religion are (1) the segregation of men and women in religious services and (2) male privilege. Chalfant et al. (1987, p. 116) point out that most literature in the sociology of religion suggests that Jewish and Christian documents and practices reflect the traditional, subservient role of women and the powerful and dominant role of men. Daly (1975), Russell (1976), Driver (1976), and others have alluded to how the Old and New Testaments of the Bible support discrimination against and domination of women. Women have been defined as the property of males, are told by Paul to be quiet in church, and instructed not to hold authority because Eve had been the downfall of mankind. The language and symbolism of the Bible clearly assign low status to women, portraying men as leaders and women as their servants. Even today, with the exception of statements of national policy, "the Church has given little impetus for change in the status of women" (Chalfant et al. 1987, p. 117).

One possible exception, though relatively uninfluential, to male dominance in religion in the United States is female leadership in some few urban Black inner-city Christian sects. Represented by store-front churches, frequently in deteriorating urban areas, these relatively informal religious organizations generally are short lived. Usually these churches are not well integrated into society and leadership is dependent upon personal qualities of the leader, who often calls for a return to pure religious beliefs and behaviors. For these and other reasons, many of these churches cease to exist once the leader is no longer capable of leading the sect. While such organizations exist, they exhibit relatively little influence on society, and the women leaders have minimal impact on religion as a societal institution.

Gender and Religious Functions

Religion is many things to many people. Despite the broadness and generality of religion, however, it is possible to point out several basic functions which religion seems to serve. The works of Durkheim (1965), Berger (1967), O'Dea and Aviad (1983), and others show that religion serves several functions: meaning and purpose for one's life, social solidarity, social control, and social criticism. Let us explore each of these functions and their relationship to maintenance of the traditional male sex role. The approach taken here is general and considers the dominant religious influences in American society. From the work of Stark and Bainbridge (1985), it may be possible to understand such influences by recognizing the degree of tension existing between the environment (American culture) and various religious organizations. For example, Stark and Bainbridge allude to the idea that some churches are well accommodated to American culture and thus low to moderate tensions exist between the two. Examples include the Protestant Episcopal church, the United Church of Christ, and the Methodist and Presbyterian churches. Somewhat less accommodated to our culture but still characterized by low tension with it are the American Lutheran church, the American Baptist church, and the Roman Catholic church.

Still, there are numerous religious organizations in America characterized by high tension with American culture, ranging from those that remain physically within the culture, including those challenged legally by the society or frequently subjected to numerous informal negative sanctions (e.g., ridicule from society), to those that opt for as much physical separation from mainstream society as possible. On the one hand, those religious organizations experiencing high to extreme tension with society include Jehovah's Witnesses, Reverend Moon's Unification Church, Hare Krishna, the Amish, Mennonites, and polygamous Mormon communes (Reichley 1985, p. 134; Stark and Bainbridge 1985, p. 135). Even when there is high tension between the religious organization and the society, religious influence on the society can still be quite strong as long as the religious organization does not physically separate itself from the society and simultaneously engage in proselytizing activities to win adherents. Such has been the case since the 1970s with various Pentecostal religious groups. But what functions do the various and sundry religious organizations serve in America?

Religion as Support for Traditional Sex Roles

It is more than a coincidence that there has been a religious revival in the United States. In the late 1970s, as women began more and more to initiate movements toward sex equality in many areas of society, Pope John Paul II issued the following dictum:

I want to remind young women that motherhood is the vocation of women. It was that way in the past. It is that way now and it will always be that way. It is a woman's eternal vocation. (*Washington Post*, 1979)

In the same vein, conservative religious organizations across America in the 1980s have voiced loud opposition to the Equal Rights Amendment, abortion, affirmative action, and other ideals and practices which would move the society toward sex role equality and away from male dominance. Often using religion to shield efforts to maintain male superiority in many areas of society, many Christian organizations provide either support for traditional sex role ideology or justification for maintaining traditional sex role distinctions. Quite frequently religion provides social support for traditional relationships between the sexes and this leads to a kind of socially constructed rationale which enhances social solidarity in society. Nowhere is this more evident than in the testimonies of women who previously had careers outside of the home but returned to the home to assume child-rearing and homemaking duties exclusively. Such women are seen as ''proof'' that social arrangements between the sexes were ordained by God and are fixed, permanent, and beyond the control of the individual.

Religion and Social Solidarity Between the Sexes

In addition to serving as means of controlling men as well as women by emphasizing traditional sex role distinctions as God-inspired, religious groups also enhance solidarity between men and women by stressing traditional sex roles. However, it is important to recognize that many mainline Protestant denominations have supported sex role equality in religion, the E.R.A., the pro-choice movement, and egalitarian family structures. Even many Roman Catholics have adopted pro-choice ideals (D'Antonio 1985). Yet, conservative forces within American religious organizations remain powerful influences in American culture. Those influences attempt to unite men and women in the society by emphasizing traditionally shared values and norms, but, of course, such values and norms support female oppression, submissiveness, and oppose equality for women. Popular strategies of such religious organizations include extolling the traditional significance of family life while opposing feminism and women's gains. McNamara (1985) points out that frequently fundamentalist religious groups in America use Biblical scriptures as literal guides for social life.

When religious groups support traditional sex role distinctions, they are attempting to minimize conflict between men and women, albeit at the expense of women. D'Antonio (1983) and Hargrove (1983) note that when women are submissive to their husbands, nurturing them, and obeying them, they are seen as doing what God intended for them to do. Conversely, women involved in activities that separate them from their husbands and often result in "disobedience" are acting unscriptural and against the will of God. The former ideals, attitudes, and behaviors are seen as solidarity building, while the latter are seen as disruptive to solidarity between men and women.

Religion Providing a Sense of Meaning and Purpose for Men and Women

It is not unusual for people who find themselves oppressed to find solace in a religion that speaks eloquently to their lowly status, indicating that it is God's will and that their status serves a greater purpose. Such is the case with some groups' interpretation of Christian ideology concerning the role of women in social life. In the same vein religious validation of traditional role definitions for males by some groups serves to justify male domination in social life. Validity of both sets of beliefs is not the important point here. What is important is that men and women share the beliefs which lead to social cohesion and/or social stability. This seems to be the rationale underlying some Christian fundamentalist and evangelical Protestant ministers' strategies to drum up popular support for federal legislation which is essentially "pro-family." Brewster (1984, pp. 237–38) points out that such legislation involves, among other things, denying federal funds for school textbooks that fail to show women in traditional sex roles and, in addition, prohibiting federal funding for abortions and divorces. It is recognized that while members of some religious groups loudly condemn sex role changes, other members sometimes opt for compromise and negotiation in their own personal relationships (McNamara 1985). What many members of conservative religious groups realize, however, is that further changes in sex roles and legislation supporting change will, in the long run, undermine much of the meaning and purpose of traditional male dominance and female submissiveness.

Religion as a Basis for Critiquing Men's and Women's Roles

We know already that many Christian fundamentalists, evangelicals, and other religious conservatives believe in literal interpretations of Biblical scriptures and that this means support for male dominance and female subjugation. Some other religious groups, however, have modified their views on traditional male and female sex roles. Some mainline Protestant denominations, reform Jewish groups, and many Roman Catholics (who defy church authority on gender related issues) have challenged the oppression of women and have been quite supportive of sex role equality, adopting an attitude of egalitarianism on family issues and in other areas of social life. It cannot be denied that changes throughout society pose interesting dilemmas for religious institutions. Yet, in all likelihood, religious institutions will make the necessary adjustments which will not only accommodate the changes but probably act as catalysts to some. Chalfant et al.'s (1987) remarks are instructive at this point.

Today, however, many first marriages do not last, and an increasingly significant segment of families in the United States consist of second spouses and children from previous marriages. Most religious groups are attempting to adjust to this new trend, and to an increasing number of single-parent families, two-income families, and gender-role changes, but the process is not easy. As a result, the religious institution is presently struggling with its interrelationship with family life.

The traditional male sex role in America, with its emphasis on achievement, has been very consistent with aspects of Protestantism. Concentrating on the doctrines of John Calvin, Weber argued that Calvinist principles which emphasize honoring and glorifying God dictated that such honor and glorification should occur during weekdays as well as on Sunday. According to Weber's line of thought, during weekdays, a good Protestant was devoted to a life of individualism, hard work, and discipline, and those individuals "who worked hardest would do the most to glorify God" (Chalfant et al., 1987, p. 262).

In the same vein, it is instructive to point out that traditional male sex roles in the United States are powerful supports for our capitalist economic system. In fact, religious groups as producing units in the economy directly support the capitalist economic system, employing thousands upon thousands of workers. The major influence of religious groups, however, remains indirect—*support for the male sex role emphasizing competition and success in our economic system.* Religious support of the white male dominated economic institution comes not only from Protestants but also from Catholic and Jewish groups. This leads Chalfant et al. to conclude that "what was once the Protestant work ethic has become a generalized work ethic followed by a majority of members (especially expected of males) from all three major religious traditions (Protestant, Catholic and Jewish) as well as by the religiously nonaffiliated" (p. 263).

The 1980s in America ushered in a new era with respect to fundamentalist and conservative Protestant traditions. Following the turbulent 1960s and on the rise since the middle 1970s, a large minority within most, if not all, of the mainline Protestant denominations emerged in America calling for Christian renewal and a return to religious conservatism. The Christian revival emphasizes, among other things, literal interpretation of biblical scripture, theological conservatism, personal morality, personal evangelism, and axiomatically, traditional sex roles for Christian men and women (according to biblical scriptures).

Headed chiefly by white males, four major denominations of contemporary evangelicalism can be identified: Evangelicals, Fundamentalists, Pentecostals, and Charismatics. Ostling (1987) offers the following glossary of the denominations:

A Gospel Glossary

Evangelicals. An umbrella term for U.S. Protestants who stress conservative doctrine and morality, a traditional or even literal interpretation of the Bible, missionizing, and individual commitments to Jesus Christ. They belong to many churches; the biggest evangelical body is the Southern Baptist Convention (14.6 million members, including Billy Graham and Jimmy Carter). Evangelicals hold a wide range of political views. One subgroup, the New Religious Right, is noted for conservative activism on social issues (abortion, school prayer) and foreign policy (U.S. defense, Israel).

Fundamentalists. Militant Evangelicals (example: Jerry Falwell) who hold to the inerrancy of the Scriptures, taken literally, and keep their churches strictly separate from Christians with differing views, even moderate Evangelicals.

Pentecostals. A group, dating from the turn of the century, that holds evangelical or fundamentalist views and is notable for such miraculous Holy Spirit "gifts" as speaking in tongues (glossolalia), faith healing and uttering of prophecies. Jim Bakker's and Jimmy Swaggart's Assemblies of God is one of the nation's fastest-growing denominations (up 34 percent, to 2.1 million members, since 1975). [Since Ostling constructed this glossary, numerous developments related to the denomination have occurred. Jim Bakker was ousted, and Jerry Falwell, who has his own ministry based in Lynchburg, Virginia, became PTL chair for a period of time on March 19, 1987, when Bakker turned the ministry over to him following publicity surrounding the Jessica Hahn incident. On October 8, 1987, Jerry Falwell announced his ten-member board resignation saying that he feared Bakker's return would make the PTL ministry "the greatest scab and cancer on the face of Christianity in 2,000 years" (*Columbus Dispatch*, Oct. 9, 1987). In addition, on February 18, 1988, elders of the Assemblies of God confronted Jimmy Swaggart in a four-hour special session with allegations that he had been in the company of a prostitute, as evidenced by photographs. On Sunday, February 21, 1988, Swaggart tearfully begged God's forgiveness, his wife and children's forgiveness, and his congregations' forgiveness for publicly unspecified sexual misconduct. Just eleven months earlier, this minister had scathingly denounced Jim Bakker for committing adultery. Swaggert has since resigned from the Assemblies of God.]

Charismatics. This fluid term usually designates those of Pentecostal-style faith within non-Pentecostal denominations (example: Oral Roberts, a United Methodist) or in independent congregations. Some Roman Catholics are charismatics. (P. 60).

It is estimated that there are 46 million Evangelicals in the United States. Hunter's (1983) Analysis of Princeton Religious Research Center survey data found that evangelicals in that study were predominantly white (88.2%), married (77.2%), and women (59.9%). Evangelicals also were found to be disproportionately represented in rural areas (43.7%) with a high concentration in the southern region of the United States (45%). What is significant about the demographic characteristics specified above is that while women seem to be overwhelmingly involved in contemporary evangelicalism, their involvement is supportive rather than in leadership. Perhaps this would seem insignificant if equality between men and women were stressed in evangelical denominations. Clearly this is not the case. A classic characteristic of these denominations seems to admonish women to assume traditional submissive roles with men. Nowhere has this been made more emphatic than in the unfortunate scandals which tarnished electronic evangelism in 1987 and 1988. Initially attempting to rebound from his confession that he had committed adultery with New York secretary Jessica Hahn in 1980, television minister Jim Bakker (with wife Tammy) appeared on his T.V. network to explain his decision to relinquish control of his $129 million-a-year P.T.L. (for Praise The Lord or People That Love), a thriving religious business. Amid charges and countercharges hurled by numerous electronic ministers and aides directly and indirectly involved in the scandal, additional comments by Bakker have implications for the role of women.

An eye-opening statement allegedly made by Jim Bakker following his public exposure may very well give us a glimpse of the status of women as seen by some evangelical religious leaders. The official statement released by Bakker during his resignation as head of P.T.L. was: "I was wickedly manipulated by treacherous former friends and then colleagues who victimized me with the aid of a female confederate" (Ostling, 1987 p. 63). This statement was followed by another from a friend who recounted that Bakker supposedly told him that he "was very surprised that this gal was able to perform the way that she did. . . . He described her as very professional for twenty-one years of age. . . . She knew all the tricks of the trade." Thus, the righteous tautology was complete. Jim Bakker, the Pentecostal, was "innocent" because he was a leader in the Assemblies of God denomination with an estimated 2.1 million members. Jessica Hahn, on the other hand, was guilty because she was simply a female church secretary.

Just as revealing about the perception some evangelical ministers have or have had of women was the public revelation by a New Orleans prostitute that Swaggart offered her $10 to enter his car, which she rejected. As the prostitute implied, here was a man who made hundreds of thousands of dollars offering her $10 to satisfy his lust. Such an incident is a reflection of how women are perceived by the would-be procurer. What all of this means for the new religious consciousness in the United States is impossible to assess at the present time. One thing that does appear certain, however, is continued efforts on the part of evangelical minorities to spread their messages without fundamental changes in the statuses of females and males. After all, such messages are derived literally from the Bible, and salvation, from this perspective, lies in following such dictates, even if this means male domination and female oppression.

Educational Institutions

The school is an arena in which new kinds of masculinity and femininity are being arbitrated. Knowledge and curriculum, as well as the kinds of gender behaviors that are allowed, encouraged, or discouraged, are related to the patterned power relations of gender in the larger society.
—Persell 1987

In the beginning there were few social institutions outside of the family in the United States. Those that did exist essentially were comprised of men, while women's interests and domain centered around the care of the household (Pleck and Pleck, 1980, pp. 9–10). Men were totally in control of the few economic and religious institutions despite economic interdependence between the sexes.

Formal education in the United States was not normative in early American history. In fact, Ritzer et al. (1987) note that initially in America, education took place in the "real world" rather than in schools and emphasized "reading, 'riting, 'rithmetic, and religion" (p. 313). In the year 1647, formal education began in the United States with the establishment of the Massachusetts Bay Colony school system. It can be said that 1647 also marks the point in America when men began to assume control of the emerging formal educational institution. Ballantine (1983) observes that the sex role distinction in education is historical, and points out that literacy for women was discouraged by the Puritans except to ensure salvation through reading the Bible. Following the American Revolution, according to Ballantine, a limited amount of education for women was deemed necessary in order for them to fulfill "their responsibility" for teaching young children and transmitting moral standards.

In seventeenth-century New England prior to the American Revolution, according to Pleck and Pleck (1980), women were only slightly more likely to be illiterate than men. However, the gap widened with the introduction of common schooling, which decreased male illiteracy as few women were sent on to school.

Perhaps a quick review of the peculiar way in which the educational system developed in the United States will shed additional light on traditional sex distinctions in education. Harvard College was established in 1636 for sons of the colonial elite to be trained as future leaders (Ritzer et al., 1987). It was not until several years later, in 1647, that the first public elementary schools were established. Between this period and the 1870s, elementary education of girls as well as boys became widespread. The mid-nineteenth century ushered in the founding of the first public high schools, attended by both sexes. It should be noted that by this time Oberlin College had opened its doors officially to women despite the fact that women's education was restricted to domestic subjects. Still, the mid-nineteenth century did see the development of women's colleges which produced women reformers, professionals, and intellectuals. In 1837, over two hundred years after the founding of a men's college, the first college for women was established. Prior to that time, a few women did receive higher education provided for them, starting in 1742, by Bethlehem Seminary at the Moravian settlement in Pennsylvania (Parelius and Parelius, 1978). Still, the following quotation, summarizing the observations of a school observer in the 1880s, pointedly illustrates early sex differences in the educational process:

> We noticed the boys all writing, but none of the girls; turning to our friend Tullis for an explanation, he said it was not safe for girls to learn to write, as it would culminate in love-letter writing, clandestine engagements, and elopements. He said women were allowed to study arithmetic, though, for Miss Polly Caldwell studied as far as long division, and Mrs. Kyle, while a widow, got as far as reduction. He says Polly Caldwell was a weaver, and required the aid of figures to make her calculations for warping.

It seems, then, that social processes operating within today's educational institution which produce structured social inequality between the sexes have their origins in the early establishment of formal educational systems.

Effects and Functions of Formal Education Structures on Females' and Males' Sex Role Socialization

The transmission of a society's way of life, its technical and specialized knowledge, is considered to be a basic function of the educational institution in America. Because our society is technologically advanced, facts must be taught. But in addition, learning must also occur in a way that will enable persons to adapt to unanticipated changes in the future.

A large part of learning involves the inculcation of cultural values, norms, and standards. For example, one of the most important cultual values transmitted via formal educational systems is achievement. Schools transmit this value explicitly by rewarding students with specific grades (e.g., A's and B's) for their accomplishments in studying. The value of achievement also is transmitted in more subtle ways, as when students are assigned to read the biographies of famous people who have achieved by American standards.

Very much an aspect of the learning of cultural values and norms are the social expectations associated with being female and male. Sex role socialization begins in the family at birth, as we have seen. The process continues beyond the family when the child enters a formal educational system. Both nonmaterial as well as material aspects of education in our culture tend to reinforce stereotypical sex roles and traditional interaction patterns between the sexes even today, despite recent changes. While some researchers have found education to be positively related to liberal political and social attitudes, others (e.g., Jackman and Muha, 1984) have failed to find such an association. Jackman and Muha found that educated people tend to show greater support for individual rights, not equal rights, and this was manifested by the lack of a significant association between men's educational level and liberal orientation toward women, among other liberal attitudes. This, along with research findings showing that teachers promote and support different behavior for the sexes (Kaminski 1985), indicates the contribution that education makes to stereotypical cultural sex role expectations.

Social integration between females and males. Another function of the educational institution is to construct a unified society, bringing together persons of diverse interests, values, and tastes. Certainly, social integration of the sexes is a difficult proposition for most educational systems in the United States, because of the necessity for the systems to fulfill the social placement function, to be discussed next. Increasingly, less traditional and more progressive schools seem to be at least paying lip service to principles fostering equality between the sexes while simultaneously instructing students in the positive value of sex equity. Undoubtedly, such a strategy has the potential to unify females and males if adopted widely by school systems in the United States.

At the very least we have seen in recent years some concern about sex equity in education despite the Reagan administration's position that schools need be concerned about sex discrimination only in programs receiving federal funds directly (Persell, 1987). While great concern about sex equity in education has not come from the Reagan administration, women educators, like Susan Klein (1985), are working tirelessly to ensure that women continue their trek toward educational equality. Whether this trek will mean greater unity between men and women depends, in part, on maintaining prohibition on sex discrimination to the point where less formal expectations held by members of society are also anti-sex discrimination.

Social placement. The identification and production of talent in females and males are functions of the educational institution. Education selects and allocates females and males to social positions in society. Social position in an avowed open-class system is supposed to reflect personal achievement and/or merit. Ideally, then, the educational institution selects certain persons as possessing characteristics which make them eligible to be considered for certain positions in the society. Closer analysis, however, reveals that the educational institution does not fulfill this function, or to be more precise, it is prevented from fulfilling this function. Some researchers (Bowles and Gintis 1976) believe that the educational institution is an instrument used by power holders in society to create inequality. It is through the educational institution that persons are unequally placed in positions, and a legitimate rationale for this placement is provided by test scans which purportedly measure merit but actually are of questionable validity. Traditionally, sex has been a powerful determinant of assignment to societal positions, and despite minor changes in recent years, it continues to mediate the relationship between education and social placement.

Generation of knowledge about females and males. Despite the caution that must be taken in discussons about society's progress toward female and male liberation from outdated and stereotypical sex roles, some recent changes in sex roles must be acknowledged. Many of these changes have been due, either directly or indirectly, to knowledge generated by the educational institution. The proliferation of Women's Studies departments across the country during the 1970s and 1980s certainly has affected what we know about sex roles. The fledgling Men's Studies in the late 1980s also promises to make an impact on the knowledge about gender produced by the educational institution.

The fact that the generation of knowledge about gender often has had to take a back seat in the 1980s to the pursuit of knowledge in areas like the natural sciences and defense technology attests to the educational institutions' knowledge generating function. But new gender information continues to be generated in educational systems all over the United States and abroad. We hope that such information eventually will find its way into policy decisions affecting females and males in this society as well as other societies throughout the world.

What Education Does Not Do

In the previous section we considered some of the things that the educational system does. In this section we still consider the effects of education, but the emphasis is on what the institution does *not* accomplish for females and males. By implication, we explain the relationship between the educational institution and the male sex role. Gender-related issues to be discussed are income, job mobility, educational tracking, and faculty and staff composition in the educational institution.

Education and income. Ordinarily we think that education enables people to earn more money. According to the U.S. Census Bureau there does seem to be a positive linear relationship between education and income. An increase in education is likely to result in an increase in income, though there are broad ranges of income at each educational level. Examination of median income by sex and education for all females and males over fifteen years of age working full time in 1984 reveals a pattern of particular interest to us! For example, the median incomes for all women and men completing high school were $14,569 and $23,269, respectively. Women and men college graduates had median incomes of $20,257 and $31,487; and, women and men who had five-plus years of education beyond high school had median incomes of $25,076 and $36,836. At each of the educational levels, then, men's median income was greater than women's. Women who completed high school had a median income which was only 63 percent of their male counterparts' median income. The pattern continues at the upper educational levels; college graduate womens' median income is 64 percent of men's median income, and for the five years plus beyond high school educational level, women's median income is 68 percent of men's. Just as revealing is that women who graduate from college have a median income which is only 87 percent of male high school graduates' median income; and male high school graduates have a median income which is 93 percent that of women with five years or more of education beyond high school. While there is some attempt to explain all income disparities as being due to occupational patterns (e.g., childbearing interruption), sex discrimination seems to be the real culprit. The educational institution has not been able to close the gender gap on the income issue.

The educational institution itself is not innocent on income and power issues. Women in educational institutions typically earn much less than men and are found in less powerful positions than men. The

U.S. Bureau of the Census reports that in 1980 only 21 percent of secondary school officials and administrators were women, and only 18 percent of the principals and assistant principals were women. In contrast, 57 percent of the high school teachers were men; only 16 percent of the elementary teachers were men; 6 percent of the teachers aides were men, and 2 percent of the clerical and secretarial staff were men.

In the upper echelons of education, faculties also reflect sex stratification; relatively few women earn the rankings of associate professor and full professor in colleges and universities across the country. Questions have been raised about women's productivity and their role conflict resulting from combining a career with family obligations. Hess et al. (1988) alludes to research discovering differences in the quantity and quality of men's and women's productivity. Pointing out that male career longevity and a merit system that favors men place and maintain men in positions superior to women even within the institution that some feel has a major responsibility for decreasing sex role inequality.

Gender, education, and occupation. What is the relationship between gender-based economic stratification and education in terms of sex differences in occupations? Some feel that most women working for pay outside of the home are to be found in a limited number of occupations, such as elementary and secondary school teaching, nursing, social work, clerical jobs, and service workers, all of which have relatively low pay. In the more highly paid positions, such as the math/science-/computer technical areas, women make up only 10 percent of workers (Kaminski 1985). This is so despite the fact that through junior high school, girls and boys do equally well on math and science ability examinations. Following junior high school, however, girls begin to fall behind boys. In terms of actual academic performance, girls consistently earn better grades (including math and science) throughout the school years. Still, there is a gender gap in the number of females to be found in math and science-based occupations, and the educational institution seems to be doing relatively little to close this gap. It is instructive to point out that the distribution relationship to be found between gender, education, and occupation is related to another issue in education—gender tracking.

Educational tracking by gender and status stratification. By inference, the obvious conclusion to be reached based on the above discussion is that males in the United States are in a disproportionate number of high income occupations which in some way is related to their disproportionate numbers in areas such as math, science, engineering, and computer technology. Given that the relationships exist and discounting that the gender gap in certain occupations and preparation for the occupation are due to innate sex differences, the educational institution must be looked to for an explanation. We have stated before that the educational institution to a great extent mirrors the society in which it finds itself. While some changes in sex roles have occurred in recent years, the changes have not been sufficient to substantially affect female entrance into those school courses which would prepare them for entrance into college courses leading to nontraditional occupational careers. Girls in high school still are encouraged, openly and subtly, by counselors and teachers as well as by parents to select traditional female careers. Of course, perception of women's roles by adolescents remains somewhat traditional, with the emphasis placed on women's home and child-care responsibilities. This means that many girls are quite unlikely even today to recognize the importance of math, science, and computer courses as they relate to the adult role they are to assume. Schools, parents, and most of society seem quite willing to continue, both blatantly and latently, the gender tracking process which produces sex segregation in occupations and contributes immensely to sex disparities in earned income.

Major sex differences have been noted in educational systems, including the preponderence of female teachers concentrated at the elementary school level and the gradual decrease in the female percentage as one moves through the educational system. Beginning at high school, instruction in the educational institution gradually becomes male dominated. Moreover, power differences between the sexes in education become apparent when one views school administrators, who are overwhelmingly male throughout the United States.

Experiencing the Education Process

Ballantine (1983) implies that the classroom environment is one where many activities appear to be sex linked, with teacher actions often reinforcing sex stereotypes. This means that boys have a decided advantage in their preparation for adult roles. For example, while boys receive more and harsher discipline, teachers also devote more time to them, praise them more, and have more flexible expectations regarding their behavior. Such sex differences carry over into school playground activities, where boys' play, relative to girls' play, tends to be: (1) outside of school buildings; (2) in larger groups; (3) in more age-heterogeneous groups; (4) in less sex segregated groups; (5) a longer period of time; and (6) decidedly more competitive (Lever 1978).

As boys and girls continue into high school, sex differences in the educational process continue, complete with the previously discussed gender tracking process. It seems, then, that the male experience in education has far more positive consequences than the female experience. Yet, there is an experience many males have that has deleterious effects on many of them which has not been discussed. This experience has its roots in Hartley's (1959) early findings that boys experience greater pressure for conformity than girls. The exact experience, however, is the sports experience—the ultimate socializer of competitiveness that the educational institution has to offer.

Because of the early pressure placed on males to conform and to be competitive, many become involved in sports quite early (e.g., Little League sports such as baseball, basketball, football, and soccer). While most males do not continue full-scale participation in sports, many eventually end up trying to excel in the sports arena or lamenting the fact that they do not excel. For those who do excel, the educational institution supports, promises, and delivers handsome rewards. It is not necessary to go into specific details about the relationship between males and sports in educational systems, but certainly most of us are aware of its inimical effects on many males. Sacrificing scholarship, personal development, maturity, and/or growth, many males, beginning in elementary school, float through educational systems (including four years of college) participating in a sport but gaining little else from the experience. What is so debilitating about the process is that its effects, like some physical disorders, are not immediate. Only after the system has no further use for the males and/or the athletes are unable to make a professional career out of the sport (and the overwhelming majority are not) do the effects become fully apparent. Frequently, the discarded male has no occupational skill, no social skills, little motivation, and generally is personally disorganized. The problem is especially acute for poor Black males and other poor minority group males who learn early to view sports as a possible means of access to riches. Placing all their confidence in their athletic skills and, more importantly, being allowed to do so by an educational system that demands little from them academically, some males unwittingly learn to fail directly from the educational institution.

Economics and Politics

While all of the institutions are interrelated in American society, no two are more closely interwoven than the economy and the polity. In our society, like all others, decisions must be made about goods and services to be produced for the people and how much of those goods and services is to be produced. In addition, economic decisions specifying use of resources to produce the goods and services, as well as for whom the goods and services should be produced and who is to produce them, must also be made. The fact that some people in American society seem to participate in the economic decision-making processes and others have very little say means that power is being exercised. Of course, controlling the means of economic production is only one resource for exercising power. Distinct dimensions of power in American society include those found in religion, science, the arts, media, medicine, and education (Vander Zanden 1986 p. 238). While this seems to imply that each sphere has its own set of power-holders or strategic elites operating within specialized areas, Vander Zanden's discussion of the nature of political institutions should be considered. Vander Zanden believes that the political institution consists of people who exercise an effective monopoly in the use of physical coercion within a given territory. Pointing out that some form of centralized government seems indispensable to modern society, Vander Zanden believes that the possession of the means of administration, insured by the threat of force, defines the political institution in America. In the following paragraphs, we will look at the roles of men and women in both the American economy and the American polity.

Gender and the American Economy

A prominent feature of American economy most relevant for this volume is sex stratification and its effects on men's and women's positions in society. Sex stratification in occupations and jobs means that men and women routinely are assigned occupations and jobs of different value partly on the basis of sex, with men being assigned to the more valued positions and women being assigned to the less valued ones.

While a great deal of attention is devoted to women's contemporary labor force participation, their participation has been important to the

American economy for a long time. In fact, Stockard and Johnson (1980) note that the sharp rise in women's labor force participation began in 1900, and married women's increased participation was the primary cause. They note that from 1900 to 1940 the number of married women in the labor force more than doubled, and from 1940 to 1970, it almost tripled. This trend continued, and in 1985, over 68 percent of married women with school-age children were in the labor force. The trend is expected to continue. The sex composition of the labor force overall appears to be changing, with women constituting an increasing proportion. In 1984, men were 57 percent of the sixteen-year-old-plus labor force, and women were 43 percent. Because women are an even larger proportion of younger segments of the labor force, their overall labor force participation proportion is likely to increase in the future.

While more and more women continue to enter the labor force, and there is some convergence with men in work statuses, men still are overrepresented in those occupations with greater prestige, rewards, and power. Moreover, when the sex composition of occupations changes, the power, privileges, and rewards associated with the occupations change. Men tend to successfully take over those occupations that call for greater skills and give greater rewards, and they tend to leave those occupations that are downgraded in skills and rewards. The trend started and was dramatically represented in the nineteenth century by the replacement of male clerks by women clerks and male elementary education school teachers by female elementary school teachers. Also, in the nineteenth century, male doctors took over midwife work, which of course had been performed by women. Oppenheimer (1985) has discussed the process by which clerical work in the labor force became the primary domain of women, and sex stratification became an entrenched aspect of the American labor force:

> A new male managerial stratum took over the quasi-managerial activities of the clerks, leaving the detail work to the now predominantly female office staffs. . . . Two distinct occupational hierarchies evolved: a male one, made up of many layers of managers, and a female one of file clerks, typists, stenographers, clerical supervisors, and secretaries.

As if the changing sex composition of occupations and professions inimical to women were not enough, increasingly complex technology actually eliminates jobs in traditionally female-dominated areas and in those which have been vehicles of upward mobility for women (e.g., secretaries replaced by word processors, department store buyers replaced by computerized inventory systems, etc.). Forces impeding women's equality and supporting men's superiority in labor force participation have created a glaringly uneven sex distribution among occupations in the American economy. For example, according to the U.S. Department of Labor, in 1986 males overwhelmingly dominated the following professions: engineers (94%), natural scientists (85%), lawyers and judges (85%), precision, production, craft, and repair (91%), engineering and science technicians (81%), health diagnosing (84%), farming, forestry, and fishing (79%), operators, fabricators, and laborers (74%), execution, administrative, and managerial (64%), and mathematical and computer scientists (63%). Female dominated occupations included health assessment and treatment (86%), health technologists and technicians (83%), administrative support, including clerical (80%), teachers excluding college and university (69%), and service occupations (60%). A cursory glance at the occupations dominated by men reveals instantly that the male dominated occupations are the most prestigious, powerful, and rewarding jobs. But even when females and males in the same occupational category are compared in terms of rewards, some rather interesting findings emerge. In 1985, for example, women executives, administrators, and managers earned only 67 percent of men's income. The U.S. Bureau of the Census also reveals for the same year the following disparities in median incomes by occupational category: professionals, men—$29,692, women—$21,216; technicians and related support, men—$24,544, women—$17,212; sales occupations, men—$22,412, women—$11,752; administrative support including clerical, men—$20,332, women—$14,040; service occupations, men—$14,144, women—$9,620; precision, production, craft, and repairs, men—$21,216, women—$13,936; operators, fabricators, and laborers, men—$16,900, women—$11,232; and farming, men—$11,232, women—$9,620. Thus, in all occupations, even those female dominated ones, men outearn females. To say that men are at a decided advantage in the American economy is an understatement.

Gender and the Polity

Of all the social institutions in the United States, the polity is perhaps the most male dominated. This should not be surprising given the patriarchal nature of politics in America. Despite the adoption and support of a women's right to vote resolution put forth at the Seneca Falls Declaration of Principles in 1848, suffrage was not easily won by women. In fact, it was not until 1920 that the Nineteenth Amendment to the Constitution was finally ratified, extending to women the right to vote. Some believe that the denial of suffrage to women until 1920 helps to account for the limited representation of women in politics today. This may be so; however, such an explanation obscures the extent to which female participation in politics has been male determined.

If female participation in politics were not uneven, a time explanation of women's representation devoid of male dominance would seem feasible. To the contrary, however, women's participation in the political arena seems quite uneven. From the beginning of their participation in politics, women have been assigned primarily "support roles" which have ranged from voting to consorting. Stockard and Johnson (1980) point out that when women first were extended the right to vote, few actually voted; however, in recent years the proportions of men and women voting have grown to about equal. In fact, because there are more adult women than men, women outnumber men at the polls. Thus, on one level, women's participation in politics is very much on a par with men's.

On still another level of participation in the polity, the proportions of men and women supporting political candidates, attending political meetings, and participating in such activities as working to elect candidates to political office are about the same. Naomi Lynne (1978) has pointed out that there is one sex difference and that is monetary contributions to political parties. She attributes this difference to sex differences in monetary resources (the ability to make such contributions).

Women also are active in politics in another way. They are likely to participate in local politics, become local political candidates, and hold local political office. At state and national levels, however, men still overwhelmingly dominate political participation. While women's participation on these levels is increasing, women still are likely to assume support roles (e.g., stuffing envelopes, answering phones, etc.), while men devise campaign strategies and develop political policy.

Geraldine Ferraro's vice presidential candidacy in 1984 notwithstanding, men remain in charge of the political arena on the national level in the United States. In 1986, out of 100 members of the U.S. Senate, there were only 2 women members. In the House of Representatives in 1986, of the 435 members, 23 were women. On the state level, too, women remain greatly under-represented. Between 1978 and 1984, for example, women's representation among state representatives and senators only rose from 9.3 percent to 14 percent of the 7,400 state legislators. Their representation in state governorship is no better. Prior to

1974, only 3 women had been elected state governors (all after their husbands had been governors—Nellie Ross of Wyoming in 1925, Ma Ferguson of Texas in 1926 and 1932, and Lurleen Wallace of Alabama in 1966). Two of the women elected to office following their husbands—Ma Ferguson and Lurleen Wallace—were widely believed to be stand-ins for their husbands, and the election of the third, Nellie Ross, followed her husband's death. Between 1974 and 1985, 4 women were elected to state governorships: Ella Grasso of Connecticut, Martha Layne Collins of Kentucky, Dixie Lee Ray of Washington, and Madeline Kunin of Vermont.

It is easy to see that the polity in the United States is still dominated largely by the 49 percent majority. Not only is the domination reflected in state and national legislatures, but it is also reflected in high level appointive posts. Sandra Day O'Connor, like Geraldine Ferraro, does not make up for years of under-representation in power positions. Moreover, their appearances, as well as the scant appearances of others like Jean Kirkpatrick, should convince few that a new era of women's participation in politics beyond the "Donna Rice" mode of participation is upon us. The distribution and exercise of power in the United States, involving the ability of some people to control other people's behavior, still are processes enjoyed primarily by white males.

8

Gender Norms
and Social Change

Most of us will agree that over the past decade and a half or so gender-related attitudes and behaviors, like the rest of the world, have changed to some degree. Just how much change has occurred, some feel, is a matter to be debated. One must be cautious when discussing change in gender-related attitudes and, more importantly, change in gender-related behaviors. The more liberal attitudes related to gender issues reflect changing norms regarding gender issues rather than changes in gender evaluations or feelings.

Ashmore, Del Boca, and McManus (1986) raise three concerns regarding changes in attitudes toward gender-related issues. They point out that intuitively gender-related attitude change seems to be occurring in American society; however, extant measures of gender-related attitude change are reactive, and purported liberal gender attitudes may be, in actuality, reports about social norms existing in American society today. Ashmore et al. question whether values of sex role equality have been internalized despite the fact that some people may be complying with antisexist norms. Just as critical in considering attitude change and behavior change are the effects of time period, age, and cohort. The key issue becomes whether gender-related changes are period-specific, age-specific, or cohort-specific. Are changes in gender-related attitudes and behavior occurring today related basically to the time period in American history? Are they products of persons' ages in the life cycle? We have discussed findings which suggest that middle-age men undergo periods wherein they become "more human" in their interactions with others.

Just as importantly, Ashmore, Del Boca, and McManus explain the possibility that changes in gender-related attitudes and behaviors may be related to a cohort effect; large numbers of persons born during a particular time period exhibit attitudinal and behavioral similarities due to certain social/environmental factors.

According to Ashmore et al., a final question of key concern in exploring change in gender-related attitudes involves the types of effects supposedly occurring. What is the nature of the gender-related attitudes undergoing change? The authors feel that gender-related attitude change in America essentially is not uniform and centers around change in gender equality as a value. Americans are much more likely today than a few decades ago to verbally oppose sex discrimination in occupations and to pay lip service to economic and political opportunities for women. Of course, if such change *is* attitudinal, it still may not be necessarily commensurate with actual behavior change.

The fact that attitude-behavior discrepancy occurs and that attitudes may not be good predictors of behavior is extremely important when considering ''harm-doing'' behaviors between people. Harm-doing behaviors can be: (1) between the sexes, individual to individual; (2) contextual, where an individual hurts another as an aspect of an organization; or (3) supportive, where an individual supports societal-level arrangements that put some groups at a disadvantage. Relative to men in American society, women are likely to be victims of all three kinds of harm-doing, and the perpetrators overwhelmingly are men. However, assessing gender-of-target effects, alone, may not reveal what we want to know about behavioral change related to gender issues. Both contextual and supportive harm-doing are subtle forms of aggressive behaviors found among many people in American society which oppress women and thereby deny them social equality. This is not to say that private violence between men and women where women are disproportionately victimized, such as spouse battering, marital rape, and incest, should go unemphasized. Such acts are heinous personal injustices, but it is important to see them within the framework of societal arrangements concerning the sexes. Nowhere are such sexist acts to be seen as parts of the fabric of a culture more than within the basic institution of American society—the family.

It has become apparent that one of the most dangerous places for a female to be is in her home, and some of the most dangerous people for her to be around are supposed loved ones. Within the last twenty years the prevalence of family violence in the United States gradually has become recognized as a serious social problem. Despite the difficulty in researching the problem, it is estimated that the proportion of couples who use violence during the course of their marriages is around 50 to 60 percent (Queijo 1984). The problem is extensive, cuts across social class, and not surprisingly, females are the most likely victims. Wife abuse, elder abuse, incest, and other forms of family violence are not new phenomena. In fact, Caplow, Bahr, Chadwick, Hill, and Williamson (1982) in findings from a fifty-year study of Middletown, a midwestern city, point out that conversations with Middletown police and social workers suggested that wife beating had always gone on in Middletown. The difference now, according to the sources, was that the women's rights movement and women's growing economic independence have made women less willing to endure interpersonal harm-doing, more likely to call public attention to the problem, more likely to obtain outside assistance to attenuate the problem (e.g., psychological counseling for abusive husbands), and when all else fails, to escape from physically punishing relationships. As Caplow et al. point out, a high divorce rate need not imply the disintegration of one of society's basic institutions; it can signal unhappy partners attempting and finding more satisfying marriages with others and, thus, increased happiness in families.

Changes in two other societal institutions seem much slower, however. One institution, the religious institution, as pointed out in chapter 7, was rocked by scandal in 1987 and 1988. While the majority of Americans perhaps were not followers of T.V. ministries, most church leaders, increasingly those leaders of so-called mainstream churches, lamented the effect that the sex-and-money scandal tarnishing electronic evangelism would possibly have on their own congregational participation. One midwestern state-wide poll taken a few weeks following the 1987 scandal showed that by a 2-1 margin, it was felt that T.V. evangelists do religion more harm than good. The concern would seem to be a rational one given the relatively high rate of church participation by females and the dubious status of women generally in the religious institution. How long women will remain content to be used as "money givers," Sunday school teachers, sex objects, and generally as supporters of men in powerful church positions remains to be seen. It seems likely, however, that the religious institution, like others in American society, will continue to undergo change in the direction of sex role equality despite efforts to thwart such change.

A beacon of progressive light has pierced another social institution highly resistant to sex role changes—the political institution. Columnist

Suzannah Lessard chronicled this change in a May 1987 *Newsweek* article entitled "The Issue Was Women." Lessard, who in 1979 wrote a controversial article on Senator Edward M. Kennedy and "womanizing" behavior as a political issue in the *Washington Monthly,* suggests that remarkable changes had occurred in political candidacies since Kennedy's and even Gary Hart's fiasco in 1987. Lessard pointed out that for a long while there has been an unwritten agreement between the media and political institution to overlook "womanizing" behavior. She suggested further that the tradition had its roots in: (1) the phenomenon being "beneath the dignity" of serious people to consider in a presidential candidate and (2) the attitude of male solidarity and "do not judge lest ye yourself be judged." Lessard contends that with the Hart episode all inhibitions gave way, suggesting to her that our society is in a transition period. This transition period seems to imply that the full humanity of women is being recognized. Believing that there is increased awareness of the dignity and equality of women, Lessard reasons the controversy was not one of Hart's judgment or morals, but rather the question of his womanizing. She states:

> As long as women were regarded as less than full-fledged human beings, a man's behavior toward them was not a good gauge of his attitude toward human beings. It was not descriptive of his moral texture, not a sounding of his emotional depth. As long as women were assumed to be creatures of a generally lesser caliber than men, it made little sense to draw conclusions about a man's character from his relationships with them—any more than you could from his relationships with his pets. Unless of course, he was doing something extreme like beating or starving them. A pet was there to please and fulfill its owner, whose life was viewed as infinitely more significant. So it was with wives of politicians. The wives' pain wasn't significant, wasn't even real. And as for the women a politician dallied with, they were truly insignificant. What they felt or how they were affected by these liaisons was of no account. This began to change in the '70s. Mary Jo Kopechne's death at Chappaquidick and Joan Kennedy's devastation made an impression—though not enough of one to dissolve that magical protective circle around Kennedy, whose political life continued. (1987, p. 32)

A revelation by Judith Campbell Exner suggests that support roles for high-level public political officials sometimes go beyond a sexual or emotional refuge. *People* magazine (Feb. 29, 1988) reported that Exner, who admitted over a decade earlier having an affair with President John F. Kennedy when he was in the White House, claimed to have been a courier for Kennedy to alleged Mafia figures. She said that she had arranged meetings between the president and Mafia figures and speculated that her courier services involved attempts to influence a state political primary prior to the 1960 election and CIA collaboration with the Mafia to assassinate Cuban Premier Fidel Castro (Kelley 1988, p. 108). Exner's revelations probably will tarnish Kennedy's image as a historical leader of America. Moreover, they illuminate the inferior and sometimes degrading positions women are placed in by men in our society's political institution.

Some may feel the above are isolated incidents and unrelated to societal institutional change. In contrast, the position offered here is that societal transition is slow, but the demise of the Hart candidacy may be, as Lessard contends, transition in its early stage. The Hart episode and others like it, where men tend to deny their lives with women as well as their own dysfunctional so-called masculine traits, will begin to decrease. Such occurrences undoubtedly will move this society toward sex role equality, because men will be unable to "hold split versions of reality" and increasingly will come to accept their own misogynist and disorganizing behaviors as problematic. In 1987 and 1988, men in high religious and political positions have had to do this publicly. We await further change on the part of substantially more men in society.

Changes in Men's Sexuality

The sexual revolution, which has been so pronounced in the past twenty years, undoubtedly is undergoing alteration as the spectre of AIDS casts a gloomy shadow over the United States and many other countries. Yet, the male sexual script remains intact, although some males express more concern about the safety of heterosexual sexual conquests. Does this mean that men's motives, values, and orientations related to sexuality are changing? It may be too early to say, but signs do not indicate that slight changes in some men's sexual behavior are accompanied by changes in men's attitudes and values related to sex.

Studies by Bailey, Hendrick, and Hendrick (1987) and McCabe (1987) reported somewhat different sexual orientations for men and women. Bailey et al.'s study reported that while females seem to be more relationship oriented, friendship-oriented, practical, communal, and responsible, males were more goal oriented, instrumental, game-playing, and sexually permissive. McCabe found that while men desired sex within a caring relationship when dating, women tended to want intercourse only when there was a greater level of commitment. Both sets of findings were congruent with Foa et al.'s (1987) cross-cultural conclusions that males tend to differentiate love and sex more strongly than females, linking sex with services provided.

As Feather (1984) and Carroll, Volk, and Hyde (1985) found in the early 1980s, masculinity and feminity are associated with quite different values and orientations about sex. Fun, pleasure, physical release, and so on may be chief reasons why men engage in sex, but women's sexual values and orientations remain tied to love, commitment, and emotion. Apparently, appreciable changes in men's sexual orientations and values in line with gender equality are yet to come.

Popular Culture and Sex Role Changes

A glimpse of impending changes in a society frequently is provided by "popular culture"—songs, magazines, and movies. Are changes between males and females occurring as depicted in popular song, movies, and magazines? If these are expressions of current values and attitudes, then America has a long way to go before sex and gender equality is reached. One of the most popular movies in 1987 was Paramount's *Fatal Attraction*, starring Glenn Close and Michael Douglas. The movie portrays Glenn Close as Alex, a competent businesswoman who has an affair with Dan (Michael Douglas), becomes pregnant by him, falls in love with him, and threatens his family (wife, Beth, and daughter). After a series of macabre attempts to woo Dan, Alex invades his home, fights with Dan and his wife, Beth, until finally Beth kills Alex and Dan's unborn child. The message seems clear. Alex is a monster who has tempted Dan and wants to destroy the dream family. Dan is relatively blameless. Beth, who is in "a woman's place," protects her family by killing the invader and the illegitimate child inside her. A competent, independent woman loses, and the man is held blameless.

Popular songs glorify female inferiority, sexually denigrate women, and in fact, perpetuate sex role inequality by exalting male dominance. George Michael's 1988 song "I Will Be Your Father Figure" says that women desire and need men to look up to, that they are pitiful, lost creatures who must be directed and dominated in life by men. In essence, women are inferior, and men are superior.

A final word should be said about an aspect of popular culture in America not ordinarily discussed—pornography. John Stoltenberg states: ''Being put down or treated in a second-class or subhuman way on account of the social meaning of one's anatomy is what the bulk of pornography is for'' (1988, p. 12). Stoltenberg feels, and I concur, that pornography reveals the political reality of the gender hierarchy in a wretched way. Much pornography depicts women in degraded ways, showing them gagged or trussed up. An obvious latent message to men is that women are ''supposed to respond orgasmically to power and powerlessness, to violence and violatedness'' (1988, p. 11). Pornography teaches men ''a reverence for supremacy, for unjust power over and against other human life'' (p. 11).

While pornography proliferates, much is being said about our efforts to become a society where females and males are equally valued. While modicum changes in some of our basic institutions portend a gradual move towards sex role equality, simultaneous retrenchment and in some instances regression in our popular culture inform us that the war for sex role egalitarianism must be continually fought.

References

Allen, B.
1983   The price for giving it up. *Essence* (Feb.), p. 60–62.
Altman, D.
1971   *Homosexual oppression and liberation.* New York: Outerbridge and Lizard: Avon.
Ashmore, R. D., F. K. Del Boca, and M. A. McManus
1986   Gender-related attitudes. In *The social psychology of female-male relationships,* edited by R. D. Ashmore and F. K. Del Boca. New York: Academic Press.
Astin, A. W.
1984   *The American freshmen: National norms for fall, 1984.* Los Angeles, Calif.: Higher Education Research Institute, U.C.L.A.
August, E. R.
1982   Modern man, or men's studies in the 80's. *College English* 44(5): 585.
Bailey, W.C., C. Hendrick, and S. S. Hendrick
1987   Relation of sex and gender role to love, sexual attitudes, and self-esteem. *Sex Roles* 16 (11/12): 637–48.
Ballantine, J. H.
1983   *The sociology of education.* Englewood Cliffs, N.J.: Prentice-Hall.
1985   *Schools and society: A reader in education and society.* Palo Alto, Calif.: Mayfield.
Bandura, A.
1977   *Social learning theory.* Englewood Cliffs, N.J.: Prentice-Hall.
Barnett, R. C., and G. K. Baruch
1978   *The competent woman: Perspectives on development.* New York: Irvington.
Basow, S.
1980   *Sex role stereotypes: Traditions and alternatives.* Monterey, Calif.: Brooks/Cole.
Beam, J.
1986   Editorial. *Black/Out* 1(2):5–6.
Beame, T.
1983   Racism from a black perspective. In *Black men/White men,* edited by M. J. Smith. San Francisco, Calif.: Gay Sunshine Press.

235

Becker, H.
1963   *Outsiders: Studies in the sociology of deviance.* New York: Free
            Press.
Bell, A. P., and M. Weinberg
1978   *Homosexualities: A study of diversity among men and women.*
            New York: Simon and Schuster.
Bell, D.
1976   *The cultural contradictions of capitalism.* New York: Basic
            Books.
Belsky, J.
1979   Mother-father-infant interaction: A naturalistic observation
            study. *Developmental Psychology* 15:601–7.
Bem, S. L.
1974   The measurement of psychological androgyny. *Journal of Con-
            sulting and Clinical Psychology* 42:155–62.
1983   Gender schema theory and its implications for child development:
            Raising gender aschematic children in a gender-schematic soci-
            ety. *Signs: Journal of Women in Culture and Society*
            8(4):598–616.
Benokraitis, N. V., and J. R. Feagin
1986   *Modern sexism: Blatant, subtle, and covert discrimination.*
            Englewood Cliffs, N.J.: Prentice-Hall.
Berger, P.
1967   *The sacred canopy: Elements of a sociological theory of religion.*
            New York: Doubleday.
Berman, P. W.
1980   Are women more responsive than men to the young? A review of
            developmental and situational variables. *Psychological Bulletin*
            88:668–95.
Bijou, S. W., and Baer, D. M.
1978   *Behavioral analysis of child development.* Englewood Cliffs,
            N.J.: Prentice-Hall.
Biller, H. B.
1981   The father and sex role development. In *The role of the father in
            child development,* edited by M. E. Lamb. New York: Wiley.
Block, J. H.
1973   Conceptions of sex roles: Some cross-cultural and longitudinal
            perspectives. *American Psychologist* 28:512–26.
1976   Issues, problems, and pitfalls in assessing sex differences.
            Merrill-Palmer Quarterly 22:283–308.
1983   Differential premises arising from differential socialization of the
            sexes: Some conjectures. *Child Development* 54:1335–54.
Blumberg, R. L.
1977   Women and work around the world: A cross-sex division of labor
            and sex status. In *Beyond sex roles,* edited by A. Sargent. St.
            Paul, Minn.: West.

Blumer, H.
1969   *Symbolic interactionism: Perspectives and method.* Englewood
            Cliffs, N.J.: Prentice-Hall.
Blumstein, P. W., and P. Schwartz
1976   Bisexuality in men. *Urban Life* 5(3).
1977   Bisexuality: Some social psychological issues. *Journal of Social
            Issues* 33:30–45.
Bowles, S., and H. Gintis
1976   *Schooling in capitalist America: Educational reform and the con-
            tradiction of economic life.* New York: Basic Books.
Bozett, F.W.
1987   *Gay Parents.* New York: Praeger.
Brabant, S., and L. Mooney
1986   Sex role stereotyping in the Sunday comics: Ten years later. *Sex
            Roles* 14(3–4):141–48.
Brannon, R.
1976   The male sex role. In *The forty-nine percent majority,* edited by
            D. S. David and R. Brannon. Reading, Mass.: Addison-Wesley.
Brewster, L. G.
1984   *The public agenda.* New York: St. Martin's Press.
Brigham, J. C.
1986   *Social psychology.* Boston, Mass.: Little, Brown.
Brod, H.
1986   New perspectives on masculinity: A case for men's studies. In
            *Changing men: New directions in research on men and masculin-
            ity,* edited by M. Kimmel. Beverly Hills, Calif.: Sage.
1987   The case for men's studies. In *The Making of masculinities: The
            new men's studies,* edited by H. Brod. Boston, Mass.: Allen &
            Unwin.
Burgess, R. L., and R. L. Akers
1966a   A differential association-reinforcement theory of criminal be-
            havior. *Social Problems* 14:128–47.
1966b   Are operant principles tautological? *Psychological Record* 16,
            305–12.
Canter, R. J.
1982   Family correlates of male and female delinquency. *Criminology*
            20:149–68.
Caplow, T., H. Bahr, B. Chadwick, R. Hill, and H. Williamson
1982   *Middletown families: Fifty years of change and continuity.* Min-
            neapolis: University of Minnesota Press.
Carlson, R.
1971   Sex differences in ego functioning. *Journal of Counseling and
            Clinical Psychology* 37:267–77.
Carrigan, T., B. Connell, and J. Lee
1987   Toward a new sociology of masculinity. In *The making of mascu-
            linities: The new men's studies,* edited by H. Brod. Boston,
            Mass.: Allen & Unwin.

Carroll, J. L., K. D. Volk, and J. S. Hyde
1985   Differences between males and females in motives for engaging
             in sexual intercourse. *Archives of Sexual Behavior* 14:131–39.
Chalfant, H. P., R. E. Beckley, and C. E. Palmer
1987   *Religion in contemporary society.* Palo Alto, Calif.: Mayfield.
Cherry, L.
1975   The preschool teacher-child dyad: Sex differences in verbal inter-
             action. *Child Development* 46:532–35.
Chodorow, N.
1974   Family structure and feminine personality. In *Woman, culture,
             and society,* edited by M. S. Rosaldo and L. Lamphere. Stanford,
             Calif.: Stanford University Press.
Clarke-Stewart, K. A.
1980   The father's contribution to children's cognitive and social devel-
             opment in early childhood. In *The father-infant relationship: Ob-
             servational studies in the family setting,* edited by F. A. Pederson.
             New York: Praeger.
Cloward, R. A. and L. E. Ohlin
1960   Delinquency and opportunity: A theory of delinquent gangs. New
             York: Free Press.
Cohen, A. K.
1966   *Deviance and control.* Englewood Cliffs, N.J.: Prentice-Hall.
Conklin, J. E.
1987   *Sociology.* New York: Macmillan.
Constantinople, A.
1973   Maculinity-femininity: An exception to a famous dictum. *Psy-
             chological Bulletin* 80:389–407.
Cullen, F. T., K. M. Golden, and J. B. Cullen
1979   Sex and delinquency: A partial test of the masculinity hypothesis.
             Criminology 17:283–301.
Daly, M.
1975   *The church and the second sex.* 2d ed. New York: Harper and
             Row.
D'Antonio, W. V.
1983   Family life, religion, and societal values and structures. In *Fami-
             lies and religions: Conflict and change in modern society,* edited
             by W. V. D'Antonio and J. Aldous. Beverly Hills, Calif.: Sage.
1985   The American Catholic family: Signs of cohesion and polariza-
             tion. *Journal of Marriage and the Family* 47:395–405.
Darwin, C. R.
1859   *On the origin of species by means of natural selection.* London:
             John Murray.
Datesman, S. K., F. R. Scarpitti, and R. Stephenson
1975   Female delinquency: An application of self and opportunity theo-
             ries. *Journal of Research in Crime and Delinquency* 12:107–23.
David, D. S., and R. Brannon
1976   *The forty-nine percent majority.* Reading, Mass.: Addison-
             Wesley.

Deutsch, C., and L. Gilbert
1976   Norms affecting self-disclosures in men and women. *Journal of Consulting and Clinical Psychology* 44:376–80.
Doyle, J. A.
1983   *The male experience.* Dubuque, Iowa: W. C. Brown.
Drabman, R. S., S. J. Robertson, J. N. Patterson, G. J. Javie, D. Hammer, and G. Gordua
1979   Children's perception of media portrayal of sex roles. *Sex Roles* 7:379–89.
Drass, K.A.
1986   The effects of gender identity on conversation. *Social Psychology Quarterly* 49 (4): 294–301.
Driver, A. B.
1976   Religion. *Signs* 2:434–42.
Durkheim, E.
1965   *The elementary forms of religious life.* New York: Free Press. (Originally published 1902)
Easton, B.
1986   Personal note written to Clyde W. Franklin II.
Egley, L.
1985   The third gender. *Changing Men: Issues in Sex, Gender and Politics* 14:5–8.
Ehrenreich, B., and D. English
1978   *For her own good: One hundred fifty years of experts' advice to women.* New York: Doubleday/Anchor Books.
Eisenberg, N., S. A. Wolchik, R. Hernandez, and J. F. Pasternack
1985   Parental socialization of young children's play: A short-term longitudinal study. *Child Development* 56:1506–13.
Eitzen, S. D.
1986   *Social problems.* 3d ed. Boston, Mass.: Allyn and Bacon.
Eysencek, H.
1977   *Crime and personality.* London: Routledge and Kegan Paul.
Fagot, B. I.
1977   Consequences of moderate cross-gender behavior in preschool children. *Child Development* 1:563–68.
1978   The influence of sex of child on parental reactions to toddler children. *Child Development* 49:459–65.
1981   Male and female teachers: Do they treat boys and girls differently? *Sex Roles* 7:263–71.
Fagot, B. I., R. Hagan, M. D. Leinbach, and S. Kronsberg
1985   Differential reaction to assertive and communicative acts of toddler boys and girls. *Child Development* 56:1499–1505.
Fasteau, M.
1974   *The male machine.* New York: McGraw-Hill.
Feather, N.T.
1984   Masculinity, femininity, psychological adrogyny, and the structure of values. *Journal of Personality and Social Psychology* 47:604–20.

Feinman, S.
1974   Approvals of cross-sex-role behavior. *Psychological Reports* 35:643–48.
Felson, R. B., and A. E. Liska
1984   Explanation of the sex-deviance relationship. *Deviant Behavior* 5:1–10.
Femiano, S.
1986   Some thoughts on Petzke's article. *Men's Studies Newsletter* 3(3).
Field, T.
1978   Interaction behaviors of primary versus secondary caretaker fathers. *Developmental Psychology* 14:183–84.
Fling, S., and M. Manosevitz
1972   Sex typing in nursery school children's play interests. *Developmental Psychology* 7:146–52.
Foa, U.G., B. Anderson, J. Converse, W.A. Urbansky, M.J. Cawley III, and S.M. Muhlhausen
1987   Gender-related sexual attitudes: Some cross-cultural similarities and differences. *Sex Roles* 16(9/10): 511–19.
Franklin, C. W.
1982   *Theoretical perspectives in social psychology.* Boston, Mass.: Little, Brown.
1984   *The changing definition of masculinity.* New York: Plenum Press.
1985   The Black male urban barbershop as a sex-role socialization setting. *Sex Roles* 12:965–79.
Freimuth, M. J., and G. A. Hornstein
1982   A critical examination of the concept of gender. *Sex Roles* 8:515–32.
Frencher, J. S., and J. Henkin
1973   The menopausal queen: Adjustment on aging and the male homosexual. *American Journal of Orthopsychiatry* 43:670–74.
Fu, V. R., and D. J. Leach
1980   Sex role preferences among elementary school children in rural America. *Psychological Reports* 46:555–60.
Gagnon, J. H., and W. Simon
1973   *Sexual conduct: The social sources of human sexuality.* Chicago, Ill.: Aldine.
Garfinkel, P.
1985   *In a man's world.* New York: New American Library.
Gibbons, D. C., and M. D. Krohn
1986   *Delinquent behavior,* 4th ed. Englewood Cliffs, N.J.: Prentice-Hall.
Glueck, S., and E. Glueck
1950   *Unraveling juvenile delinquency.* New York: Commonwealth Fund.
Goldberg, H.
1976   *The hazards of being male,* New York: New American Library.

1979   *The new male: From macho to sensitive, but still all male.* New York: New American Library.

1983   *The new male-female relationship.* New York: New American Library.

Goring, C. B.

1972   *The English convict: A statistical study.* Montclair, N.J.: Patterson Smith. (Originally published 1913)

Gove, W. R.

1980   *The labelling of deviance: Evaluating a perspective.* 2d ed. Beverly Hills, Calif.: Sage.

Gross, A. E.

1978   The male role and heterosexual behavior. *Journal of Social Issues* 34:87–107.

Hall, J. A., and A. G. Halberstadt

1981   Sex roles and nonverbal communication skills. *Sex Roles* 7:273–87

Hanson, S. M. H.

1986   Parent-child relationships in single-father families. In *Men in families,* edited by R. A. Lewis and R. E. Salt. Beverly Hills, Calif.: Sage.

Hargrove, B.

1983   The church, the family, and the modernization process. In *Families and religions: Conflict and change in modern society,* edited by R. A. Lewis and R. E. Salt. Beverly Hills, Calif.: Sage.

Hartley, R. F.

1959   Sex role pressures in the socialization of the male child. *Psychological Reports* 5:458.

Hartup, W. W.

1983   The peer system. In *Handbook of child psychology.* Vol. 4: *Socialization, personality, and social development,* edited by E. M. Hetherington and P. H. Mussen (series ed.). New York: Wiley.

Hays, H. R.

1972   *The dangerous sex.* New York: Basic Books.

Heilbrun, A. B.

1981   Gender differences in the functional linkage between androgyny, social cognition, and competence. *Journal of Personality and Social Psychology* 41:1106–14.

1986   Androgyny as type and androgyny as behavior: Implications for gender schema in males and females. *Sex Roles* 14(3/4):123–39.

Heilbrun, A. B., and B. A. Bailey

1986   Independence of masculine and feminine traits: Empirical exploration of a prevailing assumption. *Sex Roles* 14(3/4):105–22.

Heilbrun, A. B., and Y. Han

1985   Androgynous behavior versus androgynous type: An explanation for differential gender benefits from androgyny. Unpublished paper.

Herek, G. M.
1986   On heterosexual masculinity. *American Behavioral Scientist*
            29(5).
Hess, R. B., E. W. Markson, and P. J. Stein
1985   *Sociology.* 2d ed. New York: Macmillan.
1988   *Sociology.* New York: Macmillian.
Hirschi, T.
1968   *Causes of delinquency.* Los Angeles, Calif.: University of Cali-
            fornia Press.
Hite, S.
1981   *The Hite report on male sexuality.* New York: Ballantine.
Hoffman, M. L.
1970   Moral development. In *Carmichael's manual of child psychol-
            ogy,* vol. 2, 3d ed., edited by P. H. Mussen.
1981   The role of the father in moral internalization. In *The role of the
            father in child development,* edited by M. E. Lamb. New York:
            Wiley.
Horney, K.
1967   The dread of women: Observations on a specific difference in the
            dread felt by men and women respectively for the opposite sex. In
            Feminine psychology, edited by H. Kelman. New York: Norton.
1967   The flight from womanhood: The masculinity complex in women
            as viewed by men and women. In *Feminine psychology,* edited by
            H. Kelman. New York: Norton.
Humphreys, R. A. L.
1970   *The tearoom trade: Impersonal sex in public places.* Chicago,
            Ill.: Aldine.
Hunter, J. D.
1983   *American evanagelicalism: Conservative religion and the quan-
            dary of modernity.* New Brunswick, N.J.: Rutgers University
            Press.
Imperato-McGinley, J. R., E. Peterson, E. Gautier, and N. Sturla
1979   Androgens and the evolution of male gender identity among male
            pseudohermaphrodites with 5a-reductase deficiency. *New En-
            gland Journal of Medicine* 300:1233–37.
Jackman, M. R., and M. J. Muha
1984   Education and intergroup attitudes: Moral enlightenment, super-
            ficial democratic commitment, or ideological refinement? *Ameri-
            can Sociological Review* 49:751–69.
Jones, E.
1948   *Papers on psychoanalysis.* Baltimore, Md.: Williams and
            Wilkins.
1957   *The life and work of Sigmund Freud.* Vol. 3. New York: Basic
            Books.
1966   The early development of female sexuality. In *Psychoanalysis
            and female sexuality,* edited by H. M. Rutterbeck. New Haven,
            Conn.: College and University Press.

Jourard, S.
1969   Some lethal aspects of the male role. In *The transparent self*, rev.
            ed., edited by S. Jourard. New York: Van Nostrand.
1971   *Self-disclosure: An experimental analysis of the transparent self.*
            New York: Wiley.
Julty, S.
1980   Men's health issues for the '80s. *American Man* 1(4):40.
Kaminski, D.
1985   Where are the female Einsteins? The gender stratification of math
            and science. In *Schools and society: A reader in education and
            sociology,* edited by J. H. Ballantine. Palo Alto, Calif.: Mayfield.
Katz, P.
1986   Gender identity: Development and consequences. In *The social
            psychology of female-male relations: A critical analysis of central
            concepts,* edited by R. D. Ashmore and F. K. Del Boca. New
            York: Academic Press.
Kelly, J. A., and J. Worell
1977   New formulations of sex roles and androgyny: A critical review.
            Journal of Consulting and Clinical Psychology 45:1101–15.
Kimmel, D. C.
1978   Adult development and aging: A gay perspective. *Journal of So-
            cial Issues* 34:113–30.
Kimmel, M. S.
1987   Real man redux. *Psychology Today* (July), pp. 48–52.
Kinsey, A. C., W. B. Pomeroy, and C. E. Martin
1948   *Sexual behavior in the human male.* Philadelphia, Penn.: W. B.
            Saunders.
Kirkham, G. L.
1971   Homosexuality in prison. In *Studies in the sociology of sex,* edited
            by J. M. Henslin. New York: Appleton-Century-Croft.
Klein, M.
1960.   *The psychoanalysis of children.* New York: Grove Press.
Klein, S. S.
1985   *Handbook for achieving sex equity through education.* Baltimore,
            Md.: Johns Hopkins University Press.
Kohlberg, L.
1966   A cognitive-developmental analysis of children's sex role con-
            cepts and attitudes. In *The development of sex differences,* edited
            by E. E. Maccoby. Stanford, Calif.: Stanford University Press.
Kolata, G. B.
1974   Kung hunter-gatherers: Feminism, diet, and birth control. *Sci-
            ence* 185:932–34.
Komarovsky, M.
1973   Presidential address: Some problems in role analysis. *American
            Sociological Review* 38:649–62.
LaFrance, M., and B. Carmen
1980   The nonverbal display of psychological androgyny. *Journal of
            Personality and Social Psychology* 38:36–49.

Lamb, M. E.
1977   Father-infant and mother-infant interaction in the first year of life.
               Child Development 48:167–81.
1981   The development of father-infant relationships. In *The role of fa-
               thers in child development,* edited by M. E. Lamb. New York:
               Wiley.
1986   The changing roles of fathers. In *The father's role: Applied per-
               spectives,* edited by M. E. Lamb. New York: Wiley.
Lamb, M. E., M. A. Easterbrook, and G. W. Halden
1980   Reinforcement and punishment among preschoolers: Character-
               istics, effects, and correlates. *Child Development* 51:1230–36.
Lamb, M. E., J. H. Pleck, E. L. Charnov, and J. A. Levine
1985   Paternal behavior in humans. *American Zoologist* 25:883–94.
Lamb, M. E., J. H. Pleck, and J. A. Levine
1985   The role of the father in child development: The effects of incre-
               saed paternal involvement. In *Advances in clinical child psychol-
               ogy,* vol. 8, edited by B. S. Lakley and A. E. Kazdin. New York:
               Plenum Press.
1986   Effects of increased paternal involvement on children in two-
               parent families. In *Men in families,* edited by R. A. Lewis and R.
               E. Salt. Beverly Hills, Calif.: Sage.
Langlois, J. H., and A. C. Downs
1980   Mothers, fathers, and peers as socialization agents of sex typed
               play behavior in young children. *Child Development*
               51:1217–47.
Lasch, C.
1979   *The culture of narcissism.* New York: Basic Books.
Lehman, E. G.
1985   *Women clergy: Breaking through the gender barrier.* New Bruns-
               wick, N.J.: Transaction.
Lehne, G. K.
1976   Homophobia among men. In *The forty-nine percent majority: The
               male sex role,* edited by D. David and R. Brannon. New York:
               Addison-Wesley.
Lemert, E. L.
1967   *Human deviance, social problems, and social control.* Engle-
               wood Cliffs, N.J.: Prentice-Hall.
1951   *Social pathology.* New York: McGraw-Hill.
Lengermann, P. M., and R. A. Wallace
1980   *Gender in America: Social control and social change.* Englewood
               Cliffs, N.J.: Prentice-Hall.
Lessard, S.
1987   The issue was women. *Newsweek* (May 18), pp. 32–34.
Lester, J.
1973   Being a boy. *Ms.* (July), pp. 112–13.
Lever, J.
1978   Sex differences in the complexity of children's play and games.
               American Sociological Review 43:471–83.

Levinson, D. J., C. Darrow, E. B. Klein, M. H. Levinson, and B. McKee.
1978   *The seasons of a man's life*. New York: Ballantine.
Liska, A. E.
1987   *Perspectives on deviance*. Englewood Cliffs, N.J.: Prentice-Hall.
Litewka, J.
1979   The socialized penis. In *The women say, the men say,* edited by E. Shapiro and B. Shapiro. N.p.: Delta Special.
Lopato, H. Z., and B. Thorne
1978   On the term "sex roles." *Signs* 3:718–21.
LoPiccolo, J.
1985   Diagnosis and treatment of male sexual dysfunction. *Journal of Sex and Marital Therapy* 11:215–32.
Lowenstein, J. S., and E. J. Koopman
1978   A comparison of the self-esteem between boys living with single parent mothers and single parent fathers. *Journal of Divorce* 2:195–208.
Luepnitz, D. A.
1982   *Child custody: A study of families after divorce*. Lexington, Mass.: Lexington.
Lynne, N. B.
1979   American women and the political process. In *Women: A feminist perspective,* 2d ed., edited by J. Freeman. Palo Alto, Calif.: Mayfield.
Maccoby, E. E., and C. H. Jacklin
1974   *The psychology of sex differences*. Stanford, Calif.: Stanford University Press.
MacDonald, A. P.
1976   Homophobia: Its roots and meanings. *Homosexual Counseling Journal* 3(1):23–33.
Macionis, J. J.
1987   *Sociology*. Englewood Cliffs, N.J.: Prentice-Hall.
MacKinnon, C. A.
1979   *Sexual harassment of working on the job*. New Haven, Conn.: Yale University Press.
Majors, R.
1986   Cool pose: The proud signatures of black survival. *Changing Men: Issues in Gender, Sex and Politics* 17 (Winter):5–6.
Mamay, P. D., and R. I. Simpson
1981   Three female roles in television commercials. *Sex Roles* 7:1223–32.
Masnick, G., and M. J. Bane
1980   The nation's families: 1960–1990. Cambridge, Mass.: M.I.T. and Harvard Joint Center for Urban Studies.
Matteson, D.R.
1988   Married and Gay. *Changing Men: Issues in Gender, Sex, and Politics* 19 (Spring/Summer):14–16,45.

McCabe, M.P.
1987 Desired and experienced levels of premarital affection and sexual intercourse during dating. *Journal of Sex Research* 23(1):23–33.

McHenry, P., S. J. Price, P. B. Gordon, and N. Rudd
1986 Characteristics of husbands' family work and wives' labor force involvement. In *Men in families,* edited by R. A. Lewis and R. E. Salt. Beverly Hills, Calif.: Sage.

McNamara, P. H.
1985 The new Christian right's view of the family and its social science critics: A study in differing propositions. *Journal of Marriage and the Family* 47:449–58.

McWhirter, D. P., and Mattison, A. M.
1984 *The male couple.* Englewood Cliffs, N.J.: Prentice-Hall.

Mead, G. H.
1934 *Mind, self, and society.* Chicago, Ill.: University of Chicago Press.

Mercer, G. W., and P. M. Kohn
1979 Gender differences in the integration of conservatism, sex urge, and sexual behaviors among college students. *Journal of Sex Research* 15:129–42.

Merton, R.
1957 *Social theory and social structure.* New York: Free Press.
1966 Social problems and social theory. In *Contemporary social problems,* edited by R. K. Merton and R. A. Nisbet. New York: Harcourt, Brace and World.
1968 Manifest and latent functions. In *Social theory and social structure,* rev. ed. New York: Free Press.

Miller, B.
1978 Adult sexual resocialization: Adjustments toward stigmatized identity. *Alternative Lifestyles* 16:1–42.

Miller, W. D.
1958 Lower-class culture as a generating milieu of gang delinquency. In *The sociology of crime and delinquency,* edited by M. E. Wolfgang, L. Savitz, and N. Johnston. New York: Wiley.

Money, J., and A. L. Ehrhardt
1972 *Man and woman/Boy and girl.* Baltimore, Md.: Johns Hopkins University Press.

Money, J., and P. Tucker
1975 *Sexual signatures: On being a man or a woman.* Boston, Mass.: Little, Brown.

Morin, S. F., and E. Garfinkel
1978 Male homophobia. *Journal of Social Issues* 34(1):29–47.

Mosher, D. L.
1980 Three dimensions of depth of involvement in human sexual response. *Journal of Sex Research* 16:1–42.

Nacci, P. L., and T. R. Kane
1983 The incidence of sex and sexual aggression in federal prisons. *Federal Probation* (Dec.):31–36.

1984   Sex and sexual aggression in federal prisons. *Federal Probation* (March):46–53.

Nahas, R., and M. Turley
1979   *The new couple: Women and gay men.* New York: Seaview Books.

Nash, S. C., and S. S. Feldman
1981   Sex role and sex-related attribution: Constancy or change across the family life cycle? In *Advances in developmental psychology,* vol. 1, edited by M. E. Lamb and A. Brown. Hillsdale, N.J.: Erlbaum.

Nichols, J.
1978   *Men's liberation.* New York: Penguin.

Nordstrom, B.
1986   Why men get married: More and less traditional men compared. In *Men in families,* edited by R. A. Lewis and R. E. Salt. Beverly Hills, Calif.: Sage.

O'Dea, T., and J. O. Aviad
1983   *Sociology of religion.* 2d ed. Englewood Cliffs, N.J.: Prentice-Hall.

O'Neil, J. M., B. J. Helms, R. K. Gable, L. David, and L. S. Wrightsman
1986   Gender role conflict scale: College men's fear of femininity. *Sex Roles* 14(5/6):335–49.

Oppenheimer, M.
1985   *White collar politics.* New York: Monthly Review.

Osherson, S.
1986   *Finding our fathers.* New York: Free Press.

Ostling, P. W.
1987   TV's unholy row. *Time* (Apr. 6), pp. 60–65.

Parelius, A. P., and Parelius, R. J.
1978   *The sociology of education.* Englewood Cliffs, N.J.: Prentice-Hall.

Parke, R. D., and Suomi, S. J.
1980   Adult male-infant relationships: Human and non-primate evidence. In *Behavioral development: The Bielefeld interdisciplinary project,* edited by K. Immelmann, G. Barlow, M. Main, and L. Petrinovitch. New York: Cambridge University Press.

Parsons, T., and R. F. Bales
1953   *Family socialization and interaction process.* London: Routledge & Kegan Paul.

Pederson, F. A., B. J. Anderson, and R. L. Cain
1980   Parent-infant and husband-wife interactions observed at age 5 months. In *The father-infant relationship: Observational studies in the family setting,* edited by F. A. Pederson. New York: Praeger.

Pederson, F. A., R. L. Cain, M. J. Zaslow, and B. J. Anderson
1982   Variation in infant experiences associated with alternative family roles. In *Families as learning environments for children,* edited by I. Sigel and L. Laosa. New York: Plenum Press.

Persell, C. H.
1987   *Understanding society.* New York: Harper and Row.
Petzke, D.
1986   Men's studies catches on at colleges, setting off controversy and infighting. *Wall Street Journal* (Feb. 1), p.1.
Phillips, B. D.
1982   Sex role socialization and play behavior on a rural playground. Unpublished master's thesis, Department of Sociology, Ohio State University, Columbus, Ohio.
Piven, F. F.
1985   Women and the state: Ideology, power, and the welfare state. In *Gender and the life course,* edited by A. S. Rossie. New York: Aldine.
Pleck, E. H., and J. H. Pleck
1980   *The American man.* Englewood Cliffs, N.J.: Prentice-Hall.
1975   Masculinity-femininity: Current and alternate paradigms. *Sex Roles* 1(2):161–78.
1976   The male sex role: Definition, problems and sources of change. *Journal of Social Issues* 32:155–64.
Pleck, J. H.
1973   Psychological frontiers for men. *Ruff Times* 3(6):14–15.
1981   *The myth of masculinity.* Cambridge, Mass.: M.I.T. Press.
1985   *Working wives/Working husbands.* Beverly Hills, Calif.: Sage.
Pleck, J. H., and J. Sawyer
1974   *Men and masculinity.* Englewood Cliffs, N.J.: Prentice-Hall.
Polatnick, M.
1973–74   Why men don't rear children: A power analysis. *Berkeley Journal of Sociology* 18:45–86.
Ponte, M.
1974   Life in a parking lot: An ethnography of a homosexual drive-in. In *Deviance: Field studies and self-disclosures,* edited by J. Jacos. Palo Alto, Calif.: National Books.
Popenoe, D.
1986   *Sociology.* 6th ed. Englewood Cliffs, N.J.: Prentice-Hall.
Power, T. G., and R. D. Parke
1982   Play as a context for early learning: Lab and home analysis. In *The family as a learning environment,* edited by I. Sigel and M. Laosa. New York: Plenum Press.
1983   Patterns of mother and father play with their 8-month-old infants: A multiple analyses approach. *Infant Behavior and Development* 6:453–59.
Pruett, K. D.
1983   Infants of primary nurturing fathers. *Psychoanalytic Study of the Child* 38:257–77.
Queijo, J.
1984   The paradox of intimacy. *Bostonian Magazine* (July), pp. 1–25.
Radin, N.
1981   The role of the father in cognitive, academic, and intellectual de-

velopment. In *The role of the father in child development,* edited by M. E. Lamb. New York: Wiley.

1982   Primary care-giving and role-sharing fathers. In *Non-traditional families: Parenting and child development,* edited by M. E. Lamb. Hillsdale, N.J.: Erlbaum.

Rebecca, M., R. Hefner, and B. Oleshansky
1976   A model of sex role transcendance. *Journal of Social Issues* 32(3):197–206.

Reckless, W. C., and S. Dinitz
1967   Pioneering with self-concept as a vulnerability factor in delinquency. *Journal of Criminal Law, Criminology, and Police Science* 58(4):515–23.

Reich, C. A.
1970   *The greening of America.* New York: Random House.

Reichley, A. J.
1985   *Religion in American public life.* Washington, D.C.: Brookings Institute.

Reynolds, B.
1985   *Jesse Jackson: America's David.* Washington, D.C.: JFJ Associates.

Ritzer, B., K. C. W. Kammyer, and N. R. Yetman
1987   *Sociology: Experiencing a changing society.* 3d ed. Boston, Mass.: Allyn and Bacon.

Ross, H. L.
1971   Modes of adjustment of married homosexuals. *Social Problems* 8(Winter):385–93.

Rossler, J.
1987   Unmarried fathers victimized by false stereotypes. *Columbus Dispatch,* Aug. 17, p. A1.

Rowe, D. C.
1983   Biomedical genetic models of self-reported delinquent behavior: A twin study. *Behavior Genetics* 13(5):473–89.

Rowe, D. C., and D. W. Osgood
1984   Heredity and sociological theories of delinquency: A reconsideration. *American Sociological Review* 49(4):526–40.

Rubin, J. Z., E. J. Provenzano, and Z. Luria
1976   The eye of the beholder: Parents' views on sex of newborns. *American Journal of Orthopsychiatry* 44:512–19.

Russell, G.
1982   Shared care-giving families: An Australian study. In *Non-traditional families: Parenting and child development,* edited by M. E. Lamb. Hillsdale, N.J.: Erlbaum.

1983   *The changing role of fathers?* St. Lucia, Queensland: University of Queensland Press.

Russell, L.
1976   *The liberating word.* Philadelphia, Pa.: Westminster.

Saghir, M. T., and E. Robbins
1973   *Male and female homosexuality: A comparison investigation.*
            Baltimore: Md.: Williams and Wilkins.
Sanik, M. M., and Stafford, K.
1985   Adolescents' contributions to household production: Male and fe-
            male differences. *Adolescence* 20(77):207–15.
Santrock, J. W., R. A. Warshak, and G. L. Elliott
1982   Social development and parent-child interaction in father-custody
            and stepmother families. In *Non-traditional families: Parenting
            and child development,* edited by M. E. Lamb. Hillsdale, N. J.:
            Erlbaum.
Sapir, E.
1949   Selected writings of Edward Sapir. In *Language, culture, and
            personality,* edited by D. G. Mandlebaum. Berkeley: University
            of California Press.
Scarf, M.
1976   *Body, mind, behavior.* Washington, D.C.: New Republic Book
            Co.
Schau, C. G., I. Kahn, J. H. Diepold, and F. Cherry
1980   The relationship of parental expectations and pre-school chil-
            dren's verbal sex typing to their sex typed toy play behavior.
            Child Development 51:266–70.
Scheff, T.
1966   *Being mentally ill.* Chicago, Ill.: Aldine.
Schofield, M. G.
1965   *Sociological aspects of homosexuality: A comparative study of
            three types of homosexuals.* Boston, Mass.: Little, Brown.
Schuessler, K. F., and D. R. Cressey
1950   Personality characteristics of criminals. *American Journal of So-
            ciology* 55:476–84.
Schur, E.
1984   *Labeling women deviant: Gender, stigma, and social control.*
            Philadelphia, Pa.: Temple University Press.
Schwartz, H. L.
1982   Sex differences in social competence among androgynes: The in-
            fluence of sex role blending, nonverbal information processing,
            and social cognition. Unpublished doctoral dissertation, Emory
            University, Atlanta, Ga.
Seyfried, B., and C. Hendrick
1973   When do opposites attract? When they are opposites in sex-role
            attitudes. *Journal of Personality and Social Psychology*
            25:15–20.
Shaw, C. R., F. M. Zorbaugh, H. D. McKay, and L. S. Cottrell
1929   *Delinquency areas.* Chicago, Ill.: University of Chicago Press.
Shover, N., S. Norland, J. James, and W. E. Thornton
1979   Gender roles and delinquency. *Social Forces* 13:411–17.
Skinner, B. F.
1974   *About behaviorism.* New York: Knopf.

Slater, P. E.
1976   Sexual adequacy in America. In *Readings in human sexuality: Contemporary perspectives,* edited by C. Gordon and G. Johnson. New York: Harper and Row.
Smilqis, M.
1987   The big chill: How heterosexuals are coping with AIDS. *Time* (Feb. 16), pp. 50–59.
Smith, A. L.
1983   Editorial. *Chicago Men's Gathering Newsletter* 37 (March):2
Snow, M. E., C. N. Jacklin, and E. E. Maccoby
1981   Sex-of-child differences in father-child interaction at one year of age. *Child Development* 54:227–32.
Spencer, J. T., R. Helmreich, and J. Stapp
1974   The personal attributes questionnaire: A measure of sex-role stereotypes and masculinity-femininity. *ISAS Catalogue of Selected Documents in Psychology* 4:127.
Staines, G. L., and P. L. Libby
1986   Men and women in role relationships. In *The social psychology of female-male relations: A critical analysis of central concepts.* New York: Academic Press.
Stark, R., and W. S. Bainbridge
1985   *The future of religion.* Berkeley, Calif.: University of California Press.
Stockard, J., and M. M. Johnson
1979   The social origins of dominance. *Sex Roles* 5:199–218.
1980   *Sex roles.* Englewood Cliffs, N.J.: Prentice-Hall.
Stoltenberg, J.
1988   You can't fight homophobia and protect the pornographers at the same time. *Changing Men: Issues in Gender, Sex, and Politics* 19 (Spring/Summer):11–13.
Sutherland, E. H., and D. R. Cressey
1970   *Criminology.* 8th ed. Philadelphia, Pa.: Lippincott.
Tavris, C.
1982   *Anger: The misunderstood emotion.* New York: Simon and Schuster.
1986   Nine myths about men—and one truth. *Cosmopolitan* (March), pp.229–31.
Tennenbaum, D. J.
1977   Personality and criminality. *Journal of Criminal Justice* 5:1–9.
Thompson, D. N.
1985   Parent-peer compliance in a group of preadolescent youths. *Adolescence* 20(79):501–7.
Thompson, E. H., C. Grisanti, and J. H. Pleck
1985   Attitudes toward the male role and their correlates. *Sex Roles* 13(7/8):413–27.
Thompson, R. A.
1986   Fathers and the child's 'best interests': Judicial decision making

252 *References*

in custody disputes. In *The father's role: Applied perspectives,* edited by M. E. Lamb. New York: Wiley.

Thorne, B.
1980   Gender: How is it best conceptualized? In *Methodological issues in sex roles and social change,* edited by J. Wirtenberg and B. Richardson. New York: Praeger.

Tiefer, L.
1986   In pursuit of the perfect penis. *American Behavioral Scientist* 29(5):579–99.

Tiger, L.
1969   *Men in groups.* New York: Random House.

Tiger, L., and R. Fox
1971   *The imperial animal.* New York: Holt, Rinehart, and Winston.

Tischler, H. L., P. Whitten, and D. E. K. Hunter
1986   *Introduction to sociology.* 2d ed. New York: Holt, Rinehart and Winston.

Turner, J. H.
1982   *The structure of sociological theory.* Homewood, Ill.: Dorsey Press.

Vander Zanden, J. W.
1986   *Sociology: The core.* New York: Knopf.

Waldo, G. P., and D. Dinitz
1967   Personality attributes of the criminal: An analysis of research studies, 1950–1965. *Journal of Research in Crime and Delinquency* 4:185–202.

Wallerstein, J. S., and J. B. Kelly
1980   *Surviving the break-up: How children and parents cope with divorce.* New York: Basic Books.

Warren, C. A. B., and J. M. Johnston
1972   A critique of labeling theory from the phenomenological perspective. In *Theoretical perspectives on deviance,* edited by R. A. Scott and J. D. Douglas. New York: Basic Books.

Warshak, R. A., and J. W. Santrock
1980   Children of divorce: Impact of custody disposition on social development. In *Life-span developmental psychology,* edited by E. J. Callahan and K. A. McCluskey. New York: Academic Press.
1983   The impact of divorce in father-custody and mother-custody homes: The child's perspective. In *Children and divorce,* edited by L. A. Kurdek. San Francisco, Calif.: Jossey-Bass.

Webster, W. H.
1985   Crimes in the United States, 1985. In *Uniform Crime Reports.* Washington, D.C.: U.S. Government Printing Office.

Weinberg, G.
1972   *Society and the healthy homosexual.* New York: Doubleday.

Weinberg, M. S., and Williams, C. J.
1974   *Male homosexuals: Their problems and adaptations.* New York: Penguin.

Williams, J. E.
1982   An overview of findings from adult sex stereotype studies in 25
            countries. In *Diversity and unity in cross-cultural psychology,*
            edited by R. Rath, H. S. Asthana, D. Sinha, and J. B. Sinha.
            Lisse, The Netherlands: Swets and Zeitlinger.
Williams, R. M.
1970   *American society: A sociological interpretation.* 3d ed. New
            York: Knopf.
Wilson, J. Q., and R. J. Hernstein
1985   *Crime and human nature.* New York: Simon & Schuster.
Winter, A.
1986   The shame of elder abuse. *Modern Maturity* (Oct./Nov.), pp.
            50–57.
Yankelovich, D.
1981   *New rules: Searching for self-fulfillment in a world turned upside
            down.* New York: Random House.
Yogman, M. W.
1977   The goals and structure of face-to-face interaction between in-
            fants and fathers. Paper presented at meeting of Society for Re-
            search in Child Development, New Orleans, La.
Zilbergeld, B.
1981   *Male sexuality.* New York: Bantam Books.
Zimmerman, D. H., and C. West
1975   Sex roles, interruptions, and silences in conversations. In *Lan-
            guage and sex: Difference and dominance,* edited by B. Thorne
            and M. Henley. Rowley, Mass.: Newbury House.

Index